Rousseau, Burke, and Revolution in France, 1791

"Reacting to the Past" Series

Rousseau, Burke, and Revolution in France, 1791

Mark C. Carnes
Barnard College
Columbia University

Gary Kates
Pomona College

PEARSON
Longman

New York Boston San Francisco
London Toronto Sydney Tokyo Singapore Madrid
Mexico City Munich Paris Cape Town Hong Kong Montreal

Publisher: Priscilla McGeehon
Editorial Assistant: Stephanie Ricotta
Executive Marketing Manager: Sue Westmoreland
Managing Editor: Bob Ginsberg
Senior Cover Design Manager/Designer: Nancy Danahy
Cover Illustration: "French National Guardsmen Swear to Uphold New Constitution, September 1791,"
    painting by Le Sueur/The Granger Collection, New York.
Senior Manufacturing Buyer: Alfred C. Dorsey
Printer and Binder: Phoenix Color Corporation
Cover Printer: Phoenix Color Corporation

Library of Congress Cataloging-in-Publication Data
    CIP data is on file with the Library of Congress

Please visit our website at http://www.ablongman.com

ISBN 0-321-33229-6

12345678910—PBT—07060504

Table of Contents

Introduction: A Cloud on the Horizon

"There! To the left. Along the Champs-Elysee!"

You lean out the window and peer toward the north, where the great boulevard begins. In the distance, beyond the ancient walls of Paris, a cloud of dust smudges the horizon. You hear a faint rumble, like a distant waterfall. The people in the street, confused, look up. For once, you are glad that you chose an apartment on the fourth floor which, though cheap and hot, provides a panoramic view of the neighborhood near the Tuileries [TWEE-lhur-EE].

A little over two years' ago, in the spring of 1789, after you had been elected to the *Estates-General*, you had rented a room in Versailles, a dozen miles to the west. You had wanted to be near the court and the king, where the business of the realm was transacted. You had no idea that Paris would become your home, and indeed your life. But who ever knows when an earthquake is about to knock their world off its foundation?

But shortly after you arrived at Versailles, an earthquake struck, and hard. The first jolt came in June 1789, when the Estates-General, in open defiance of the King, declared itself to be a "National Assembly"—the legislative body of France. Then came the aftershocks: The King's failed attempts to crush the National Assembly by force; the mob's takeover of the *Bastille* (July); and the Great Fear, when the countryside was turned upside down, and peasants burned castles and manors and drove noblemen from the land (August).

Yet, there were more shocks to come: in October 1789, the market women of Paris, numbering in the thousands, marched to Versailles and forced the royal family back to Paris, and to the Tuileries Palace. The National Assembly came to Paris, too, and commenced meeting in a great hall that had been the King's riding stables at the Tuileries. You took this apartment because it was also near the major clubs. The radical Jacobin club meets just across the way, in what had been the Jacobin convent—thus their name. Recently some members of the Jacobins, alarmed by the mounting chaos on Paris, formed a moderate club; it met in what had been the Feuillant [feh-yawn] monastery, and so is called the Feuillants. The Cordeliers [KOHR-DEE-lee-AY] Club, which attracts the leaders of the working poor of Paris, meets across the Seine River, about ten minutes away. You are fortunate to live near the vortex of the churning political life of Paris, and thus of France.

Last month you told the landlord that you would keep this apartment for another six months, by which time the National Assembly should have finished a constitution. But who, in the chaos that is Paris, can predict what will happen a half year from now? For that matter, who can predict what will happen in the next half hour, as the cloud of dust looms ever larger to the north?

Now you can make out individual people, running ahead of the cloud. You see that the cloud has been caused by an immense sea of people whose footsteps have kicked up the dust from the streets, baked dry by the summer sun. Bisecting the dusty smudge is a thin green thread. Then it comes to you: the National Guardsmen in their new uniforms. The uniforms have provoked debate and considerable comment. The National Guard emerged spontaneously back in 1789, when the King demanded that the National Assembly disperse. Then the people of Paris, workers especially, poured into the streets carrying pikes, clubs, knives, and muskets. Their militancy saved the revolution. The Marquis de Lafayette, a hero of the America Revolution, took command of the armed rabble and molded it into a fighting force: the National Guard of Paris, it was called, and its colors were red and blue—the colors of the city of Paris—and, at Lafayette's insistence, white as well, symbolizing the monarchy. Towns and municipalities throughout France formed their own volunteer militias, all of which took to calling themselves the National Guard. Below, in the street, many wear red, white, and blue ribbons; some fasten the ribbons onto the red caps that have become the symbol of revolution. But now things have changed. The National Guard of Paris has new uniforms—green and white, the colors of King Louis XVI and the Bourbon monarchs—and Lafayette has pushed the rabble out of the National Guard by requiring that all Guardsmen pay for their own uniforms and possess enough property to pay taxes. The poor do not qualify. The radicals say that Lafayette is no longer the hero of the revolution, but its enemy. You squint at the green line and try to find Lafayette's great white horse, but cannot.

At one dark point, however, you spot frenzied activity.

A shout from the roof: "Over there! The King's carriage! They've got him. They've brought him back!"

In the street below, a crowd has gathered. They look up for directions. Some race down the street toward the rumble.

Then you see it, enveloped in dust, proceeding slowly down the Champs Elysee toward the Tuileries. Another shout. You spot the King's carriage.

"Look at the size of that thing."

"Gotta be, to haul that Pig!" someone calls from the street.

Laughter and more shouts.

"And Antoinette, that pig of an Austrian whore."

"With all the little royal piglets."

"Gron. Gron. Gron," Chanting and more laughter.

One young girl, in a high-pitched voice, begins the "Ca Ira," [SAH-ee-RAH], a bouncy, roguish tune that is heard everywhere nowadays.

> Ah, ça ira! Ca ira! Ca ira!
> Les aristocrates a la lanterne.
>
> ["Ah! It'll happen! It'll happen! It'll happen!"
> To a lamppost, send the aristocrats.]

A roar of approval in the street, and most take up the song.

> Ah, Ca ira! Ca ira! Ca ira!
> Les aristocrates on les pendra."
>
> [Ah, it'll happen! It'll happen! It'll happen.
> There we'll hang the aristocrats."]

The next verse peters out. Is it the one about Lafayette leading the people to liberty? Have people forgotten the words, or do they no longer trust him? Since the King's departure, many of the rumors center on Lafayette, who promised the National Assembly that he would keep the King in Paris. Did Lafayette conspire with those who abducted the King? Or did Lafayette connive to help the King flee? Or did he just bungle and allow him to do so?

"News! News here! Queen kidnaps the King!" Another voice from below.

"What, boy?"

"The Queen stole the King away. Says so right here!" The newsboy taps a stack of newspapers.

"She can keep him!"

"What'll she do WITH him?"

"Roast him, and serve 'em with potatoes."

More laughter. A throng gathers around the newsboy, reaching for papers.

You recall reading such a report in Stanislas Freron's radical newspaper last week, just before the King's—departure. Marat, editor of the radical *The People's Friend,* had said something similar: That Queen Marie Antoinette had abducted the King from Paris so that Leopold, her brother, Emperor of Austria, would be free to attack France and crush the revolution. But there are other theories. One holds that the Comte d'Artois [KOHN-DAHR-TWAH], the King's youngest brother, in league with émigré noblemen, had seized and deposed the King for failing to crack down on the revolutionaries. The moderate papers associated with the Feuillants continue to defend the King, describing him as a good man and fair king who had endorsed the revolutionary reforms. "If the King has made errors," one Feuillant added, "it is because he has been ill-advised."

You notice that someone has crossed out the word "Crown" on the sign of the Golden Crown Inn across the street.

Questions hang in the air like the dust, and the answers are as plentiful as the questions.

Another newsboy runs down the street, waving newspapers.

"King Repudiates Revolution! Never supported it."

"Says who?"

"Even left a note, he did," the boy shouts, and a crowd gathers round.

Then, a deep and resonant voice from the rooftops: "Vive le Roi! Long live the King!"

Howls of protest from the street.

"Ain't our King."

"No King flees his people."

"That fat bastard deserves. . ."

A scuffle breaks out. Several men brandish pikes. One hard-looking man, in the short blue trousers that people call *sans-culottes*, pries a paving stone loose and hefts it onto his shoulder. He swaggers toward several well-dressed gentlemen. One raises a wood cane, but his friends tug him up the steps and pull him into a building across the street. The man with the paving stone runs up the same steps and hurls it through a casement window, bashing it in, frame and all. Glass shards cascade down the steps. Others on the street bend over for paving stones and rocks. You're sure your door is locked, but you fear fire: the old wood building would burn in an instant. The scuffle is turning into a riot, again.

Again! All spring riots have flared throughout Paris. The National Guardsmen, it seems, are always running from one section to another, attempting to restore order. No one seems to pay taxes anymore. The government pays its bills with paper money, whose value depreciates continuously. Food prices have risen more sharply than wages, and this has sparked hundreds of strikes, many of them violent. Riots erupt, too, when noblemen walk through poor districts, or when priests and bishops speak against the revolutionary government. Just a few weeks ago you were there when the National Assembly, to crack down on worker-initiated violence, passed the Le Chapelier law, which outlawed workers' associations. Paris is hot, dry, and about to burst into flames. Will the cloud of dust soon become a cloud of smoke?

Was this the sort of anarchic world that Thomas Hobbes, the English philosopher, envisioned when people lack the restraint of government? Hobbes held that human beings are mere brutes who, if left to their own devices, will run amok. For their own good, people make a deal—a contract of sorts—with a strongman. He and his soldiers provide people with security; and they provide him with loyal support and money. That strongman evolves into a hereditary monarchy, which is everywhere the way of the world. In exchanging their liberty for security, people get the better of the deal, or so Hobbes claimed.

As you survey the scuffle below, you wonder if he was right. Yours is a different century, and perhaps a more enlightened one. Jean-Jacques Rousseau was its prophet. Rousseau, who was alive when you were a child, declared that Hobbes was wrong. Human beings are naturally inclined to goodness. If men nowadays act like brutes, it is because repressive human institutions—many of them formed by tyrants—have made them so. In the *Social Contract,* Rousseau suggested that human beings could attain a society that was at once free and just if they would only be willing to join together in selfless pursuit of the common good. On Friday evenings you sometimes go to the club with the funny name Cercle Social to hear a sermon by a patriotic priest on a chapter from Rousseau's tract.

And you resolve to read another book. It is by Edmund Burke, a famous member of the English Parliament who established a career as a liberal by opposing British tyranny against the Irish and the American colonists. Just six months ago, however, he published a book denouncing the French revolution, called *Reflections on the Revolution in France*. Your English is not strong, but you were unsettled by his blistering indictment of the National Assembly and the revolution they have wrought. He called the National Assembly a bunch of crooks who stole land from the Church. That's what happens, he added, when a bunch of lawyers, filled with foolish notions by the *philosophes*, try to invent a government from scratch. History, he wrote of revolutionary France, is about to enter a new and terrifying era.

The radicals hope to build a new France, free of the oppression of the *ancien régime*. And the conservatives maintain that the revolution is pushing France over a cliff into an unfathomed oblivion. Nearly everyone agrees, however, that France—and perhaps all humanity—approaches a crossroad.

The cloud is now in the next block, but the nearby buildings block your view. Two days ago you had witnessed another procession along nearly that street. It was supposed to be the Corpus Christi parade, led by the local parish, but it took on a political tone. People from various political clubs marched together, arms linked, singing songs. You worried that it would erupt in violence, but when the processions from parishes throughout Paris converged on the Place Vendome, just beyond the King's Riding Stables, the marchers were greeted by Lafayette and the National Guard. Lafayette allowed the leaders to submit a petition, signed by 30,000, calling on the National Assembly to ferret out conspirators against the nation.

The National Guardsmen have taken up positions along the street. They hold their guns pointed downward, an expression of disrespect for the King. Several people run down the street, toward your building.

"No cheers! No catcalls! Nothing!"

The crowd becomes still. As the carriage rounds the corner, it approaches slowly, and passes in silence.

You can make out some faces inside, mostly men. The King must be there, but you cannot see him. One woman stares straight ahead: the Queen, surely, but you can scarcely recognize her. Her hair has turned grey, it seems, almost overnight. A young child leans against her shoulder. Perhaps it is the dauphin, Louis XVI's successor.

What, you wonder, is to become of the boy? Of yourself? Of France? Always more questions.

A shudder runs through you when you realize that, beginning tomorrow, you—and the National Assembly—must answer them.

Historical Context

NOW: PARIS, 1791

The place: Paris. The time: June 26, 1791. Few people have ever lived, as you do, amidst such earth-shattering changes. You are likely a member of the National Assembly. [In history, the National Assembly had by now been identified as the Constituent Assembly, because its chief duty was to make a constitution; to simplify matters, the game retains the name, National Assembly.] As a delegate to the National Assembly, you may be a Jacobin, on the radical Left; or, on the Right, a nobleman or a Catholic clergyman; or perhaps you have recently abandoned the Jacobins to form the moderate faction, the Feuillants (Feh-YAHHN); or perhaps you are King Louis XVI, confined to your palace at the Tuileries; perhaps you are Lafayette, hero of the American Revolution and now a leading figure of the new government; or perhaps you are a leader, male or female, of the Parisian poor and thus one who possesses, some say, more power than even the King or Lafayette. Whatever your role, your words and actions will forever change the course of human affairs, not just in France but throughout the world.

Yesterday King Louis XVI, who five days earlier had disappeared from his palace, has just been returned to Paris, having been located—or apprehended—at the village of Varennes, near the northeastern border of France. Rumors abound as to the circumstances of his departure, or abduction. The issue has profound constitutional implications. Over the past twelve months, a majority in the National Assembly has been forming in support of a constitutional monarchy; the draft of the existing constitution [its key provisions are included in Appendix A] retains the monarch, but sharply curtails his powers. Aside from his traditional role as the military commander-in-chief, his chief remaining power is the "suspensive veto"—the ability to veto a law passed by the National Assembly for a period of up to six years. But the departure of King Louis XVI, who had repeatedly affirmed his support of the moderate revolution and the reforms it accomplished, calls into question the viability of this constitution. If this constitution is rejected, what is to replace it? A few radicals, especially among the leaders of the clubs, demand the elimination of the monarchy, and they are increasingly supported by the far-Left faction in the National Assembly known as the Jacobins. And then there are the parties of the Right, chiefly consisting of Catholic clergy and the nobility; they may seek to repeal the revolutionary acts and decisions of the past two years.

For some time prior to the King's departure, preparations have been underway for the second anniversary of what nearly all agree were some of the most momentous events in the history of man: the Fall of the Bastille—July 14, 1789—an astonishing insurrection that precipitated the collapse of a system of government, and of a way of life, that had endured for countless centuries. The pace of events swept passed so quickly that now the sequence is unclear in your own mind. You must think hard to put it back in its proper order. But the story goes something like this.

INTELLECTUAL ORIGINS OF THE REVOLUTION, AND THE AMERICAN EXAMPLE

For as long as you can recall, France has been troubled by episodic bread riots in Paris and occasional flare-ups of violence in the countryside; the extraordinary happenings of the past two years represent a wild escalation of earlier disturbances.

You recall the foreshadowings: One was the brutal winter of 1788, when the Seine froze past Le Havre, canals throughout France were locked in ice, and grain shipments could not make it to Paris. The price of bread doubled, and many went hungry. Artisanal workshops, deprived of cloth and leather to make garments and sew shoes and of wood for furniture and construction, closed down for several months. Workers were thrown out on the streets. Peasants, who comprised some 20 million of the nation's total population of 25 million, worked nearly always in poverty. In lean seasons, some starved. But had it not always been thus?

New ideas, though, were in the air. Most had germinated when you were young and have since been carried by the winds of change throughout France, and even abroad: Voltaire's witty scorn for organized religion and feudal institutions [for example, *Candide* (1759)]; the advance of science and knowledge, most obviously manifested in Diderot's multi-volume *Encyclopédie* (1751-1772); and especially the profound iconoclasm of Jean-Jacques Rousseau, whose two great works, *The Social Contract* and *Emile*, both published in 1762, illuminated a utopian vision, and provided hints on how to attain it. Books such as these got people talking, and changed the way they looked at things. Some imagined that the world could be different, and far better, and such thoughts were exciting and unsettling. What a different world would look like, no one could say for sure.

Then, amidst these inchoate musings, a remarkable story unfolded on the other side of the Atlantic. In 1776 you watched with fascination as the upstart American colonists took up arms against the British empire, France's traditional and formidable foe. Your interest turned to delight in 1777 when, against all odds, plucky American volunteers defeated the British redcoats at Saratoga, in the swampy wilds of a place called New York. You applauded King Louis XVI's subsequent decision to send money and later ships and troops to aid the American insurgents. When the French fleet in 1781 trapped the English army on a peninsula in Virginia and forced it to surrender, you cheered lustily.

In recent years, you have been impressed with how the leaders of that untamed and crude land in the Americas have devised a new "democratic" form of government whose principles are embedded in a Constitution (1787). You recall reading somewhere that the last state had ratified that Constitution, and thus it would go into effect. Would it work?

The example of the Americans has helped inspire your own labors as a member of the National Assembly, which for the past two years has been drafting a constitution for France. But unlike the Americans, who have been erecting a new government in a trackless wilderness of America, the National Assembly of France is attempting to reshape a political and social system—*the ancien régime*—whose foundations were laid in stone many centuries ago. And therein lies the problem: although most agree that the ancien régime has its faults, some now seek to preserve the architectural essentials of that system; others seek to retain its basic structure but add many new rooms; and still others seek to burn down the entire edifice, pulverize the foundation, and build something entirely new.

The Americans are relevant to your current labors for yet another reason. The cost of supporting the American Revolution—over one billion livres—bankrupted the treasury of King Louis XVI. Four years' ago, even before the horrible winter of 1788, he called on the noblemen of France (Assembly of Notables) to accept higher taxes; they refused, citing the fact that their obligations and relations to the monarch had long been fixed. Desperate for the revenue that could only be generated by new taxes, Louis in 1789 summoned the Estates-General, an ancient three-tiered institution that embodied the major constituent elements of the ancien régime: the First "estate" consisted of representatives of the Catholic Church (cardinals, bishops, monks, and priests); the Second "estate," of the nobility; and the Third "estate," the remainder of the French people. The Estates-General had not met since 1614, and its legal function and procedures were unclear.

THE ANCIEN RÉGIME: *PRIVILEGES AND RECIPROCITY*

To the King and his advisers, the principle was simple: France was a prosperous country but its government was insolvent. New taxes had to be raised from people who preferred not to pay. The King could not simply impose new taxes and demand that they be paid. For all of the descriptions of the French monarchy as absolutist, the reality was much more complicated. The King reposed at the center of a web of interdependent relations, each party being bound by oaths of obligation and mutual responsibilities. Each group won from the king special privileges (literally the word privilege means private law); in turn, the privileged groups acknowledged the king as the source of all legitimate privileges. For example:

King and Church

Louis XVI received his crown during a coronation at the cathedral in Rheims. He then took a vow to protect the Catholic Church. He even agreed to "extirpate heretics" (i.e., Protestants). The Catholic Church, for its part, anointed him with sacred oil, which had been supplied to King Clovis by a dove sent from heaven. The Catholic Church thus acquired special privileges: Though it owned about a tenth of the arable land of France, it was exempt from the two main land taxes— the *taille* and the *vingtième*. The Catholic Church was also the only legal church in the realm. The King received from the Church the moral legitimacy for his powers; and the Church, whose credit sources were superb, often loaned money to the king's treasury. The Church had acquired from the King its own legitimacy as a public agency: Insofar as the children of France were educated, it was at schools run by the Catholic Church; the Church also operated the nation's poor-relief system and its hospitals;

King and Nobility

The monarchy existed in a similarly mutual relationship with the nobility. In ancient times, the king made permanent grants of land to those soldiers and magnates who had served him best. They promised the monarch their continued military protection and loyalty, and he extended them special privileges: freedom from corporal punishment and also from land taxes; the right to be tried by special courts; and the right to impose certain taxes on the peoples who worked the noblemen's lands. Over time, the genealogies of the hereditary nobility became confused and sometimes lost. During the past century, thousands of commoners (those lacking noble birth) who had acquired wealth in finance or trading, attained noble rank through military service in the officer corps, or they acquired noble title and rights by paying for positions in various local *parlements* (Nobility of the Robe). Some of these "new" nobility merely desired the distinction of noble rank, while others bought noble positions to make money from the customary fees paid by peasants and others. In any case, nobility was a legal privilege whose rights could not be terminated by monarchical fiat. The nobility were entitled to rights they held by tradition or for which they had paid good money, or so they believed;

King and Guilds and Universities

The monarchy had, for hundreds of years, extended special privileges to guilds which organized and supervised various crafts, ranging from the huge silk workers' guild of Lyons (which had 60,000 members) to the smaller guilds, such as stone-masons, furniture-makers, bakers, and the like. The monarch conferred on the guilds the authority to supervise their trades, and in return the monarch imposed certain licensing fees and taxes. A similar arrangement governed the monarch's relations with the universities. Many activities, and nearly all involving skilled labor, were subject to royal regulations and fees, and the guilds received in return the right to exclude non-guild members from practicing such tasks and trades.

King and the Cities

The monarchy had also long exempted urban dwellers from the usual land tax, the *taille*. City dwellers were obliged to pay some special taxes and fees, but in the main they were commonly exempted from many of the older feudal obligations derived from a mostly agricultural economy;

King and the Royal Chartered Companies

The King also granted trading monopolies to certain companies, usually in return for payments made to the treasury.

Thus in the late 1780s, when confronted by a need to seek broad new sources of revenues, Louis XVI was obliged to call together "all" of France, as embodied in the traditional assemblage of its constituent elements: the three "estates." He preferred to conceive of France as a constellation of discrete bodies, each of whose orbit was regulated by the monarchy.

CONVENING THE ESTATES-GENERAL (MAY 1789)

After a complicated electoral process, conducted for each estate at the provincial level (see, for example, the section on "Lafayette"), the delegates convened at Versailles in May 1789. It was a memorable spectacle: the clergy processing in their vestments, the nobility in silk breeches, with gilt swords, gold waistcoats, and white-plumed hats; and the Third Estate following in sober plain black. But trouble surfaced over how the Estates-General would conduct their deliberations. The King had assumed that the estates would meet separately, and that each estate's collective voice would count as one; this ensured that on any matter on which a majority of the First and Second Estate were in agreement, the Third Estate would be outvoted, two to one. King Louis XVI's real task, he imagined, was to find a common ground between the first two estates.

But some prominent figures in the Third Estate, and even some in the First and Second as well, disputed this arrangement. In *What is the Third Estate?* the Abbé Sieyès [see-YEHZ] answered his own question with an extraordinary declaration: the Third Estate was "everything." The First and Second Estates represented small privileged interests at odds with the French people; only the Third Estate, Sieyès declared, represented the will of the nation. [See Censer and Hunt, http://www.chnm.gmu.edu/revolution/.]

The members of the Third Estate agreed from the outset not to conduct any votes or deliberations unless they met with the other estates and voted collectively, by head. Insofar as the delegates of the Third Estate more than equaled the combined First and Second Estates, and insofar as some members of the clergy and nobility sided with the Third Estate, this ensured that the Third Estate would control the proceedings. The First Estate voted, 188 to 46, to continue to meet separately, as did the nobility, the latter by a surprisingly close vote of 133 to 114. Subsequent negotiations among the estates for a collective meeting dragged on, with no resolution in sight. On June 10 the Third Estate voted, 493 to 41, to constitute itself as the sole collective deliberative body of France. Several days later, a handful of parish priests, delegates of the First Estate presented themselves for admission to the Third, amidst jubilant cries of approval. Two days later sixteen more clerical delegates slipped over to the Third. Then, by a scant majority, the First Estate voted to join with the Third.

No longer merely the Third Estate, that group declared itself to be the National Assembly, much as Sieyès had proposed earlier. Some members of the Assembly declared a moratorium on tax collection until the Assembly had authorized such payments.

The claims of the National Assembly unsettled the monarchy. You well recall the rumors back then that the King had deployed tens of thousands of troops in and about Paris and Versailles: even then the King's firebrand younger brother, the Comte d'Artois [cohn-dahr-twa], and the King's Austrian wife, Marie Antoinette, made no secret of their disdain for the changes that were sweeping France. Rumors of a royalist crackdown were seemingly confirmed when a royal edict ordered that the chambers of the National Assembly be locked.

Rumor had it that thousands of peasants, starving and armed with pikes, were moving into the outskirts, clamoring for food and preparing to attack. Within Paris, too, some sections were ready to explode, as high food prices and bread lines maddened thousands. In the evenings, throngs of poor gathered in the parks of Paris and listened to the speeches of radicals: Georges-Jacques Danton [dahn-tohn], a king's court lawyer with a voice that bellowed fury; Camille Desmoulins [day-moo-lawn], who stuttered in conversation but spoke flawlessly while addressing a multitude; and, more recently, Dr. Jean-Paul Marat, radical editor of *The People's Friend.*

Many expected the king's army to move into Paris at any moment, perhaps to protect the city from ruffians or perhaps to crush the National Assembly.

THE TENNIS COURT OATH (JUNE 20, 1789)

You were perhaps among those delegates of the National Assembly who proceeded to a nearby tennis court where you vowed not to disperse until "the constitution of the Realm and public regeneration are established and assured." Then, some 47 nobility joined. The "National" Assembly could now fairly claim to embody a substantial proportion of the traditional "Estates." Finally, the King appeared before the Assembly and proposed concessions on taxation. But what the King gave, he also seemed to withhold: if the "National Assembly" passed any legislation abrogating existing rights of the clergy or the nobility, either body could veto it; moreover, the King asserted a right to veto any action of the Assembly, a threat punctuated by the presence of thousands of soldiers outside. When the King subsequently dismissed Necker, a popular reformist minister of finance, rumors swept Paris: that the Comte d'Artois was organizing an army to march on the Assembly; that royalists were withholding bread so as to provoke riots that would bring about the downfall of the National Assembly; and that the Queen was fornicating with beasts and king's ministers alike. Concerned about anarchical violence breaking out in the city, the King ordered several thousand troops to surround Paris, included his feared Swiss and German mercenaries.

Then, on July 12 Desmoulins, standing on a table outside the Café de Foy, gave a speech that started the revolution. He concluded, "Tonight all the Swiss and German battalions will move from the Champ-de-Mars [a field in Paris] to cut our throats. We have only one recourse left—to take up arms!"

Riots erupted in one district after another and turned bloody. Sometimes mobs rampaged through the streets, threatening the houses of the rich and slaughtering aristocrats, clergy, and others. More than a few rowdy groups broke into gunsmiths' or sword-cutlers' shops. The royal officials of the city proved powerless to deal with the unrest, and another group increasingly filled the void and asserted the right to do so. These were the Electors for Paris, the lawyers, doctors, merchants and a few others who had been elected to choose delegates for the Third Estate. The Electors met at the Hôtel de Ville and formed an unofficial Permanent Committee to manage the affairs of the city. Similar groups were popping up in cities, towns, and villages throughout France. One of the first acts of the Permanent Committee of Paris was to call on the people to serve in a citizens' militia to restore order (and to protect the National Assembly and Paris from the king's troops). Most of the Electors, themselves prominent citizens, further decided that only those who had paid property taxes equal to three days' work would be eligible for this new military body. The Permanent Committee did not want to give the rabble more weapons.

THE FIRST JOURNÉE: THE FALL OF THE BASTILLE (JULY 14, 1789)

Fears of the expected, and long rumored, royal onslaught provoked several vividly memorable *journées* ("days" [JHOOR-NAY). No one can forget the first. The sky was overcast, with a cold morning rain. Six royalist regiments from the eastern frontier had arrived on the outskirts of Paris, and then came another ten mercenary divisions. Here, it seemed, was the long-awaited royalist attack on the Hôtel de Ville, aimed to oust the Permanent Committee and doubtless proceed to Versailles to arrest the delegates of the National Assembly. Paris was swept by panic.

In nearly every neighborhood of Paris, crowds had seized the most prominent places— the churches. Now bells throughout the city tolled, attracting tens of thousands. At the Church of the Couvent des Cordeliers, Danton climbed upon a table and shouted above the din:

> Citizens! Let us arm ourselves! Let us arm ourselves to repel the 15,000 brigands assembled in Montmartre, and the 30,000 military who are ready to descend on Paris, to loot the city and slaughter its inhabitants!. . . The sovereign people is rising against despotism!

A crowd of volunteers surged forward and soon the Battalion des Cordeliers had nearly 600 men. This group, joined by others from many other districts, moved toward the Hôtel de Ville. There the Permanent Committee called on the assembled groups to barricade the streets of Paris with carriages, carts, and furniture. It also instructed soldiers of the king's troops—especially the French Guard—to desert and report for service with the citizens' militia, which was taking defensive positions behind the barricades at the Hôtel de Ville. Within an hour, tens of thousands of Parisians had gathered there and began digging ditches in front of the barricades and fashioning weapons from iron grates and wooden posts. Few imagined that such weapons would repel the trained and well-armed soldiers of the King.

Some realized that firearms were kept at the soldiers' hospital, the *Invalides*, and within several hours some 40,000 people had surged onto its parade grounds. The Governor of the Invalides ordered his men to dismantle its cache of weapons—they refused—while he tried to buy time by negotiating with representatives of the mob. Finally, the mob pushed through the gates and clambered across the moat. The guards walked away from their cannon. (Royal officers commanding the troops refused to march their men from the barracks, because they feared that their men would more likely join the rioters than fire on them.) The crowd surged through the Invalides, gathering up some 28,000 muskets. But they found few cartridges and little gunpowder.

"There's gunpowder at the Bastille," someone shouted, and the crowd moved. Within minutes the huge assemblage, by now perhaps 60,000, brandishing muskets and pikes and clubs, was streaming toward the Faubourg Saint-Antoine. As the crowd passed through Saint-Antoine, one of the poorest neighborhoods of Paris, more people joined in. Then the torrent spilled toward the Bastille. Once a formidable fortress, with eight round towers and stone walls eight feet thick and eighty feet high, the Bastille had become an unimportant prison that held a handful of prisoners. Yet it had once imprisoned Voltaire and many regarded it as a symbol of the worst excesses of the ancien régime. And, as had been rumored, the Bastille held hundreds of barrels of gunpowder.

The Governor of the Bastille, the Marquis de Launay, had feared an attack such as this, for in recent weeks many of his soldiers had deserted. As the mob approached the Bastille, de Launay raised the drawbridges, ordered the cannon loaded, and prepared to drop tons of paving stones upon the besiegers. A delegation from the Permanent Committee arranged to meet with de Launay, who obligingly served them a meal. He also instructed his men to withdraw the cannon from the walls, lest they provoke the crowd. But he refused to surrender the king's fortress. When the cannon were pulled back from the walls, however, the crowd outside assumed that this was preparatory to their being fired. Tens of thousand of people surged over the moat and into the courtyard. Then the shooting began, and paving stones were hurled from the battlements. The citizens' militia fired back and some regular soldiers, defectors from the king's army, managed to bring cannon from the Invalides right up to the drawbridge doors. At this point, de Launay surrendered. When the doors opened, the mob went on a frenzy, slaughtering the defenders. Within minutes the heads of de Launay and his second-in-command had been stuck upon pikes, and were brandished on the celebratory procession back to the Hôtel de Ville.

Later that evening, the Permanent Committee voted to demolish the Bastille, stone by stone. The King, who had been hunting and retired early, was awakened with news of the fall of the Bastille. "Is this a rebellion?" he asked. "No," responded the Duc de La Rouchefoucauld-Liancourt. "It is a revolution." The King then sent word to the Third Estate: he would withdraw all of his troops from Paris. The National Assembly was saved.

THE FOURTH OF AUGUST DECREES (1789)

The National Assembly, still in Versailles, applauded the King's decision, as did the Permanent Committee in Paris, which decided to constitute itself more formally as the Commune of Paris. Bailly, head of the Permanent Committee, was elected Mayor of Paris and Lafayette was elected commander general of the citizens' militia, which he renamed the National Guard of Paris. Its uniforms were originally to include a cockade, to be attached to their hats, in red and blue, the colors of Paris; but Lafayette added white, the color of Louis XVI, forming the revolutionary tricolor: red, white, and blue.

The good will did not last. Louis refused to bring back the popular Necker. On July 16, the King met with his Ministers, the Queen, and his brothers; what transpired there is still debated in Paris. Rumor had it that the Comte d'Artois, a firebrand, wanted to order the royalist armies against the Commune and then against the National Assembly. The Queen evidently suggested that the royal family withdraw from Versailles to Metz, a military fortress in the northeastern frontier. When the War Minister doubted that the King's soldiers would protect him during a departure to Metz, Louis decided to ride out the storm in Versailles. What is beyond doubt is the fact that the National Assembly, working several blocks away in Versailles, began to write a constitution (the work that you seek to finish within the next few months).

The situation back in July 1789 was monumentally confused (as it remains today). The King was monarch. Sometimes government officials did as he commanded and sometimes not. Sometimes, and in some places, the King's intendants and his army officers and police authorities were in control. At other times and places, ad hoc municipal communes possessed power, backed by the local National Guard. In some districts of Paris, armed bands were in effective control. The National Assembly voted "decrees" that many assumed had the force of law; others disagreed.

In August, bread prices crept higher, straining the meager resources of the working poor. Townspeople claimed that farmers and millers were withholding grain, hoping for further price increases. Many demanded the return of Necker. Then came more violence. Groups of sans-culottes attacked and burned the government posts on the bridges along the Seine, where taxes were imposed on incoming shipments of grain. In other parts of Paris, especially the poorer districts, or sections, people rioted against royal and municipal authorities alike.

Elsewhere in France, similar groups rose up, almost as if in imitation of what was transpiring in Paris. At Troyes, a mob seized and killed the mayor. At Rennes, the royal garrison deserted. In Marsailles, armed citizens disbanded the royal garrison. Food stores and prisons were stormed and looted. In many places, the King's chief officials—the intendants—simply disappeared. Arsenals were seized and customs duties withheld, and gangs of beggars roamed the countryside.

Rural folk worried that hungry and heavily armed sans-culottes from the urban slums would flock to the countryside in search of food. And town dwellers imagined that hungry peasants would flood into the cities or would turn against the revolutionaries. Royal officials nearly everywhere were in danger: Some were murdered and decapitated, their heads placed upon pikes as a warning to others.

A paroxysm of terror seized the countryside; what set it off, no one can say for sure. But in hundreds, perhaps thousands, of villages, peasants invaded the manor houses and castles of the nobility, destroying the books on which their age-old feudal dues and obligations were recorded. Others swarmed into church abbeys and monasteries, again destroying tithing books and records. Generally these were focused attacks of sabotage against property; relatively few people were killed.

Then on the Fourth of August, the National Assembly witnessed an orgy of selflessness, wholly unprecedented in French history, and perhaps in human affairs. It all began when the Duc d'Aiguillon, the wealthiest landowner in all France, with annual income from feudal dues of some 100,000 livres, proposed that the aristocracy renounce **all** feudal obligations (and thus much of its income)! Others seconded the motion and suddenly, almost before anyone could catch their breath, the National Assembly passed a decree ending feudal obligations to the nobility. The delegates had no sooner taken their seats when several church prelates proposed that the Catholic Church renounce **its** feudal dues, too. After brief debate, this passed the Assembly. In a few short minutes, the chief representatives of the feudal regime had eliminated feudalism. Delegates, some of whom had voted away their own income, wept with joy. "What a nation!" another declared. While the National Assembly would soon step back from the radical nature of the proposal, in many cases compensating noblemen with money for the loss of their privileges, "feudalism" was never again restored in France.

Later that month, the National Assembly passed the Declaration of the Rights of Man and Citizen, a set of principles that were to supersede the ancient notion that all political rights were a monarchical privilege; the Declaration insisted that all men possessed rights as citizens from birth. Perhaps most important for current events, the Declaration enshrined in law what had become since 1788 an unusually free freedom of the press. Almost overnight, scores of news sheets appeared in Paris, more than 400 in 1789 alone. Desmoulins now found his calling: as editor of a revolutionary broadsheet, first called the *Courrier of Brabant*, whose title was an obscure reference to the insurrection of a Belgian province. Then came the violent and even scatological rhetoric of Marat's journal, *L'Ami du Peuple* [The People's Friend].

THE JOURNÉE OF THE MARKET-WOMEN (OCTOBER 5, 1789)

Meanwhile, the King refused to accept either the Fourth of August Decrees or the Declaration of the Rights of Man and Citizen. He maintained that such measures violated long-standing rights and obligations among the First and Second Estates. His obduracy was seemingly punctuated by an intensification of the bread crisis, which resulted in long lines and riots. On October 5, huge crowds of women at the central markets in the Faubourg Saint-Antoine began shouting for bread. Then bells were rung at the nearby Sainte-Marguerite church, and some 6,000 women—fishwives, market stall-keepers, prostitutes, and even well-dressed *bourgeois*—marched toward the Hôtel de Ville, where the Mayor and the leaders of the Paris Commune were attempting to administer the city. The women crowded around the National Guards, taunting, teasing, cajoling, and eventually disarming them. The women swarmed up the stairs and charged into the municipal offices, flinging papers and demanding bread. At the desperate insistence of the officials of the Commune, they agreed to leave. "On to Versailles," one woman cried and the others took up the chant.

Then ensued one of the most remarkable spectacles of the entire Revolution: Thousands of women pouring through the crowded streets of Paris, heading for Versailles, twelve miles away, to the palace of the King and the halls of the National Assembly. Along the way, they gathered up more women, and plenty of men, too. The throng bristled with muskets, swords, pikes, crowbars, bludgeons. The march took all day. When they arrived at Versailles, the palace shone brilliantly in the setting sun.

Mounted officials—of the Commune and of the monarch—had raced ahead to warn the King, who hastily conferred with his ministers. Many counseled him to flee Versailles; but Necker, returned to office, urged him to stay. Again, the King's officers were not sure that their military escort could be trusted to take him to safety.

As the mob of market-women approached the courtyard, the Bishop of Langres shouted, "Order! Order!"

"We don't give a fuck for order," one woman declared. "We want bread!"

The King reluctantly agreed to meet with a delegation and it was ushered into the palace. He told them that he would gather up all the bread at Versailles and distribute it to the group outside. Mollified, these delegates reported the King's proposal to the assemblage outside, but some denounced it. Probably they were agents of the Duc d'Orléans, a cousin of the King whom many thought to be exploiting the revolution to enhance his own monarchical claims. The women remained in the courtyard, shouting and chanting, while the troops who constituted the King's bodyguards, many of them Swiss mercenaries, watched with alarm as the shadows of the palace lengthened into evening.

Meanwhile, in Paris, contingents of the National Guard had been pressuring Lafayette, their commander, to join the procession of the market women. Lafayette feared that his untested and untrained men might themselves attack the King's palace, and for several hours he extemporized. Finally, when it became clear that many of his men would leave even without their commander, he agreed to march to Versailles. They arrived before midnight, some 20,000 strong. The market-women, who were finding whatever shelter they could, cheered.

Alarmed by this new threat, the King again considered flight; but instead he received Lafayette, who explained that he was not fully in control of his men. Outside the shouting recommenced. Lafayette, and some of the King's ministers, urged the King now to declare his acceptance of the Fourth of August decrees and the Declaration of the Rights of Man and Citizen. At two in the morning, the King wearily assented to these demands. Lafayette went to the balcony, managed to quiet the multitude, illuminated by torchlight, and announced the King's concessions. He then made arrangements for the National Guard to protect the palace and proposed that the King's mercenaries withdraw, less their presence provoke the mob. The King agreed. Exhaustion took over, as people milled about and slept as best they could.

But before sunrise, some of the mob sneaked through an unattended gate and raced into the palace, seeking to kill Marie Antoinette. They slaughtered some of her bodyguards, whose screams alerted the Queen. She dashed through a secret passageway to the King's rooms. Lafayette raced to the palace with his most trusted men and managed to save the King and Queen and evict the intruders. But the shots and screams had alarmed the multitude outside, which began to riot. "The King to Paris!" they shouted. Lafayette stepped upon a balcony and attempted to address the people, but they shouted him down and demanded to see the King. The King obligingly appeared, as did the Queen, who serenely gazed on the churning mob below, many of whom taunted her with obscenities and demanded her death. Some raised muskets and took aim. Then came Lafayette's famous gesture, which people talked about for weeks: He saluted the crowd, bowed to the Queen, took her hand, and kissed it. This stunned nearly everyone into silence, and then came some cheers. Finally, the King announced that he and the royal family would immediately return to Paris. The crowd roared its approval.

Lafayette made the best of this impromptu drama. As fearful palace officials crowded together close to the King (and especially to Lafayette's troops), Lafayette hastily arranged a procession. Lafayette and the National Guard surrounded the carriages of the King and his retainers, and these were followed by wagonloads of flour from the palace, and, last, by the market-women. When they arrived at the outskirts of Paris, 60,000 strong, the Mayor made a nervous welcoming speech, and the haggard King managed some suitable responses. Finally the King and Queen were established in the old palace called the Tuileries [TWEE-luhr-ee]. National Guardsmen patrolled the premises, though it was unclear whether their function was to keep the mob out, or the King in.

DRAFTING THE CONSTITUTION AND THE DECLARATION OF THE RIGHTS OF MAN AND CITIZEN

You were perhaps among the National Assembly when it followed the King, leaving Versailles and reconvening in Paris, meeting in what had been the King's Riding Stables at the Tuileries. And you began, in earnest, the work you hope to finish in the next few months: France's constitution [The Constitution of 1791, most of which appears in Appendix A].

You are well aware of the main provisions **as they currently stand,** though nothing has yet been finally approved. The National Assembly's task is complicated by the fact that in addition to writing a constitution, it must also deal with problems of the moment. The government must raise money, ensure public order and services, and otherwise fill the void caused by the paralysis of the bureaucracy of the royal government. Moreover, the National Assembly has necessarily held that some provisions of the constitution, when approved by the National Assembly and signed by the King, have the force of law right now, even before the entire constitution has been passed. As a member of the National Assembly, you may choose to change, modify, or eliminate these provisions or add new ones entirely.

The Constitution in fact consists of two documents, the Declaration of the Rights of Man and Citizen and the Constitution itself.

Declaration of the Rights of Man and Citizen [Summary]

This document, approved by the National Assembly on August 26, 1789, outlines the basic principles on which the constitution is to be based.

Its main provisions are as follows:

> Article 1. Men are "born free and equal in rights," with social distinctions based "only upon public utility." This marks a sharp rupture with the ancien régime's notion of society as an aggregation of separate orders (estates, guilds, municipalities, corporations, etc.) each possessing special duties, rights, and privileges.
>
> Article 2. Political associations exist to promote the rights of man, those being enumerated as, "liberty, property, security, and resistance to oppression." This entitles people to come and go as they choose and to own the property they possess. [A complication here concerns the "right to property": Does this include property, such as the estates of the nobility, that some regard as institutionalized repression? Does the right to resist "oppression" entitle someone to attack a tax collector?]
>
> Article 3. Sovereignty resides in the Nation, which confers political rights. The Nation may choose to confer special rights upon a monarch [as in the current draft of the constitution]. It cannot be the other way around.

Article 6. Law is the expression of the general will. [Although much of the Declaration is derived from principles outlined in the writings of Rousseau, especially his *Social Contract*, this article is the most obvious manifestation of Rousseau's centrality to the Declaration. This article helps identify the Nation with law (i.e., a constitution) and further declares that the Nation emerges from the "general will" of the citizens. The use of the term "general will," echoing Rousseau's term, implies the disinterested, virtuous action of the people. In Rousseau's view, the selfish will of a majority of citizens is what he calls, "the will of all." That is not the same as the "general will," which emerges only when citizens acts disinterestedly, heeding only of the needs of the polity. The implication here is that a citizen is a citizen only when being virtuous. The general will is the collective will of the virtuous citizenry.]

Article 7. Those members of a Nation who resist or oppose its law (i.e., the virtuous "general will" of the Nation) are guilty of a political crime that warrants punishment.

Articles 8-9. Those charged with a crime should receive due process, and punishments should not be excessive.

Articles 10-11. Freedom of worship and speech is a right of all citizens, "provided their manifestation does not derange the public order established by law." [The freedom of worship is something of a dig at the Catholic Church, which had campaigned, sometimes successfully, to outlaw Protestant worship. Some of those in England who embraced the French revolution did so because it weakened the power of the Catholic Church.]

Article 13. Taxes are to be apportioned "equally" and "according to the means" of citizens. No longer will privileged orders receive preferential tax treatment (as with the clergy and nobility and special corporations).

Article 15. People have the right to demand an accounting of public officials, and even to charge them with crimes. [Officials serve the people; it cannot be the other way around.]

Article 16. "Any society in which the guarantee of the rights is not secured, or the separation of powers not determined, has no constitution at all." [This echoes Montesquieu's famous writings on the need for a separation of powers between the judicial, executive, and legislative branches; it suggests, further, a constitutional structure akin to the tripartite structure of the recent American Constitution. On the other hand, this article exists in considerable tension with those articles that locate sovereignty within the Nation and define the Nation in terms of the general will of the people as a whole, which implies the supremacy of the legislature over all other branches of government.]

Article 17. Reinforces the "property" clause (Article 2) by defining property as "a sacred and inviolable right." "No one can be deprived of it, unless a legally established public necessity evidently demands it, under the condition of a just and prior indemnity."

Having passed the "Declaration," the delegates proceeded to begin deliberations on the constitution, still unfinished.

Special Issues: What of the Rights of Women?

One subject ignored by the Assembly but intensely debated in some important Paris clubs was the extent to which women would have full civic rights under the constitution. Despite the obvious participation of women at critical moments such as the October Days, when their political contribution to freedom was beyond dispute, the all-male National Assembly had trouble envisioning a formal political role for women. Consequently, a burgeoning feminist movement was not hard to notice, especially in the capital. Perhaps you were at the Cercle Social club in December 1790, when Etta Palm rose to the podium to demand an end to "unjust laws which only accord us a secondary existence in society and which often force us into the humiliating necessity of winning over the cantankerous and ferocious character of a man." Perhaps your hometown was one of the sixty cities around the country that established Jacobin clubs specifically for women between 1789 and 1793. If so, the odds are that you agree with the radical left-wing journalist Louis Prudhomme, who commented in February 1781, perhaps in response to Palm's speech, "civil and political liberty is in a matter of speaking useless to women and in consequence must be foreign to them."

Special Issues: What of the Rights of Slaves in Caribbean Colonies of France?

Another issue is the political situation in France's highly lucrative Caribbean colonies. While it may seem obvious that the Declaration of the Rights of Man and Citizen contradict the legitimacy of slavery and the slave-trade, many colonists, including free persons of color, resist any plans to emancipate slaves. They argue that without slaves working the plantations, the colonial economy will collapse, throwing France itself into economic recession, and jeopardizing the revolution. Rather, as one of the moderate Jacobin leaders of the Assembly, Antoine Pierre Barnave, warned in March 1790, "the interest of the French nation" lies in "supporting its commerce" and favoring the prosperity of its colonies.

Early Debates on the Constitution [Summary]

Some issues have already been resolved, such as those subsumed by the Fourth of August Decrees (1789) renouncing feudal obligations and many traditional church prerogatives.

Such matters appear in the **introduction** to the constitution: "There is no longer nobility, nor peerage, nor hereditary distinctions, nor distinctions of orders, nor feudal regime, nor patrimonial jurisdictions, nor any titles, denominations, or prerogatives derived therefrom, nor any order of chivalry, nor any corporations or decorations, etc. . ."

Title I roots the constitution not in manmade institutions or traditions, but in "natural law," which transcends human agency. An assumption is that natural law, rather like Newton's laws of gravity, is bound up with the underlying principles of the cosmos. Because of "natural law," people possess "natural rights", including the liberty "to move about, to remain, and to depart without liability," and the liberty to "speak, to write, to print and publish," and so on, as in the Declaration of the Rights of Man and Citizen. Such rights, however, are subject to certain constraints. For example, citizens retain the freedom to meet "peaceably and without arms," but they are obliged to obey "the police laws." Similarly, the legislature cannot infringe on a citizen's natural rights, but it can "establish penalties against acts which. . . may be injurious to society." The constitution also reiterates the "inviolability of property." Education, too, is to become an obligation of the state, not of private charity or the Catholic Church.

Title II pertains to marriage, which ceases to have legal significance as a matter of the Catholic Church. That is, marriage is transformed into a civil contract, subject to laws set by the National Assembly. Couples can still choose to consecrate their relation through the rites of the Catholic Church, but that religious ceremony will have no **legal** significance.

Title III outlines the fundamental principle that sovereignty resides with the people of France as expressed in their legislature (the National Assembly). Thus the introduction of Title III explains, with Rousseau, that sovereignty is "one, indivisible, inalienable, and imprescriptible: it belongs to the nation: no section of the people nor any individual can attribute to himself the exercise thereof."

Title III. Chapter 1, "Of the Legislature" further explains that the legislature's power itself is not to be divided: [unlike the British legislature (House of Lords and House of Commons) or the American Congress (Senate and House of Representatives), the French legislature is to remain paramount, a true expression of the will of the French people. It will therefore consist of an "indivisible" unicameral (one body) legislature, re-elected every two years. This measure was hotly debated, but eventually passed by a vote of 499-89, with 122 abstentions.]

Title III. Chapter 2, "Of the Royalty" explains that the new government is nevertheless a constitutional monarchy. [The king's person is, like property, "inviolable"; and it is also "sacred." The king's authority derives from the constitution, and not the other way round. Whenever a new monarch is crowned, he or she is obliged to swear loyalty to the constitution. The king's lands are to be transferred to the nation, and the king is to be supported (given a salary from a "civil list") according to the dictates of the National Assembly.]

Title III. Chapter 3, "Of the Exercise of Legislative Power" gives the legislature the right to propose and enact laws, to set government revenues and budgets, and to declare war and ratify peace treaties. The monarch's relationship to all such matters is merely "suspensive": He can postpone implementation of legislation; he cannot kill it forever. [After protracted debate, the National Assembly voted 733 to 143 to grant the king a veto. There ensued a debate over the nature of the veto; finally, a smaller majority (673 for, 143 against) voted that the king's veto was merely "suspensive." That is, the king cannot initiate legislation but he can "veto" it (imposing his "royal sanction").] In that case, the measure does not become law until passed by two **subsequent** legislatures. Lastly, the king remains the head of executive matters—"the general administration of the kingdom"—and he is also the supreme head of the army and navy. But insofar as the budgets for all ministries are subject to approval by the legislature, the powers of the king and his ministers are sharply constrained.

THE DECREE ON CHURCH LANDS (NOVEMBER 1789)

One issue confronting the National Assembly on its return to Paris was the matter of the First Estate. About one-tenth of the land of France was owned by the various sections of the Catholic Church, which collected feudal dues and fees from those who worked its lands.

As the administrative functions of the King evaporated—intendants no longer reported for duty, most people ceased paying taxes, and tax collectors did not know to whom payments should be forwarded—the National Assembly assumed more administrative duties (as did local municipal governments). The most expensive of the costs of the National Assembly is the National Guard, which requires arms, uniforms, and sometimes pay. Money, too, had to be found to ensure an adequate food supply to prevent Paris from slipping into complete anarchy. The National Assembly happened upon the idea of issuing loans in small denominations, called *assignats*, which would be backed by the sale of church lands. This was first approved in November 1789; nine months later, the National Assembly decided to put all church lands up for sale. Without the income from the sale of church lands, the current government could not function.

When the National Assembly passed the Decree on Church lands, it also amended the working draft of the constitution, which in Title I had declared the "inviolability of property." The additional paragraph dealt with the expropriation of church lands: "Property intended for the expenses of worship and for all services of public utility belongs to the nation and is at all times at its disposal."

PASSING THE CIVIL CONSTITUTION OF THE CLERGY (JULY 1790)

This necessitated a complete restructuring of the government. The National Assembly therefore embarked upon a complete reorganization of the complicated overlapping religious, economic, juridical, feudal, and monarchical jurisdictions: France was now to be divided into 83 nearly uniform departments. All administration, clerical and otherwise, would conform to this geographical organization.

Moreover, lest the Catholic Church come to regard itself as separate from France and thus endanger the new government, the National Assembly decided to place the entire administration of the Catholic Church under the purview of the new state of France. To that end, the National Assembly proposed to nationalize the administration of the Church through the Civil Constitution of the Clergy [See Appendix A].

The issue proved to be even more divisive than the expropriation of church lands. Supporters of the Civil Constitution insisted, with Rousseau, that the sovereignty of the nation cannot be subdivided. The existence of the Catholic Church as a separate entity, possessing some state functions (charity, education) and obliging its leaders to swear allegiance to foreign powers (vows of ordination ultimately approved by the pope in Rome) meant that France could never cohere as a unified nation. Thus there was a need to subsume the administration of the Catholic Church, but not its spiritual beliefs or dogma, within the structure of the new French constitution. The defenders of the Catholic Church, many of them clerics or delegates from rural regions, declared that the Church must remain separate from the state.

The chief provisions of the Civil Constitution are as follows.

> Section A1. Reorganization of the Catholic Church to conform to the geographical subdivisions of the new French departments.

> Section A4. The prevention of high church officials—bishops and archbishops—from taking vows to any foreign power (i.e., the pope).

> Section B3. The election of bishops and priests by the people (rather than their being chosen by the church hierarchy), **subordinating even the clergy to popular sovereignty**.

> Section B21. Newly elected bishops must affirm, before their congregants and the lay people of the department (including government officials), their loyalty to "the nation, the law and the king, and to support with all [their] power the constitution decreed by the National Assembly and accepted by the king."

> Section C. The salaries for all clergy are to be fixed by the National Assembly, and paid by the national government. The clergy shall receive no other emoluments. [That is, the clergy are paid solely by the French government; they can receive no money from the Catholic Church itself.]

Almost exactly a year ago, on July 12, 1790, the National Assembly passed the Civil Constitution of the Clergy. The state now assumed operation of schools, hospitals, and charities; parish priests and all other Catholic clergy would be paid according to a fixed schedule by the national government.

After stalling for several months, in the fall last year (1790), Louis XVI signed the Civil Constitution of the Clergy. This, combined with the Decree on Church Lands, completely transformed the practice of religion and the role and functions of the Catholic Church in France.

OPPOSITION TO THE CIVIL CONSTITUTION OF THE CLERGY AND PASSAGE OF THE OBLIGATORY OATH (NOVEMBER 1790)

The Civil Constitution of the Clergy, even more than the seizure and sale of church lands, has precipitated considerable opposition, especially in rural provinces to the west of Paris and in the south of France. Many clergy have resigned and many parishes refuse to welcome the new "constitutional" clergy (those who accepted the Civil Constitution.) When such officials attempt to celebrate the mass or merely enter their cathedrals and churches, they are increasingly confronted with stony-eyed parishioners. Sometimes there are riots and fights, obliging the "constitutional" clergy to call on the forces of the revolutionary government—the local contingent of the National Guard—to restore order.

As religious opposition to the Civil Constitution of the Clergy threatened to become outright resistance to the revolution, the National Assembly passed an additional Section D to be appended to the Civil Constitution of the Clergy [See Appendix A]. Section D provides that all clergy must take an oath "to be faithful to the nation, to the law and to the king, and to maintain with all their power the constitution decreed by the National Assembly and accepted by the king." A failure to take the oath constitutes a *de facto* resignation, or so the law proclaims.

CONTINUED DEFIANCE OF THE CIVIL CONSTITUTION (1791)

The obligatory oath failed to silence opposition to the Civil Constitution of the Clergy. By the beginning of this year—January 1, 1791—only half of the clergy of France had taken the oath; even fewer of the highest church officials had done so. Mirabeau, a leading figure in the National Assembly until his untimely death a few weeks ago, warned that the Catholic clergy were spearheading opposition to the revolution, working in secret cabals and in concert with the pope.

The National Assembly attempted to force "refractory" (non-swearing or non-"constitutional") priests and clerics out of the new "civil" church, but this only intensified opposition at individual parishes. Some defenders of the traditional church support the radicals' harsh measures against the traditional Catholic Church because such measures will doom the revolution: "Let the decree pass; we need it. Two or three more like that and it will all be over," the Bishop Maury has said. Maury's predictions have born some fruit: In recent months, armed peasants, especially in Brittany and the Vendée, have been attacking constitutional clergy and hiding refractory priests.

ENCYCLICAL OF POPE PIUS VI: CHARITAS (APRIL 1791)

On April 13, 1791, just ten weeks ago, Pope Pius VI publicly denounced the Civil Constitution of the Clergy and rebuked King Louis XVI for signing the document. In a The Papal Bull CHARITAS, the pope flayed the National Assembly and ordered Catholic clergy to repudiate any vows taken or performed under its auspices. "Last year," the pontiff declared in the encyclical,

> we could scarcely credit the rumor . . . that the radical philosophers, joining forces and constituting the majority of the National Assembly in France, were stirring up feeling against the Catholic religion. . . In a letter dated 9 July, 1790, to Louis our son most dear in Christ, a most Christian King, we exhorted him again and again to refrain from confirming the Civil Constitution of the Clergy which would lead the nation into wrong and the kingdom into schism. . . . To be sure, the most Christian King refrained from giving the constitution his sanction; but, under the insistence and pressure of the National Assembly, he permitted himself to be carried away to the extent of lending his approval thereto. . . . [Then came] even more absurd decrees, such as those issued on 27 November, 1790

[Obligatory Oath]. These very decrees were the reason why the French bishops, priests, etc.. .took up the fight against the Constitution of the Clergy... The result of which is that. . . the civil oath [of obedience or obligation to the National Assembly, required of all clergy] is to be regarded as perjured and sacrilegious . . . and that all committing the act are to be regarded as schismatic, and as worthless, futile, and subject to greater censure. . . .

Therefore, to recall the erring to their duties, we, by virtue of the apostolic power which we exercise, declare that all cardinals of the Holy Roman Church, . . . archbishops, bishops, etc., who have taken the civil oath as prescribed by the National Assembly, shall be suspended from the tenure of any office whatsoever and liable to the charge of irregularity if they exercise such office, unless within forty days, dating from today, they have retracted said oath.

Moreover, we declare specifically that the elections of the following bishops [elected via mechanisms in Civil Constitution, and listed by name herein] are illegitimate, sacrilegious, and absolutely null and void.

We declare that the consecrations of same were criminal and illicit. . .

. . . Up to this point we have declared the infliction of these canonical penalties in order that the sins thus far committed may be corrected. . . But if it should ever come to pass that our present policy of temperate action and our fatherly admonitions should be of no avail--which God forbid!--let them realize that it is not our intention to exempt them from those more weighty penalties to which they are subject by the canons. . . For it is altogether appropriate that each one should have chosen to wallow in the mire of his own folly.

Finally, we beseech you in the Master's name, dear sons, Catholics everywhere in France, and reminding you of the religion and faith of your fathers, we, moved in our heart of hearts, urge you not to abandon your religion, inasmuch as it is the one and only true religion which bestows life eternal, and also preserves civil societies and causes them to prosper. Be steadily on guard lest you lend ear to the insidious voices of the philosophy of the century which lead to death. . .

The pope had virtually declared war on the National Assembly.

RURAL OPPOSITION INTENSIFIES

The pontiff's encyclical has spurred more resistance. In some instances, mobs loyal to their former "refractory" priests have taken up arms against those "juring" priests who took the Oath. Armed bands have driven the representatives of the National Guard from about two dozen villages in the Vendée and Maine-et-Loire. The movement appears to be gaining momentum. The following is a report forwarded from the administrator of the Maine-et-Loire department to the National Assembly:

The department's problems are so great that incalculable damage will result unless the National Assembly takes prompt and stern measures. Crowds of three to four thousand armed men have gathered in several parts of Maine-et-Loire to indulge in all the excesses which the fever of superstition and fanaticism can produce.

Pilgrimages and nocturnal processions led by seditious priests have served as the pretexts for these unlawful assemblies. They were easily dispersed while the pilgrims were still armed only with rosaries, but now they carry muskets, scythes, and pikes and have several times held out against the National Guard. Everywhere the constitutional priests [that is, those who have taken the Obligatory Oath required by the National Assembly], are being ill-treated, assassinated even at the altar steps. Priests who have not sworn the oath have taken up their office again, and could well finish by bringing about a counter-revolution through civil war.

THE PROBLEM OF THE ÉMIGRÉS

And there are more problems elsewhere. Ever since the market-women forced Louis XVI and the Queen back to Paris in October 1789, the King's younger brothers, the Comte d'Artois [KOHN-DAHR—TWAH] and the Comte de Provence [KOHN-DUH-PRO-VOHNZ] have been causing trouble. The Comte d'Artois, who fled France, has declared his opposition to the National Assembly. D'Artois has added that Louis' actions in signing various laws and decrees have no legal power because the King's assent has been coerced. More worrisome still, to the revolutionaries at least, d'Artois has installed himself at Coblenz in the German principality of Trier, just beyond the northeastern border of France. There he has assembled an army of several thousand émigrés, who spend much of their time sharpening their sabers. D'Artois now makes noisy pronouncements about leading the émigré army into France, overthrowing the National Assembly, and crushing the mob of Paris. Just two months ago, d'Artois demanded that Louis XVI repudiate the National Assembly. The Comte of Provence, the King's older brother, has also been active in counter-revolutionary circles. Together, they have put together an "army" of some 4,000 like-minded émigrés, mostly consisting of noblemen who have served as officers in the French army. Their main base of operations is Coblenz, a city in the German state of Trier.

The émigrés are busy seeking assistance from the monarchs of Europe: Catherine of Russia, various German princes, and especially Leopold II, Emperor of Austria—the brother of Marie Antoinette. Just two months ago, after the National Assembly passed a law ordering the émigrés to return to France or else forfeit any claim to their lands, Louis XVI vetoed it. This enraged many radicals, as well as the sans-culottes in the Paris crowd. Fears of foreign invasion are aggravated by reports of Catholic agitation throughout France against the Civil Constitution of the Clergy.

THE ABORTIVE JOURNEY TO ST. CLOUD (APRIL 1791)

Last April, just over two months ago, King Louis XVI declared his desire to travel to the royal chapel at St. Cloud, a palace outside Paris, during Holy Week. (Some said that he wished to repair his soul, following the pope's rebuke and therefore he sought to receive communion privately from a non-constitutional priest.) Lafayette personally attempted to escort the King from the Tuileries to St. Cloud. As the royal family entered their carriage, however, a large mob assembled. Lafayette sought to rally the National Guard to clear the way for the King's carriage, but too many soldiers ignored him. The crowd quickly grew unruly, shouting "Death to the Veto" and "Kill the Fat Pig." Some threw stones and spat at the carriage while Lafayette blustered about on horseback, waving his sword and haranguing the mob. After three hours, the carriage had not moved; so Lafayette eventually succeeded in getting it back through the gates at the Tuileries. Still more National Guardsmen were assigned to protect the king, and to watch him.

THE "TRIP" TO VARENNES (JUNE 1791)

They did not watch carefully enough. Less than two weeks ago, on the night of June 20th the King, Queen, and the King's heir, the young Dauphin, were either abducted by persons unknown, or they fled in a large carriage towards Germany. Most people in Paris believe that the King attempted flight. Meanwhile Lafayette sent mounted soldiers to save the King or apprehend him. On the morning of June 22, the National Guard caught up with him at Varennes and escorted him back to Paris. Tens of thousands lined the streets of Paris, watching the odd procession in silence. The Guardsmen installed the King in the Tuileries.

That was just last week. Now, they watch his every move.

The Game

THE CAST OF CHARACTERS

Louis XVI

Louis XVI, thirty-six years old, is the King of France, the fifth monarch in the Bourbon line. As a child (and, some say, also as an adult), he was withdrawn and taciturn. The death in 1765 of his father, the dauphin, himself the eldest son of Louis XV, left the younger Louis in direct line to succeed his grandfather. He disliked social occasions and was regarded as inept on courtly occasions; he enjoined solitary pursuits, like hunting and locksmithing. He loved horses. He took his studies seriously and became fluent in English, German, and Italian.

In 1770, when he was sixteen, his grandfather promoted France's alliance with Austria by arranging for Louis's marriage to Marie-Antoinette, daughter of Maria-Theresa, archduchess of Austria. Marie-Antoinette was fourteen. The marriage was not happy. Marie-Antoinette was vivacious, and Louis was not. Rumors abounded about the couple and many French harbored ill-will toward their Austrian queen. For several years their marriage was unconsummated due to a genital malformation on Louis' part; the lack of an heir fueled speculation about their relationship.

In 1774 Louis' grandfather died and Louis became King; he was twenty-one. He was coronated in the cathedral at Rheims. Minor surgery corrected the young King's genital problem and the couple had five children from 1777 to 1785. Louis became popular and earlier irritation toward the Queen subsided.

Louis was a student of foreign affairs and played a major role in the French decision to intervene on behalf of the American colonies in their "revolutionary war" against Great Britain. The cost of the war exacerbated perennial French budget problems. On the advice of the Swiss banker and financier Jacques Necker, Louis in 1788 decided to convene the Estates-General, which by French precedent, was necessary before the crown could impose new taxes.

Louis XVI bristled when the "Third Estate" declared itself to be the legislative body of France—the National Assembly—but his attempts to cow it into submission failed when the people of Paris, in a massive upheaval, stormed the Bastille. The emergence of the National Guard of Paris, under the command of Lafayette, provided an effective counterweight to the King's soldiers and ensured the survival of the National Assembly. In October 1789, after the market women had besieged the King at Versailles and forced him to the Tuileries Palace in Paris, he and his family became virtual prisoners.

Under pressure from the National Assembly, he began to endorse some of its revolutionary proposals. He even took an oath to support the constitution that the National Assembly was enacting. In 1790 he agreed to sign into law the Civil Constitution of the Clergy, which made all Catholic officials employees of the state, and ultimately subject to the authority of the National Assembly. It also obliged Catholic officials to take an oath to that effect. Several months ago, Pope Leopold VI repudiated the Civil Constitution of the Clergy and threatened to excommunicate those Catholics who adhered to its provisions. About half of the Catholic clergy in France have refused to take the oath. King Louis XVI, who had long been more religious than most monarchs and frequently spoke of his "Christian duty," appears to side with the "non-juring" priests and bishops and thus against the National Assembly. Rumors fly that the King takes mass privately with a non-juring priest.

Now, having been abducted from Paris, or perhaps having attempted to flee from it, the King and his family have been returned and placed "under protection" at the Tuileries.

Louis's behavior has been difficult to understand: Sometimes, perhaps influenced by his wife and brothers, he denounces the Revolution and seemingly conspires to destroy it. (There are rumors that when he left Paris he left behind a written indictment of the revolution.) At other times, perhaps when under the influence of liberal ministers such as Necker, he has supported reforms that would have struck his father and grandfather as democratic extremism.

Despite his awkward living arrangements at the Tuileries, Louis remains the titular head of the government. If the National Assembly passes a piece of legislation, it requires his signature to become law. Some government ministers are more attentive to the instructions of the Assembly than to those of the king, but the king still possesses some power, or at least some claim to power. And if the current draft of the constitution passes and he signs it into law, Louis will continue to exercise some executive functions, including the power to delay legislation by exercising a "suspensive veto." Overshadowing the political dispute over the future role of the king is the crowd of Paris which, on several occasions, has taken matters into its own hands and nearly killed the royal family.

What, though, will the king do? What does he want? Some say that having seen the sullen crowds on his ignominious return to Paris he has finally comprehended both the inevitability of revolution and the justness of accepting limits on monarchy as proposed by the current constitution. Others say that he gives mere lip service to the current constitution and plots with noble émigrés in Coblenz, with the Austrian and Prussian emperors, with the pope, and with nearly anyone else opposed to the French republic in the hopes that they will invade France, crush the revolution, and restore him to the throne of an unreconstructed ancien régime.

Lafayette

Formerly the Marquis de La Fayette, Lafayette, though only thirty-two years old, has accomplished much. While many ambitious and rich men attain noble status by acquiring a judgeship (current cost, about 100,000 livres, or $600,000) in one of the *parlements* (whose functions confer the "nobility of the robe"), Lafayette is from one of the truly noble families of France. While hereditary nobles must prove that their ancestors held noble office prior to 1400 A.D., the La Fayette genealogical charts included noble blood back to 1000 A.D. His mother's family, the La Rivieres, were courtiers with ties to the royal family in Versailles.

Lafayette's father, a captain, was shot and killed by the English at the Battle of Minden in 1759. Then Lafayette was only two. The family was sustained by the dues and rents paid by the peasants on its estates; the estates were fairly large, yielding an annual income of 25,000 livres (about $200,000). The death of his mother, and then of her father seven years later, left the young Lafayette with an annual income of 120,000 livres, or nearly a million dollars. Although he could do whatever he wished, he aspired to be a soldier like his father. At fourteen his relatives arranged for him to sign a marriage contract with Adrienne de Noailles, whose family was also among the richest in France; her dowry was about two million dollars. Three years later, they were married. Lafayette was now one of the richest men in France.

The Noailles family was also well-connected at the court at Versailles and young Lafayette became friends with the smart set of young people that gathered around the young Comte d'Artois. Lafayette, however, was not particularly smart: ungainly, ill-at-ease, and often tongue-tied, he cut an unimpressive figure. Even in the military, he left little impression on his superiors and, at nineteen, he was removed from the active military list. It was unlikely that he would ever gain a meaningful command.

Thus, when the Americans declared war on England in 1776, Lafayette volunteered to serve as an officer in the American army, an impulsive action that complicated French-British relations and initially angered the French king and Lafayette's relations. Barred from leaving France, he bought a ship, ordered it to depart secretly, and then set course for the American colonies. He vowed to fight for the American rebels! His defiant departure increased the romance of his adventure, and the young Lafayette became a hero to the French. The Americans, seeking to exploit the political implications of this seemingly well-connected and rich French nobleman, named him a major general in service to General Washington, commander of the American armies.

Lafayette's courage and enthusiasm won him the affection of the Americans and, after the British defeat at Saratoga, Lafayette's connections at Versailles helped persuade Louis XVI to enter the war on behalf of the Americans. Lafayette also served ably as a commander of American forces that helped trap Cornwallis at Yorktown.

During the years immediately following the American Revolution, Lafayette had supported reform in France. In 1787 he endorsed the concessions Louis XVI sought from the Assembly of Notables; Lafayette, like the King, was disappointed by the nobility's refusal to accept a heavier tax burden. Lafayette then became a leading figure among a group of liberals known as the Society of Thirty. They had founded the French Society of the Friends of the Blacks, which sought to eliminate slavery on the French colony of Saint-Domingue (Haiti). The Thirty also endorsed Louis XVI's decision to convoke the Estates-General. Lafayette even encouraged the king to "double" the number of delegates representing the Third Estate, raising its total to 600, so that it would be as numerous as the First Estate (clergy, 300) when it combined with the Second (nobility, 300). The King eventually agreed to this arrangement, an encouraging signal to reformers.

Lafayette's role as a liberal prompted the Comte de Provence, another brother of the King, to rebuke the Marquis at a public dinner at Versailles: "I hope, Marquis de Lafayette, that, quite republican though you are, you do not approve of the murder of Charles I of England." Lafayette, less awkward than in his youth, mumbled something about the execution being "iniquitous" but failed to repudiate the radical sentiments attributed to him: not even the Society of Thirty advocated a republic. But he did begin drafting a "declaration of rights," a statement of principles that he circulated to his American friends: Thomas Jefferson, Gouverneur Morris, and James Madison. (Madison, shortly thereafter, commenced work on adding a "bill of rights" to the American constitution.)

For the initial meeting of the Estates-General, Lafayette resolved to be elected to represent the Second Estate (nobility) for the province of Auvergne, the La Fayette's oldest estate. Many of the nobility of Auvergne wanted to resist encroachments on the traditional privileges of the nobles and to preserve the "ancient constitution" (i.e., traditions) of France; Lafayette, on the other hand, had by now acquired a nationwide reputation as an apostle of democracy and a champion of the poor. When some of the Auvergne nobles refused to support Lafayette, the local leaders of the Commons proposed that Lafayette stand for election as a delegate for the Third Estate. Finally, by a one-vote margin, Lafayette was selected as one of several deputies for the Second Estate for Auvergne; but the nobles there insisted that their representatives refuse to agree to allow the Estates-General to vote by head (1200 separate votes, totaled together) as opposed to by estate (each estate getting one vote).

Thus when the Third Estate, in defiance of the king, broke away and declared itself the "National Assembly" and refused to disband (Tennis Court Oath, June 20: see above), Lafayette made no public comment. Three days later, when many of the First Estate began to join with the Third, some of the liberal members of the Second Estate did so, too. Lafayette, however, remained faithful to his promises to the nobility of Auvergne. His dilemma was resolved when the king capitulated and instructed the first two estates to meet with the third; on July 1, 1789, Lafayette was accepted by the National Assembly as a duly accredited member of the body.

Almost immediately, he advanced his "declaration of rights" and again began circulating drafts of the document, though its tone now was far more democratic than before. These philosophical speculations were interrupted by outbreaks of mob violence and reports of royalist troop movements. Members of the National Assembly worried that Louis was about to crush the protesters; the King spoke of a need to preserve order in the capital. The National Assembly, fearing imminent attack, chose Lafayette as its vice-president. The president immediately resigned so that Lafayette could lead the National Assembly in its time of danger.

The dismissal the next week of the liberal minister, Necker, caused Paris to erupt in violence. The electors of the Third Estate for Paris (Electors of Paris) assumed power over the municipality and tried to restore order; they began to refer to themselves as the Permanent Committee. On July 14, while Lafayette was presiding over the deliberations of the National Assembly in Versailles, came the attack on the Bastille. When a delegation from the Electors of Paris arrived to inform the National Assembly of the chaos in Paris, Lafayette warned that the National Assembly had more to fear from the King's army than from the protesters. Then, nearly at midnight, came word that the Bastille had fallen and its commandant had been murdered.

The King, sobered, now addressed the National Assembly by name, announced the removal of his troops from Paris, and agreed to further procedural concessions. Lafayette, escorted by cheering delegates and the citizens' militia, returned to Paris to convey the good news. Within hours of his arrival, the Paris Electors proposed Lafayette as commander general of the citizens' militia, an announcement the crowd cheered so loudly he could not attempt a speech. He accepted by saluting the populace with his sword. Lafayette was now, simultaneously, a major general in the King's army; a deputy and president of the National Assembly, and commander general of the citizens' guard of the Permanent Committee, or, as it was now called, the Commune of Paris.

He immediately set about the work of shaping the citizens' guard into an effective force. He instituted an oath for all recruits "to be faithful to the nation, the king, and the commune of Paris." And the "citizens' guard" was renamed the National Guard. During the weeks to come, countless cities throughout France underwent similar transformations as the usual congeries of overlapping (if royally sanctioned) municipal authorities were replaced by an elected council (commune) that enforced order by means of a local **National Guard**. Authority throughout France was now being divided between elected municipal "communes" and the old royalist administration; there existed a bifurcated military/police as well, divided between the royalist army and the new National Guards.

Lafayette instructed the National Guard to confiscate weapons that had been seized during the assault on the Invalides and the Bastille, and to confiscate equipment left by royalist soldiers when they were withdrawn from Paris. Many of the King's troops, moreover, began to defect to Lafayette's National Guard (of Paris). Though technically "deserters," they were, at least initially, accepted into Lafayette's National Guard.

Lafayette sought to regularize recruitment and ensure that the men would accept discipline. To that end, he proposed and the Commune of Paris agreed that all able-bodied male taxpayers were to enroll in his militia: The National Guard would be a middle-class body, mostly unpaid. But violence persisted: there were bread riots and some aristocrats and store-owners were lynched; detachments of his National Guard failed to heed his orders and became as disorderly as the mob they were to be controlling. Lafayette threatened to resign, but was persuaded to stay.

Then came the **Great Fear** in the countryside, when peasants rose up against the nobility, attacking chateaux and burning the hated volumes that recorded ancient feudal dues. To preserve order in Paris, Lafayette took a personal loan from his bankers to help pay the National Guard. The Paris Commune voted him a large salary, which he refused.

Lafayette found time to attend some sessions of the National Assembly. His draft of the "declaration of the rights of man" bore many similarities to the final document passed by the National Assembly; and Lafayette came up with the current constitutional compromise (**suspensive veto**) whereby the king can veto any legislative of which he disapproves; if, however, two subsequent legislatures pass the legislation, it would become law.

During the riot of the market-women on October 5, 1789, Lafayette nearly lost control of the National Guard. Lafayette arrived at Versailles just in time to prevent the wholesale butchery of the King and his family. The King finally acceded to the wishes of the mob, and Lafayette tried to make the most of a difficult situation by forming up a procession to escort the now-captive King to Paris.

In January, 1790, offered command of all the National Guards in the nation, he refused. During the winter of 1789-90, Lafayette declared, time and again, that the revolution was over. In a speech in February, he called for an end to social upheaval throughout France: "For the Revolution, we needed disorders; the old order was nothing but slavery and, under those circumstances, insurrection is the holiest of duties, but for the Constitution, the new order must be stabilized, individuals must be secure. . . . The government must take on strength and energy." The speech alarmed royalists and radicals alike.

Increasingly, Lafayette was denounced in the public presses. After the National Guard put down a riot in Nancy, Jean-Paul Marat, editor of *L'Ami du Peuple* (Friend of the People), denounced the "shameful tricks used by the man Motier [Motier de La Fayette was the Marquis' full name]." Another radical editor, Camille Desmoulins, declared, "The name of Lafayette had died on our lips as that of an ambitious officer whose soul was not great enough to be a Washington and now only awaits the time when he can be another Monk" [the general who ended the English Civil War and restored the English king in 1660]. Some slanderous broadsides even claimed that Lafayette took part in sexual orgies with Marie Antoinette.

The royalist press was nearly as critical. As the author of one pamphlet put it,

> Everyone asks: is M. de La Fayette a demagogue or a royalist? Does he want to uphold or topple the throne? No one can answer the question and both parties distrust the Parisians' General equally. . . The circumstances have produced in M. de La Fayette a kind of prudence that looks very much like falseness. . . Weak and irresolute under all circumstances, his behavior is almost always characterized by timidity or hypocrisy. . . He has, in his folly, thought he could emulate Washington; but what a difference in men and circumstances.

When the mob prevented the King and Queen from celebrating mass at St. Cloud (April 1791), Lafayette barely managed to herd them back into their prison at the Tuileries. Lafayette's impotence was further confirmed by the disappearance of the royal family on June 20, 1791. Lafayette had either been inattentive to his duties to protect the King from abductors or had collaborated in his escape. In any case, Lafayette ordered the National Guard to pursue him. Radical leaders in the Assembly, especially the Jacobins, thought otherwise. Just last week M. Danton at the Jacobin club intoned, "M. the commander-general promised on his head that the King would not leave; we must have the person of the King or the head of M. the commander-general." Some radicals now call not for a constitutional monarchy but a republic. When the King and Queen were returned to the Tuileries, Lafayette greeted them, "Sire, your Majesty knows how attached I am to you; but I have always said that if you were to separate your cause from that of the people, I would remain on the people's side." This was just last week.

Lafayette, though swamped by his duties as commander of the National Guard, continues to attend sessions of the National Assembly, though he no longer presides. He also controls many votes of loyal supporters in the Assembly.

What does Lafayette want? Some on the Left say that he conspires to terminate the revolution, that he was part of the conspiracy that sought to liberate the King, and that now the Marquis de la Fayette intends to use his National Guard to crush the Jacobins, the radicals in the Assembly, and the mob outside. Some on the Right say that much as he used the National Guard to apprehend the King, he intends to install himself as President of France, rather like his mentor in the United States, George Washington. Others say that, having veered from a radical to a conservative stance, he now sides with the Feuillants as a sensible compromise and that he is willing to bow to the wishes of both the National Assembly and the King.

The Crowd of Paris: Danton

The crowd has played a major role in the revolution. Some have extolled them as "citizens of virtue," and some have denounced them as ignorant and unlettered, or even as "monsters." But the revolutionary crowd has figured in the revolution, especially in Paris.

The most visible—and certainly the most audible—figure is Danton [DAHN-THAN], a huge man whom many say possesses the loudest voice in all Paris. He organized the militants within his Cordeliers [kor-DEE-lee-aa] district of Paris during the early phase of the revolution and he founded the radical Cordeliers Club, frequented by his close friend, Desmoulins, a radical journalist.

Danton attained his radical status despite the fact that he was a lawyer in service to the King, a position for which he borrowed tremendous sums to acquire. Nowadays Danton lives in considerable comfort; some say that he received payments from the King or from the King's uncle, Philippe, the Duke of Orléans. But Danton is a formidable figure because he mobilizes the Crowd of Paris like no one else. In the summer of 1789, when the King's troops menaced the National Assembly, Danton organized the poor of the Cordeliers district into a fighting force that helped save the fledgling revolution. Where the Jacobin club sought to advance the revolution through the creation of a debating society, which imposed high dues on potential members, Danton formed the Cordeliers Club as a club for the dispossessed poor of Paris. Now, he moves between both the Jacobins and the Cordeliers, goading the former to take a more radical stand and seeking to gain weapons and power for the latter.

Danton's strength is ultimately derived from the huge numbers of sans-culottes who can be summoned by the section assemblies throughout Paris. Of the 600,000 people of Paris, probably 5,000 are—or were—members of the nobility; 10,000, officials of the Catholic Church; and 40,000, members of the financial, commercial, manufacturing, and professional *bourgeoisie* (urban dwellers who make money in such professions). Probably a half million Parisians, the overwhelming majority, are small shopkeepers, street vendors, craftsmen, journeymen, laborers, vagrants, and city poor (or the families of same); these people are now known as sans-culottes (literally "without knee breeches") because they wear trousers rather with than breeches with high silk stockings. There are a handful of textile factories that each employ as many as 800 workers, but most of the artisanal workshops—furnishings, upholstery, stocking weavers, dyers, glassmakers, building tradesmen, and the like—employ a dozen or so workers. [For the purposes of the game, the Crowd refers to the sans-culottes of Paris, but most of the smaller cities of France experienced dynamics similar to what transpired in the capital.]

Most adult laborers earn 20 to 30 *sous* a day; a journeyman mason or craftsman might earn 40 *sous*; and carpenter or locksmith, 50 *sous*. In normal times, a four-pound loaf of bread—the staple in the Frenchman's diet—costs about eight or nine *sous*. When the price of bread rises to 15 *sous*, many workers can barely feed themselves, much less their families. Thus the food riot has been more common than the wage strike. Royal officials thus took great care to ensure a regular supply of grain to the millers in and around Paris, but if the harvest was poor or speculators interfered with the market to drive the price upwards, the result could be calamitous. Turgot, a finance minister who preceded Necker, sought to improve the supply of grain by promoting trade with England, but this measure caused more harm than good: tens of thousands of French artisans lost their jobs as cheap, machine-made English goods flooded into Paris; and Turgot's free-trade measures also drove up the price of grain, promoting greater misery among the Crowd. The harvest of 1788-89 was poor and the price of bread remained above 14 *sous* for most of the spring and summer.

The Crowd, when starvation approaches, will swarm through food markets and bakers' shops and take what they want or refuse to pay more than they think is fair. Hunger is a prime motivator. Moreover, because the supply of food derives from the vagaries of nature, no government can ensure complete order at this time. Yet it is wrong to think that the Crowd consists chiefly of the riff-raff and vagrants of Paris; many of the sans-culottes, and many of the most active members of the Crowd, are small proprietors and shopkeepers, people who pay taxes and even serve in the National Guard. the Crowd may claim with some truth that it betters represents "the people" of France than the lawyers who were chosen to represent the Third Estate two years' ago.

In the spring of 1789, the talk of the "Third Estate" as constituting the entire nation cast the food shortage in political relief. A pervasive fear was that the ancien régime sought to undermine the rise of the "Third Estate" by starving it to death. Marie Antoinette and the Comte d'Artois were especially accused of arranging for shortages so as to embarrass the National Assembly, or so the demagogues charge.

Increasingly, too, knowledgeable and clever men seek to educate the sans-culottes as to their rights and responsibilities. Members of the National Assembly for the Jacobins and Cordeliers (another radical club) attempt to guide the actions of the sans-culottes. The Electors of Paris have mobilized the sans-culottes to prevent the King from crushing the revolution; and the Paris Commune now works in tandem with the militant leaders among the forty-eight sections of Paris. The King could not crush the National Assembly in July 1789 because of the tens of thousands of members of the Parisian Crowd barred the way of the royalist troops. And it was the Crowd, guided by the leaders of the Commune, who found arms at the Invalides and gunpowder at the Bastille. The march to Versailles was, of course, undertaken chiefly by the women of the Crowd.

What, now, does the Crowd want? This is hard to determine because the Crowd speaks with many different (if uniformly emphatic) voices. Some contend that the Crowd, far better than any elected representatives, best expresses the general will of the people of France. The sans-culottes actions are more virtuous, because they are less self-serving. Constitutions are mere words, an expression of political compromise and lawyerly tricks. The will of the people, when driven by virtue, is pure and irresistible. Governments should not rule the people; the people, acting together in accord with the wishes of Rousseau's general will, should rule themselves.

According to many in the Crowd, the current constitution promotes the schemes of the money-grubbing businessmen and speculators by destroying the old economic system—feudal dues and royal fees, and government control everywhere—and replacing it with a system controlled by fast-talking entrepreneurs who care mostly about property and wealth. The Crowd wants protection from these predatory market forces; they want a return to the old way of doing things, with stabilized prices and secure employment. Some in the Crowd want the Declaration of the Rights of Man and Citizen, and similar provisions in the constitution, to refrain from endorsing a "natural" right to property. If a child is about to die of hunger and another person has an extra piece of bread, the child's right to that bread is absolute. It is a natural right. The Crowd insists that the revolution is not over until such rights have been guaranteed.

Some in the Crowd also believe that elements of counterrevolution are gathering steam—the non-juring priests and bishops in the countryside; the émigré army, headed by the Comte d'Artois in Germany; the property-holding troops of the National Guard under the command of the Marquis de La Fayette; and the vengeful troops of the other European monarchs—Leopold of Austria, Frederick William of Prussia, Catherine of Russia—seeking to punish the Crowd for its actions against Louis XVI. These members of the Crowd want to destroy the enemies of the revolution before those enemies march on Paris and destroy the Crowd. Many in the Crowd do not want to see the King who has already betrayed them restored to power as a constitutional monarch.

The Jacobins: Maximilien Robespierre

Formed in 1789 by a group of delegates to the Estates-General from Brittany (i.e., far west France), the group acquired its name in October, when the National Assembly moved to Paris. Although it formally identified itself as the Society of Friends of the Constitution, it became know by the Dominican monastery in which it met—the Jacobins. The Jacobins corresponded with similar revolutionaries throughout France. Now, there are perhaps 800 Jacobin clubs in the nation, which circulate newspapers, letters, and revolutionary gossip.

The Jacobins consist mostly of lawyers, small-town notables and magistrates, and others who were familiar with the workings of the ancien régime and had thus come to despise it. The Jacobins approve of the achievements of the revolution at present, but they insist that more must be done. They applaud specifically the fact that the Catholic Church has been stripped of its feudal power and placed under the thumb of the National Assembly; and they have cheered the dismantling of noble powers and the tentative adoption of a unicameral (single) house legislature, whose powers are great. Unlike the United States and England, where the will of the people is divided into multiple houses (Senate and House of Representatives; Lords and Commons), the current constitution places great power in a single legislature. The pending constitution also protects property rights, and this matters immensely to the many lawyers and shopkeepers who belong to the Jacobin Club.

Maximilien Robespierre, a small-town lawyer from **the northern French town of Artois**, has emerged as the leader of the Jacobins, and he has pushed the club to an increasingly explicit republican position. The people are sovereign, he declares. He cites Rousseau, who insisted that sovereignty cannot be divided, to call for the elimination of the monarchy. The nation is to be governed by the general will of the people; the monarch ultimately serves no interests but his own.

The ascendancy of Robespierre, sometimes in concert with Danton, has pushed the Jacobins into seeking a larger, and far greater, revolution. The issue ceases to be who will rule France, but to be whether any government can be truly based on the general will of the people, a principle that is both universal and almost holy in its implications. Under Rousseau, the Jacobins seek to advance a utopian vision and export it throughout the world, one reason why they support the cause of slaves in Saint-Domingue [Haiti]: liberty (freedom), equality, brotherhood— these principles are to become the basis for a new order of mankind.

Now the Jacobins demand an end to the monarchy, which would plunge France into a radically different political world. The attempted flight of the King is proof, they say, of his perfidy, and all the more justification for an end to the monarchy and the beginning of a republic. Even as you read this, Jacobin leaders are circulating petitions calling for the dethronement of Louis XVI.

The Feuillants

Such actions have alarmed many Jacobins, most of whom abandoned that club and have recently begun meeting at the former Feuillant [fuh-yawn] convent, leaving the Jacobins with only a small faction of members under the spell of Robespierre. The Feuillants endorse the revolution and its accomplishments: the Civil Constitution of the Clergy; the abolition of feudalism; the replacement of monarchical power with a forceful unicameral legislature; the protection of individual freedom from royal encroachment; the defense of property; and so on. Yet they think that the elimination of the monarchy portends social chaos.

The Feuillants agree that mob violence has indisputably advanced the revolution, but now that the revolution has accomplished its objectives, violence must end. The revolution has gone far enough; it should go no farther. The task now is to reconcile the deeply divided people of all France so that they can come together and build a strong nation. This, the Feuillants feel, requires a compromise: retention of the king, whose duties will be carefully circumscribed by a constitution.

The Feuillants' goals are embedded in the current draft of the constitution. The Feuillants have an eye, too, to the future and to economic development of the nation. They believe that the "corporate" character of the ancien régime—the pervasive power of guilds, the Catholic Church, and the financial system of the French monarch—hindered the nation's economic growth. If France is to play a major role in the future, it must in some way approximate the more vigorous free-market institutions of England.

At present, the Feuillants seem to be the dominant force in the National Assembly, and the National Assembly seems to be the dominant force in contemporary France. One reason is that the chief form of income for the new government is derived by the sale of church lands, the income for which is converted into a new currency known as *assignats* [ahs-seen-yah]. Without this income, the new government could not pay the National Guard or the army, much less the Catholic Church officials who now are employees of the government.

The Clergy

Most of the Clergy who still belong to the National Assembly were initially sympathetic to the Third Estate and to the need to reform the Catholic Church. But the National Assembly, abetted by the mob of Paris, rather than effect the reformation of the Catholic Church, has nearly destroyed it. The expropriation of some church land (Decree on Church Lands), initially adopted to equalize church revenues, soon became the chief source of finances for the revolutionary government of the National Assembly. The Civil Constitution of the Clergy imposes secular control and direction over a spiritual matter. The Obligatory Oath provision, added recently, transforms half of the good and pious priests of the Catholic Church into outlaws. Pope Pius VI's encyclical now obliges all "constitutional" or "juring" clergy (those who have taken the oath) to renounce their clerical offices.

Clergymen now are either enemies of the French state or of the Holy See. Although some Catholic Jansenists long to return to the primitive life of the early Christians, most of the Catholic Clergy in the National Assembly seek to reverse the pending constitution's position on religious issues. They also value the office of the King as a traditional source of authority and stability.

The Nobility

The Nobility who belong to the National Assembly were also sympathetic to the Third Estate and were among the exuberant body that in August 1789 renounced feudal privileges (Fourth of August Decrees). But suddenly things went haywire: peasants rose up in frenzied rebellion later that month, looting chateaux, burning the registers where feudal dues were kept, and attacking the nobility and their families. This was during the Great Fear of August 1789. Then, in October, all Paris erupted in chaos as the market-women went on a rampage to Versailles. Hundreds, perhaps thousands of aristocrats fled the country. Now members of the Jacobin Clubs throughout France hold festivals when they sing the blood-thirsty ditty, "Ca Ira" ("It'll happen.")

> Ah, ça ira! Ca ira! Ca ira!
> Les aristocrates a la lanterne.
> Ah, Ca ira! Ca ira! Ca ira!
> Les aristocrates on les pendra."

("Ah! It'll happen! It'll happen! It'll happen!"
To a lamppost, send the aristocrats.
Ah, it'll happen! It'll happen! It'll happen.
There we'll hang the aristocrats."

The nobility regards the current constitution as an invitation to more bloodshed and violence. The legislature has all the real power; the King is a pitiable figurehead. The protection of property rights consists of mere words. The power is in the hands of an unstable legislature that happily condones violence.

Delegates from Languedoc, Vaucluse, Lyons, Nancy, Burgundy, or Paris

Although political clubs have popped up throughout France, reiterating the main political divisions within the National Assembly, many people in France (and in the National Assembly) remain undecided about what is best for France. These delegates read the various newspapers, looking for guidance. They also seek to determine the shape of the future and how it will affect their personal and local interests. They were elected to advance the wishes and needs of a particular geographical area, or perhaps of a particular economic group or cultural constituency, and they take this responsibility seriously.

But then, too, like people everywhere, they may be looking out, especially, for themselves.

VICTORY OBJECTIVES

Each player's goals are outlined in his/her specific "role statement," which will be distributed randomly within the next few sessions. Each player will seek to shape the momentous events that have plunged France into Revolution. Players receive "points" for achieving the objectives listed in their "victory objectives statement." Some objectives may involve actions: staying alive, getting elected to leadership posts, or putting out a newspaper on time. But most objectives will involve persuasion: Should the Civil Constitution of the Clergy be revoked? Should the Declaration of the Rights of Man and Citizen retain its protection of a "right" to property? Should the monarchy be retained and, if so, in what form?

In many cases, you will not achieve exactly or entirely the stated condition prescribed in your role, but a portion of them; those will be rated by the Gamemaster in determining the final tally. Some objectives can receive partial credit, some cannot. If, for example, your "objectives sheets" required that you abolish a right to "property" and the National Assembly abolishes property rights in "businesses: corporations, factories, bakeries" but retains property rights in farm land, the Gamemaster would regard your achievement as a "partial" victory, depending on the exact circumstances of the legislation (such as the likelihood, given the final executive structure and political alignments, that the legislation could be enforced, etc.)

Members may propose to the Gamemaster modifications in their victory conditions. The original conditions may have omitted a logical objective that warrants pursuit by the player.

The Gamemaster may also assign new conditions and objectives and alter existing ones. This is profoundly unfair—as is life.

SETUP

The game will consist of four types of classroom situations:

1) Beginning setup, where students will come to class having read all or parts of the game packet, philosophical texts, or historical context; the class will consist of discussion of those materials **without reference to any roles**;

2) Faction meetings, where students will meet with the members of their faction so as to discuss issues, choose leaders, plot strategy, allocate research and writing tasks, and the like;

3) Public meetings of the full National Assembly (some 800 members), which will normally be held in the classroom; and

4) Wrap-up classes, after the game is over, for "out of role" discussions of the game and the materials.

RULES FOR SESSIONS OF THE NATIONAL ASSEMBLY

At the first public session, the Gamemaster will ask for nominations for President of the National Assembly. The President will lead the discussions and direct the proceedings of the National Assembly. A public roll-call vote will immediately be taken to select the President. To expedite matters, the Gamemaster will determine if a run-off vote is necessary to select the President. All votes must be public; if the Gamemaster deems it necessary, votes will be conducted by roll call, with the Gamemaster calling out the roll and announcing the tally. The Gamemaster will keep public records of the resolutions and votes.

After the President has been elected, he will take a position of at the center or end of the table; the podium will be placed opposite him. All members of the National Assembly will sit at the table; the National Assembly may also extend that courtesy to the King. The Crowd leaders may be seated in the galleries (or chairs around the edge of the room, but not at the table).

The President of the National Assembly will conduct the sessions as he sees fit, though in conformity with the following rules.

1) **Any member of the National Assembly or the King may propose legislation**, make comments, or give speeches;

2) **Any member of the NA or the King may stand at the podium,** or take a place in line at it, at any time. The President is free to call on delegates and the King to speak as he sees fit. The Gamemaster will, if necessary, remind the President that someone is at the podium. If the President persists in neglecting those at the podium, the GM will issue a warning that the President must "respect the podium." If, following the warning, the President continues to neglect those at the podium, the Gamemaster may penalize the President by reducing the President's delegate total. (Note: Any member of the National Assembly who ceases to "represent" any delegates ceases to exist);

3) The main task of the National Assembly is to come up with a constitution. But the **National Assembly will also act as the legislative body** of France until a new constitution is created and put into effect. In that capacity, the National Assembly may pass whatever legislation it chooses, whether it is to declare war on the United States, to choose the squirrel as the national mammal, or to oblige all clergy to take the Obligatory Oath of the Civil Constitution of the Clergy on pain of death. But the vote of the National Assembly does not guarantee that whatever laws it passes will have force beyond the rooms in which it deliberates. One issue is practical: It is often uncertain whether the ministers who head up the government agencies will heed the directives of the National Assembly. If the King concurs in the decision, then the ministers will doubtless agree; if he publicly opposes the decision or makes no comment whatsoever, then there may be confusion in the minds of the ministers, especially if the vote in the National Assembly was close. A second issue concerns capacity: If the National Assembly has not voted funds for the navy or army, its war declaration against, say, the United States will be meaningless. The Gamemaster will attempt to alert the NA on all such matters, but may require an evening to research the matter;

4) When the President calls for a vote, he will request the assistance of the GM to call out the names of the delegates and keep tally of the votes. For example, the first delegate will say, "I cast 51 votes for [or against]" the resolution or issue at hand. She may choose to divide her vote, (i.e., "I cast 3 votes for, 48 against"), or abstain. **The Gamemaster will then tabulate the vote** and post the results;

5) The editor of any published newspaper may at one point during the game request a five-minute **recess**, which the GM will approve. This does not apply to the final game session;

6) The **President may be removed at any time by a majority vote** of the National Assembly; to avoid wasting time, a motion to request a vote to remove the President must first come in a written note to the Gamemaster bearing the signatures of members representing at least 200 delegates. The Gamemaster will then call the roll;

7) The National Assembly pointedly eschews English contrivances such as Roberts' Rules of Order in governing its deliberations; the NA may conduct itself in any manner it wishes as long as it does not contravene any of the above rules; and

8) The **podium rules do not apply to the Crowd**, although the President may choose to grant Crowd leaders the right to speak. The GM may function, at the direction of the President of the National Assembly, to preserve orderly deliberations within the King's Riding Stables—the building where the National Assembly meets.

CLUBS AND NEWSPAPERS

The French Revolution was largely the work of a new political entity: the political club. In 1789, tens of thousands of French citizens, exhilarated by their newfound liberty, banded together to protect themselves from counterrevolutionaries and other enemies, and to discuss and promote their new political ideas. They met in cafés, theatres, municipal halls, and even unused monasteries and convents; they held debates, established libraries and reading rooms, published newspapers and books (on subjects ranging from Rousseau to animal husbandry), and created thousands of affiliated clubs throughout France. Some clubs charged fees for membership; others, such as the Cordeliers, welcomed nearly everyone. Mostly the clubs debated politics. From 1789 to 1791, the number of Jacobin clubs nationwide increased from 19 to 921. Thus when leaders of the Jacobins in Paris adopt a position, one can fairly assume that that same position will be adopted and articulated by local Jacobin clubs throughout France.

Many of you will be advised, at the outset of the game, to join and establish a specific political club: the Jacobin Club, the Cordeliers Club, Cercle Social, the Feuillants Club, or Les Amis de Roi (Friends of the King). The Club will publish the names of its founding members in its first newspaper. The club will also find a place to meet near the classroom, because at various points during the game portions of class time will be devoted to separate meetings of the clubs. If a nearby tavern or monastery is unavailable, you might try any other place convenient to the meeting hall. Whatever place you choose must be announced to the entire class; and the place of meeting, at least during the regular class time, must be publicized (unless the club has been outlawed).

Each club shall make whatever rules it wishes. [These rules must not violate the U. S. Constitution or the rules of the institution hosting the game.] Although all members of the class must know where every club is located, the club may choose to admit (or expel) whomever it wishes. It may elect leaders, choose them by lot, or dispense with leaders entirely. It may schedule meetings outside of class at places it deems appropriate.

At the first meeting, every club must, in addition to posting its "founding members," choose a **Newspaper Editor** and announce the name to the entire class. The editor will have responsibility of approving every paper submitted for that club. That is to say, if the editor of the Jacobins disapproves of a paper submitted to her paper, the editor can reject it. It can be submitted to other clubs, or directly to the Gamemaster (perhaps acting in the capacity of, say, Pope Pius VI or Edmund Burke, etc). (Such a paper would have no public function and in effect would be secret.) Students who fail to adhere to their editor's deadlines not only harm their team, but also impose on the good offices of their peers.

Newspaper editors should arrange to print enough copies of each of their issues to distribute to the Instructor, to the other editors, and to the indeterminates.

The Gamemaster will evaluate the newspapers for each week. The best newspaper for each week will receive a bonus in the form of additional National Assembly members for the team. The Gamemaster will announce this bonus at the beginning of the class after the issues had been submitted. The Editor of the winning newspaper will decide how to allocate the additional delegates.

Some members of the class may not choose to join a club at the outset or even later on. They may wish to visit one club, or perhaps all of them, or perhaps chat over coffee with the Gamemaster. But members who are not part of a club may find it difficult to attain their political objectives; and they are dependent on the various club newspapers to find out what's happening. And they, too, must submit written work; sometimes they may offer it for publication to one—or perhaps all—newspaper editors. Sometimes they may submit it directly to the Gamemaster.

Anyone—or any group—may decide to leave a club at anytime or to form a new club of their own. If the club consists of only one person, that person must also serve as editor. All clubs must inform the entire class of their creation and provide a list of founding members, place of meeting, etc.

The purpose of the clubs is to transform individual sentiment into political power. This requires the carefully calculated strategy that comes from coordination and leadership. The larger the club, the more power it will command. And revolutions are all about power; on the other hand, large political organizations can become unwieldy, their ideology dulled through compromise.

The club is also a forum to consider rhetorical strategies to best explain to others what you desire and why. The first issue of each newspaper should include, at the very minimum, a statement of philosophy; it may also offer articles and editorials on the various political issues of the day. These sessions will provide the coherence that enables the views of the political faction to prevail in the sessions of the National Assembly.

The National Assembly may pass legislation regulating the clubs. The clubs may choose to abide by those rules—or not.

Preparation of Papers for the Newspapers

Most of your written work for this game will consist of what you have published in your club's newspaper. You may choose whatever topic you wish and any format that best suits your purposes. For various reasons, however, students may choose not to publish their papers.

Each newspaper will likely publish three issues. Teams must anticipate who will address what topics. Chances are that each student will complete three or four pages of material for each of the newspapers. The National Assembly must consider a host of issues, each of which itself may be rapidly changing. Writers must therefore anticipate the arguments that will likely surface in advance of the debates. To that end, effective clubs will encourage a measure of specialization.

Perhaps one will focus on issues concerning the Catholic Church; another on the relation of the monarch to the legislature; and another on property, taxation, and mob control. Many other issues will also intrude, requiring further ad hoc organization: issues of foreign policy, relating to the émigré army at Coblenz and the threat of Austrian invasion; the slave rebellion in Saint-Domingue in the East Indies; and the symbolism of the flag. Club members may wish to review these and other likely debate topics.

The game packets will not provide enough technical information on many issues. Students are obliged to conduct additional research on their own, as proves necessary. The instructor will be pleased to offer assistance.

Specialization within the Clubs

The situation confronting France is bewilderingly complex. No single person can be expected to master all of the details. For that reason, effective clubs will organize themselves so that different leaders specialize in a particular set of issues. In the actual history, much of the work of the National Assembly was done in committees. What follows is a list of the major committees and the issues each addressed. A member of each faction should be assigned to master the issues concerning at least one of the following committees; he should be prepared to write essays and speak on the topic when it surfaces in the National Assembly.

ECCLESIASTICAL COMMITTEE (REORGANIZATION OF CATHOLIC CHURCH)
1) Decree on church lands;
2) the status of Catholicism as the official religion of France;
3) the Civil Constitution of the Clergy;
4) the Obligatory Oath;
5) the salaries of clergy and their manner of selection;
6) the role of the pope in Catholic affairs;
7) the management of hospitals and schools; and
8) Title II (of Constitution): marriage as a secular institution.

CONSTITUTIONAL COMMITTEE (CHIEFLY, RELATIONS WITH KING AND NOBILITY, AND ALSO ISSUES OF PROPERTY AND SLAVERY IN COLONIES)
1) the Declaration of the Rights of Man and Citizen (note, particularly, Article 17, enshrining "property rights";
2) All Chapters in Proposed Constitution, not otherwise addressed, including: The Royal Sanction and powers of the monarch;
3) The structure and powers of the legislature;
4) The rights of slaves and free blacks in Saint Domingue (Haiti); and
5) The division between Active and Passive Citizens (those who can vote, by virtue of their being able to pay a tax equal to or greater than three-days' wages).

MILITARY COMMITTEE
1) Oversight of operations and preparations of army and navy; and
2) Role of nobility in officer corps;

FINANCE COMMITTEE

1) Economic factors concerning revenue: payment of government debts, and also issuance of *assignats* (promissory notes, converted into legal tender, secured by revenue from the sale of church lands [see Ecclesiastical Committee]); and

2) Trade and Food Supply.

FEUDAL COMMITTEE

1) Abolition of the Nobility.

COMMITTEE ON RESEARCH

1) Examines plots against the revolution, including those enemies within France and those Frenchmen, especially émigrés, who may be plotting from abroad; and

2) The National Guard, and the requirement that only Active Citizens belong.

SECRECY

In life, most people are assigned roles with conflicting obligations. We're never sure exactly how they will sort out, and thus we never really know our ultimate goals. Most of us perform as students, parents, spouses, employees, Democrats or Republicans, etc., without being fully conscious of our goals, or, more precisely, without understanding how one role may alter our performance of another. (One example: bosses may script a role that requires our total commitment to work and offer us abundant and tangible rewards for a good performance; yet we may sometimes reject this role because our friends or family demand a very different performance.) No one thus ever truly knows his or her own ultimate goals, and others who presume to know that information about ourselves are deceiving themselves.

For this reason and for some practical ones as well, no player may show his or her specific "game conditions" to anyone else. Everyone is free, as in life, to affirm verbally what she is about. And you may or may not choose to believe them. If the Gamemaster learns that a player has shown her "role sheet" to someone else (watch out for spies!), that player's role may be changed suddenly and arbitrarily.

IF THE CONSTITUTION IS APPROVED

In the event that the National Assembly completes and approves, by majority vote, of a constitution, and if it is signed by the King, then it becomes law immediately.

If any additional sessions are left in the game, the game will **not** be over. Players will continue in their roles, and members of the National Assembly are automatically presumed to have been instantly elected to serve as legislators in the new Legislative Assembly. In the event that the constitution creates a two-chamber legislature, the Gamemaster will make any necessary adjustments.

Grading: Written and Oral Work

STRATEGY ADVISORY: ADVANCE AN IDEOLOGICAL WORLD VIEW

This is a very complex game and some players may attempt to transform it into a narrow exercise in constitution-writing. This would be a mistake. The objectives of many members of the National Assembly are prescribed by their roles. It will be against their interest to act in opposition to their victory objectives. To win the game, you must either be very lucky, or you must persuade the indeterminates and others that "your" views are the right ones.

Your task is not to belabor the technical advantages of your specific legislative initiatives, for they will bore nearly everyone and turn off the indeterminates.

Rather, you must persuasively advance a philosophy of society that seems to make sense: you must reach out to the uncommitted members of the National Assembly and bring them to your side on grounds of general principles.

To that end, you need to understand the larger ideas that informed each of the main positions. For those on the Left, especially the Jacobins and leaders of the Crowd of Paris, the central philosophy has been articulated, in brilliant and beautiful language, by Jean-Jacques Rousseau. No Crowd leader or member of the Jacobins can make a persuasive argument in favor of a radical new form of social organization without understanding Rousseau's *Social Contract*. Conversely, the many and specific arguments against social experiments of the sort undertaken by the radicals in the National Assembly were brilliantly attacked by Edmund Burke, *Reflections on the Revolution in France*. Partisans of both Left and Right must internalize the arguments of these thinkers.

The Feuillants, whose position is intellectually less pure (and thus politically all the more compelling), need also to be aware of the strength of the arguments of both ideologues. The Feuillants may be inclined to argue against intellectual purity of any sort, and the need to make compromises.

For the intellectual partisans, you advance your cause best not by focusing on the particulars of any single legislative of constitutional matter, but on promoting your overall worldview; if you can win over people to your great vision for society, then the particulars of the corresponding legislative program will follow easily.

HISTORICAL GUIDANCE

In framing your arguments, you may wish to consult what "real" people said and did in your circumstances. Also included at the back of this packet is a conventional historical narrative of the French revolution, from the beginning to the flight of the King (June 1791). Leo Gershoy's *The French Revolution and Napoleon* (1964) presents detailed historical background (see selection in Appendix D). This will provide useful context for your work. But you may find it useful to look ahead. The game has been designed to reflect causal forces that operated in history. A Bibliography of possible sources is also included (see Appendix F).

An indispensable element of the game, encompassing several media, is Jack Censer and Lynn Hunt, ed., *Liberty, Equality, Fraternity* (including CD ROM). A related source of rich primary materials, including speeches, songs, maps, and pictures, can be found on line at the following website: http://www.chnm.gmu.edu/revolution/.

WRITTEN WORK

Your instructor will indicate the total number of pages of written work you must complete. For those who belong to factions, most of your written work will be in the form of articles for your club newspaper. With certain exceptions (specified in your game assignment), you must submit at least three separate pieces of written work, such as committee reports, speeches, editorials, indictments, etc. Your written work—single spaced and formatted as the editor wishes—should be submitted to the editor prior to the publication date. Students who do not belong to any clubs may submit their work to a club for publication, or they may publish their piece as a solo newsletter. (The Gamemaster will arrange photocopying.) Sometimes committee reports may be reworked as newspaper articles, which will be allowable, assuming the author has made a genuine attempt to frame each essay differently.

GRADING

Written work counts 2/3 of the grade for this section of the course. Class participation counts the other 1/3.

There are some special conditions. If you are adjudged among the winners, then your class participation grade is raised by one-half (B becomes B+). The instructor may modify the proportion of the grade comprised by writing and speaking.

ACCEPTABLE EVIDENCE

Anything that happened before July 2, 1791, or that was written prior to that date, may be added to the evidentiary basis of the game by any player and cited in papers and in class.

To do so, however, you must advise all of the players in advance of the name of the document, with at least several illustrative sentences from it. This information—a statistic, a primary source document, etc.—should be submitted to all players by being posted on the class website. Most students need not post their papers on the website, because their papers will be published (photocopied) as part of their club newspaper.

Class Schedule Overview (for 14-class version of game)

Class	Student duties before	Faculty duty	Class activities	End of class
1	Scan packet. Read on-line: Voltaire, "Selections from the Philosophical Dictionary," and some entries from Diderot's *Encyclopédie*	Introduce Enlightenment	Discuss Voltaire and Diderot	
2	Read "Student Packet," basic rules, and Rousseau's *First Discourse* (Appendix B); also read Rousseau, *Social Contract*, Books I and II.	Lead mini lecture/discussion: Rousseau	Students should have questions about "Student Packet"; Discuss Rousseau's *First Discourse*	GM Selects King Louis XVI, Lafayette (randomly)
3	Read Remainder "Student Packet," and Rousseau, *Social Contract* Books III and IV; also complete one-half of Gershoy reading (Appendix D)	Mini-lecture/ discussion: Gershoy and Fr. Revolution; Rousseau	Discuss readings	GM Distributes Remaining Roles
4	Complete Gershoy narrative. Read excerpts of Burke's *Reflections of Revolution in France* (Appendix C)	Meet with Indeterminates (separately; confirm National Assembly President, and give him special role sheet	Meeting of Factions to choose editors, articles; Indeterminates mull about	Each faction informs GM of name of Editor (leader of faction).
5	Work on essay for first newspaper	GM: unstructured oversight	Faction meetings/ First National Assembly (Civil Constitution of Clergy)	GM Distributes News Bulletin 1
6	**Newspapers, Vol. 1, Due** for each faction; indeterminates prepare "biographical" synopsis of self	GM: oversight	Second National Assembly Discussion (Civil Constitution of Clergy cont'd)	GM prepare to grade papers IMMEDIATELY
7	Students work on second essay; GM announces winner of Vol. 1 winner bonus	Confer via e-mail with editors (separately)	Third National Assembly (Topic optional)	GM Distributes News Bulletin 2
8	Newspapers Vol. 2 Due	GM: Oversight	Fourth National Assembly (Topic optional)	
9	Vol. 2 winner announced	E-mail	Fifth National Assembly	GM Distributes News Bulletin 3
10	**Newspapers Vol. 3 Due** GM announces winner of Vol. 2 Newspaper Sweepstakes	E-mail	Sixth National Assembly	

11		E-mail	Final Meeting NA	Arrange Party, Showing of movie, *Danton*
12	Uncovering the Game: Read essay by Gary Kates (appendix this packet) on French revolution historiography	Discussion "out-of-role" of game; what happened in real history		Game Evaluation Forms Completed
13	Finish Kates essay	Discussion of *Danton* (movie)	Participate in discussion	Special historiographical assignment
14	Historiographical		To be determined	

Class by Class, Reading Requirements and Questions

PRIOR TO FIRST CLASS

Students should scan this entire packet to see what is here and where.

You should read Voltaire, "Selections from the *Philosophical Dictionary*," excerpted in the Web site http://www.chnm.gmu.edu/revolution/searchfr.php.

(For keyword, type Voltaire, and select "text" at bottom, and click on Find, and then scroll down to "Selections from the Philosophical Dictionary" and read all.

Also, you are to sample articles on from Diderot's *Encyclopédie*, which is available online, on topics such as those listed below.

Atheists	Government	Natural Rights
Beast	Humanity	Observation
Bible	Idol	Political Authority
Craft	Intolerance	Political Economy
Encyclopedia	Jew	Reason
Fanaticism	Natural	Representation
Farm Laborer	Equality/Natural Law	Slave Trade

CLASS 1 (SETUP): IDEAS AND TEXTS OF THE ENLIGHTENMENT: VOLTAIRE AND DIDEROT

This game is all about ideas. You are obliged to come to terms with two thinkers, both brilliant, and both very different. First, you will grapple with excerpts from Voltaire's *Philosophical Dictionary* (1764), which are available on-line (see above). His ideas may not seem all that radical, but that reflects the power of Enlightenment thinking. Part of the challenge for modern readers is to read Voltaire freshly and especially to tease out the differences—they are profound—between his thought and thought of his contemporary, Rousseau, perhaps the intellectual cornerstone of the French Revolution. If you do not understand Rousseau, you cannot understand the French Revolution and play this game, any more than you could participate in the trial of Anne Hutchinson without understanding Puritan ideology or the importance of Confucian principles in the political and social order of Ming China.

CLASS 2: ROUSSEAU'S FIRST DISCOURSE AND GAME SETUP

Prior to class, students should read the entire game packet (not appendices) and Rousseau's *First Discourse*. They should also being reading Rousseau, *Social Contract* (i.e., Books I-II). Rousseau believed that most of the other Enlightenment *philosophes* did not go far enough in repudiating the values of the ancien régime. He is the central intellectual figure of the French revolution, though it occurred after he was dead.

Introduction and Questions: Rousseau's First Discourse

One must begin with Rousseau's *First Discourse* (1750), which he wrote in response to a question for an essay competition: "Has the restoration of the sciences & arts tended to purify morals?" The text of this *Discourse* is included as Appendix B to this booklet.

The text is important because it shows Rousseau's ingenious iconoclasm. While most of the *philosophes* championed science and knowledge as a means of overcoming superstition and outmoded tradition, Rousseau takes the opposite position. Knowledge is overvalued, and its purveyors (such as the Academy at Dijon, which sponsored the prize!) deceive themselves in imagining that "modern education" is of service to society. Rousseau's argument against the Enlightenment may hardly seem the flammable stuff to ignite a revolution; but Rousseau's point is that "modern France" (of the eighteenth century) has become materialistic, soulless, unhappy, superficial, mannered, deceitful, and unwholesome—so rotten, by implication, that it should be gutted and rebuilt entirely.

In the introduction to the essay, he allows that it may seem "contradictory" for him to advance an argument against knowledge in the hope of winning a literary prize offered by a university. But the real prize, he notes, is not the one offered by the Dijon Academy, but "the cause of truth": and this, he will assuredly receive, for "I will find it at the bottom of my heart." Thus the opposition: knowledge versus the truths of the heart. Rousseau sides with the latter, however brilliantly.

QUESTIONS: PART I

When Rousseau writes that man has, in "recent generations," risen above himself to explore both the natural world and man, what exactly is he referring to?

Rousseau alludes to the dark ages, a time when "Europe had sunk back into barbarism." Does he disapprove of the rise of learning that commenced with

Islamic scholarship and precipitated the Renaissance ("brought about its rebirth amongst us")?

Rousseau mentions the "vaunted civility" of ancient Athens and Rome and sees its echo in the salons of the leading intellectuals of contemporary Paris. What does Rousseau see as the failing of civility and good manners?

What does Rousseau say about the intellectual literati of China (remember the Hanlin Academy)?

If societies that have championed knowledge are characterized by moral debauchery, what societies does Rousseau find as exemplars of moral purity and wholesomeness?

Does Rousseau prefer the militaristic, spare culture of ancient Sparta or the opulent, brilliant culture of Athens?

The example of Sparta is important because it placed so much emphasis on the moral demands of citizenship. Rousseau writes that while the plays and sculpture and paintings of Athens have inspired contemporary French writers and artists, "of the ancient Spartans nothing is left to us except the memory of their heroic actions." What is the implication of this ironic remark?

Rousseau is perhaps the greatest democratic exponent of the modern world; yet he sides with Socrates and denounces Athenian democracy. Why?

Rousseau denounces the *philosophes*, and especially popular figures such as Diderot, whose *Encyclopédie* was to bring knowledge to the reading masses, as "arrogant attempts" to enable man to "emerge from the happy ignorance in which eternal wisdom had placed us." What does Rousseau mean by "happy ignorance" and "eternal wisdom"?

QUESTIONS: PART II

How does Rousseau criticize the Newtonian revolution in science? What does he mean when he says that the "enlightened and learned men" smile "disdainfully at the old-fashioned words of fatherland and religion, and devote their talents and philosophy to destroying and debasing all that is sacred among men"? (And ponder, again, how such seemingly reactionary pronouncements can advance a radical agenda?)

What is the relation of science to luxury? Why is the latter "bad"? How does science sap the "warlike" and "moral" qualities of young people?

What is the relationship between the advance of knowledge, and of luxury, and what is the relationship between social distinction and equality?

What is the paradox of learning (such as the professors at the Dijon Academy)? What is Rousseau getting at when he writes that Descartes and Newton, the great intellects of the previous century, themselves had no teachers?

How, as a Frenchman (or woman), have likely responded to this work?

Rousseau's Second Discourse (1755)

This, too, is available in multiple on-line sources, and it is essential for those, such as members of the Crowd, who wish to frame an argument against individual rights to property ownership.

QUESTIONS

What is the claim to legitimacy in property ownership and why is it specious? What is the relation between property ownership and inequality?

CLASS 3: OVERVIEW OF ROUSSEAU AND BURKE

Before class, you should read Rousseau, *Social Contract* (Penguin) and the selections of Edmund Burke, *Reflections on the Revolution in France* that is included in the appendix of this booklet.

***Discussion Questions for Rousseau,* Social Contract**

BOOK I

"Man was born free, and he is everywhere in chains" —this is one of the most famous quotes in all history. What does Rousseau mean by this statement? How does he argue against the existence of a "right" of domination? Rousseau sees some benefits of life in a "state of nature." What are these? What are the limitations of such a life? Why do people choose to abandon a state of nature? What are the benefits of living in society, and amongst other people? What, for Rousseau, is the chief limitation?

How does Rousseau propose to promote society and still preserve individual freedom? What does Rousseau mean when he writes, "Since each man [in the Social contract] gives himself to all, he gives himself to no one"? What is the difference between one's "private will" and the "general will"? Between the "will of all" and the "general will"? How can someone be "forced to be free"?

The answer comes three paragraphs later, in Rousseau's most famous sentence, "Man is born free, and he is everywhere in chains." In what sense are all men "free" (where, when, how?) and "everywhere in chains"?

Rousseau now returns, perhaps predictably, to the "first societies," prior to the establishment of any "government." This strongly evokes the *First Discourse*: praise for rustic simplicity and directness; denunciation of modern manners and arts. But here Rousseau has some doubts about primitive simplicity. What are its deficiencies? One crucial passage to consider: "Although in civil society man surrenders some of the advantages that belong to the state of nature, he gains in return far greater ones; his faculties are so exercised and developed, his mind is so enlarged, his sentiments so ennobled, and his whole spirit so elevated that, if the abuse of his new conditions did not in many cases lower him to something worse than what he left, he should constantly bless the happy hour that lifted him for ever from the state of nature and from a narrow, stupid animal made a creature of intelligence and a man." Consider this passage in light of the *First Discourse*: what type of "civil society" does Rousseau favor?

How does Rousseau argue that "all legitimate authority among men must be based on covenants"? Against whom is this passage aimed?

Rousseau challenges the notion of Hobbes that during times when warlords or powerful desperadoes prevailed, fearful individuals surrendered their sovereignty to a mighty warlord, who promised to protect and guide them in return for their vassalage to him. The modern king (seventeenth century, of course) is the heir to that legacy: his rule is legitimate because it was part of an earlier contract. How does Rousseau reject Hobbes?

Why is there no "right" to slavery?

What, then, gives any system of government its legitimacy?

In a crucial passage, Rousseau states the problem his book seeks to resolve: "'How to find a form of association which will defend the person and goods of each member with the collective force of all, and under which each individual, while uniting himself with the others, obeys no one but himself, and remains as free as before.' This is the fundamental problem to which the social contract holds the solution." Understand, here, that Rousseau does not mean **any** social contract, but his very special type of social contract.

Rousseau sets up several conditions that are necessary for the emergence of his special social contract. What are they?

What is the difference between a person's "private will" and his "general will"? What is the difference between the "will of all" and the "general will"?

How can this "general will" constrain the actions of some of its members and yet not deprive them of their freedom? What, in other words, does Rousseau mean by saying that the sovereign state—a product of the general will in his special social contract—can "force a man to be free"?

Civil society also gives rise to property. What are Rousseau's attitudes toward property? (On this crucial idea, compare Rousseau here with his *Second Discourse on the Origin of Inequality* (to summarize briefly: man in nature was free and equal; as soon as the first man claimed a patch of land as his own property, and managed to persuade someone else of that fact, the consequence was increasing inequality). How has Rousseau's attitude to property changed? Does he impose limits to property rights?

BOOK II

Sovereignty means the governmental power in Rousseau's special contract: the agency that emerges from the "general will" of the members of that polity. Why does Rousseau say that that "sovereignty" can never be alienated, or transferred from the contracting members to someone else (i.e., "we all decide to give up our say to a mighty warlord, or to our representative, whom we trust")? "Power may be delegated," he writes, "but the will cannot be."

Why, too, does he say that sovereignty (rule by the "general will") is "indivisible"? What would Rousseau have said of the U.S. Constitution?

Why does Rousseau oppose "factional associations"? Can they exist within the polity?

Rousseau argues that, as a practical matter, the general will is determined by counting the "disinterested" votes of those participating in the social contract. The majority of "disinterested, community-minded" votes determines the "general will" of that polity. But Rousseau argues that the virtue behind the voters is more important than the number of voters: ". . . the general will derives its generality less from the numbers of voices than from the common interest which unites them—for the general will is an institution in which each necessarily submits himself to the same conditions which he imposes on others. . ." This is why Rousseau can elsewhere describe the general will as "wholly sacred" and "infallible."

How does Rousseau reconcile his goal of ensuring the "freedom" of the members of his social contract with his declaration that the sovereign may justly decide to kill those who defy the general will?

What is the role of the lawgiver in Rousseau's system?

BOOKS III AND IV

What, according to Rousseau, are the strengths and weaknesses of democracy? Of aristocracy? Of monarchy?

Read especially carefully the section on "deputies and representatives": Why are the English unfree?

If one votes in the minority in determining the general will, why is that vote inherently wrong?

Burke's Reflections on the Revolution in France

In addition to Rousseau, you should be acquainted with Edmund Burke's scathing indictment, *Reflections on the Revolution in France*. All students should read the portions of Burke's *Reflections* that are included in the game packet. Students representing the clergy and nobility, and even Louis XVI, will want to read more of this classic text.

CLASS 4: FACTION MEETINGS

Students will assemble into their faction to decide club organization and begin planning for the first National Assembly meeting. Indeterminates will meet with the Gamemaster.

CLASS 5: FIRST COMMITTEE MEETINGS/ NATIONAL ASSEMBLY (ORGANIZATION)

CLASS 6: PUBLIC SESSION #1

First full National Assembly meeting.
Newspapers (all factions) Volume 1 aredue before class.

CLASS 7: PUBLIC SESSION #2

Meeting of the National Assembly.
At the end of class, the GM distributes GM News Services Bulletin #2.

CLASS 8: PUBLIC SESSION #3

Meeting of the National Assembly.
Newspapers (all factions) Volume 2 are due before class.

CLASS 9: PUBLIC SESSION #4

Meeting of the National Assembly.
At the end of class, the GM distributes GM News Services Bulletin #3.

CLASS 10: PUBLIC SESSION #5

Newspapers (all factions) Volume 3 are due before class.

CLASS 11: PUBLIC SESSION #6

CLASS 12: POST-MORTEM

Class will discuss their roles, experiences, and questions. The session will help the class uncover the game and unwind.

CLASSES 13 AND 14: REMEMBERING, HISTORIOGRAPHY

Key assignment will be the essay on the historiography of the French Revolution by Gary Kates, included as Appendix E to this packet.

Appendix A: Primary Documents

THE TENNIS COURT OATH (JUNE 20, 1789)

The National Assembly, considering that it has been summoned to determine the constitution of the kingdom, to effect the regeneration of public order, and to maintain the true principles of the monarchy; that nothing can prevent it from continuing its deliberations in whatever place it may be forced to establish itself, and lastly, that wherever its members meet together, there is the National Assembly.

Decrees that all the members of this assembly shall immediately take a solemn oath never to separate, and to reassemble wherever circumstances shall require, until the constitution of the kingdom shall be established and consolidated upon firm foundations; and that, the said oath being taken, all the members and each of the individually shall ratify by their signatures this steadfast resolution.

DECLARATION OF THE KING UPON THE ESTATES-GENERAL (JUNE 23, 1789)

The King wishes that the ancient distinction of the three orders of the state be preserved in its entirety, as essentially linked to the constitution of his kingdom; that the deputies, freely elected by each of the three orders, forming three chambers, deliberating by order, and being able, with the approval of the sovereign, to agree to deliberate in common, can alone be considered as forming the body of the representatives of the nation. As a result, the king has declared null the resolutions passed by the deputies of the order of the Third Estate, the 17th of this month, as well as those which have followed them, as illegal and unconstitutional.

His Majesty having exhorted the three orders, for the safety of the state, to unite themselves during this session of estates only, to deliberate in common upon the affairs of general utility, wishes to make his intentions known upon the manner of procedure.

There shall be particularly excerpted from the affairs which can be treated in common, those that concern the ancient and constitutional rights of the three orders, the form of constitution to be given to the next States-General, the feudal and seigniorial rights, the useful rights and honorary prerogatives of the first two orders.

The especial consent of the clergy will be necessary for all provisions which could interest religion, ecclesiastical discipline, the regime of the orders and secular and regular bodies.

DECLARATION OF THE INTENTIONS OF THE KING (JUNE 23, 1789)

1. No new tax shall be established, no old one shall be continued beyond the term fixed by the laws, without the consent of the representatives of the nation.

2. As the borrowing of money might lead to an increase of taxes, no money shall be borrowed without the consent of the States-General, under the condition, however, that in case of war, or other national danger, the sovereign shall have the right to borrow without delay, to the amount of one hundred millions: for it is the formal intention of the king never to make the safety of his realm dependent upon any person.

10. The king wishes that to consecrate a disposition so important, the name of taille be abolished in the kingdom and that this tax be joined either to the vingtièmes, or to any other land tax, or finally that it be replaced in some way, but always in just and equal proportions and without distinction of estate, rank and birth.

12. All property rights, without exception, shall be constantly respected, and His Majesty expressly understands under the name of property rights, tithes, rents, annuities, feudal and seigniorial rights and duties, and, in general, all the rights and prerogatives useful or honorary, attached to lands and fiefs or pertaining to persons.

13. The first two orders of the state shall continue to enjoy exemptions from personal charges, but the king would be pleased to have the States-General consider means of converting this kind of charges into pecuniary contributions and that then all the orders of the state may be equally subjected to them.

15. The king, desiring to assure the personal liberty of all citizens in the most solid and durable manner, invites the States-General to seek for and to propose to him the means that may be the most fitting to conciliate the orders known under the name of lettres de cachet, with the maintenance of public security and with the precautions necessary in some cases to guard the honor of families, to repress with celerity the beginning of sedition or to guarantee the state from the effects of criminal negotiations with foreign powers.

30. His Majesty wishes that the use of the corvée for the making and maintenance of roads, be entirely and forever abolished in this kingdom.

COMMENTS OF THE KING IN RELATION TO THE ABOVE

You have, gentlemen, heard the substance of my dispositions and of my wishes; they are conformable to the earnest desire that I have for the public welfare; and, if by a fatality far from my thoughts, you should abandon me in so fine an enterprise, alone I will assure the well being of my people; alone I will consider myself as their true representative; and knowing your cahiers, knowing the perfect accord which exists between the most general wish of the nation and my kindly intentions, I will have all the confidence which so rare a harmony ought to inspire and I will advance towards the goal that I wish to attain with all the courage and firmness that it ought to inspire in me.

Reflect, gentlemen, that none of your projects, none of your dispositions, can have the force of a law without my special approbation. So I am the natural guarantee of your respective rights, and all the orders of the state can depend upon my equitable impartiality. All distrust upon your part would be a great injustice. It is I, at present, who am doing everything for the happiness of my people, and it is rare, perhaps, that the only ambition of a sovereign is to come to an understanding with his subjects that they may accept his kindnesses.

I order you, gentlemen, to separate immediately, and to go tomorrow morning, each to the chamber allotted to your order, in order to take up again your sessions. I order, therefore, the grand master of ceremonies to have the halls prepared.

DECREE OF THE ASSEMBLY (JUNE 23, 1789)

The National Assembly unanimously declares that it persists in its previous resolutions.

The National Assembly declares that the person of each of the deputies is inviolable; that any individuals, any corporations, tribunal, court or commission that shall dare, during or after the present session, to pursue, to seek for, to arrest or detain a deputy, by reason of any propositions, advice, opinions, or discourse made by him in the States General: as well as all persons who shall lend their aid to any of the said attempts by whomsoever they may be ordered, are infamous and traitors to the nation, and guilty of capital crime [punishable by death]. The National Assembly decrees that, in the aforesaid cases, it will take all the necessary measures to have sought out, pursued and punished those who may be its authors, instigators or executors.

THE FOURTH OF AUGUST DECREES (AUGUST 4-11, 1789)

(Following the overthrow of the Bastille on July 14, and the subsequent revolution in rural areas whereby peasants sacked the homes and castles of their feudal overlords and destroyed records of their feudal obligations)

1. The National Assembly completely abolishes the feudal regime. It decrees that, among the rights and dues, both feudal and censuel, all those originating in real or personal serfdom, personal servitude, and those which represent them, are abolished without indemnification; all others are declared redeemable, and that the price and mode of the redemption shall be fixed by the National Assembly. Those of the said dues which are not extinguished by this decree shall, nevertheless, continue to be collected until indemnification takes place.

2. The exclusive right [of the nobility] to maintain pigeon-houses and dove-cotes is abolished; everyone shall have the right to kill [pigeons] upon his own land.

3. The exclusive right to hunt and to maintain unenclosed warrens is likewise abolished; and every land-owner shall have the right to kill all kinds of game on his own land.

4. All manorial courts are suppressed without indemnification.

5. Tithes of every description and the dues which have been substituted for them. . . are abolished, on condition, however, that some other method be devised to provide for the expenses of divine worship, the support of the officiating clergy, the relief of the poor, repairs and rebuilding of churches and parsonages, and for all establishments, seminaries, schools, academies, asylums, communities and other institutions. . .

7. The sale of judicial and municipal offices shall be suppressed forthwith. Justice shall be dispensed gratis.

8. The fees of the country cures are abolished, and shall be discontinued as soon as provision shall be made for increasing the minimum salary for priests and for the payment to the curates. . .

9. Pecuniary privileges [for nobility and clergy], personal or real, in the payment of taxes are abolished forever. The assessment shall be made upon all the citizens and upon all property, in the same manner and in the same form.

11. All citizens, without distinction of birth, are eligible to any office or dignity, whether ecclesiastical, civil or military; and no profession shall imply any derogation.

17. The National Assembly solemnly proclaims the king, Louis XVI, the Restorer of French Liberty.

18. The National Assembly shall present itself in a body before the king, in order to submit to His Majesty the decree which has just been passed.

DECLARATION OF THE RIGHTS OF MAN AND CITIZEN (AUGUST 26, 1789)

The representatives of the French people, organized in National Assembly, considering that ignorance, forgetfulness or contempt of the rights of man, are the sole causes of the public miseries and of the corruption of governments, have resolved to set forth in a solemn declaration the natural, inalienable, and sacred rights of man, in order that this declaration, being ever present to all the members of the social body, may unceasingly remind them of their rights and their duties; in order that the acts of the legislative power and those of the executive power may be each moment compared with the aim of every political institution and thereby may be more respected; and in order that the demands of the citizens, grounded henceforth upon simple and incontestable principles, may always take the direction of maintaining the constitution and the welfare of all.

In consequence, the National Assembly recognizes and declares, in the presence and under the auspices of the Supreme Being, the following rights of man and citizen.

1. Men are born and remain free and equal in rights. Social distinctions can be based only upon public utility.

2. The aim of every political association is the preservation of the natural and imprescriptible rights of man. These rights are liberty, property, security, and resistance to oppression.

3. The source of all sovereignty is essentially in the nation; no body, no individual can exercise authority that does not proceed from it in plain terms.

4. Liberty consists in the power to do anything that does not injure others; accordingly, the exercise of natural rights of each man has no limits except those that secure to the other members of society the enjoyment of these same rights. These limits can be determined only by law.

5. The law has the right to forbid only such actions as are injurious to society. Nothing can be forbidden that is not interdicted by the law, and no one can be constrained to do that which it does not order.

6. Law is the expression of the general will. All citizens have the right to take part personally, or by their representatives, in its formation. It must be the same for all, whether it protects or punishes. All citizens being equal in its eyes, are equally eligible to all public dignities, places, and employments, according to their capacities, and without other distinction than that of their virtues and their talents.

7. No man can be accused, arrested, or detained, except in the cases determined by the law and according to the forms that it has prescribed. Those who procure, expedite, execute, or cause to be executed arbitrary orders ought to be punished: but every citizen summoned or seized in virtue of the law ought to render instant obedience; he makes himself guilty by resistance.

8. The law ought to establish only penalties that are strictly and obviously necessary, and no one can be punished except in virtue of a law established and promulgated prior to the offence and legally applied.

9. Every man being presumed innocent until he has been pronounced guilty, if it is thought indispensable to arrest him, all severity that may not be necessary to secure his person ought to be strictly suppressed by law.

10. No one should be disturbed on account of his opinions, even religious, provided their manifestation does not derange the public order established by law.

11. The free communication of ideas and opinions is one of the most precious of the rights of man; every citizen then can freely speak, write, and print, subject to responsibility for the abuse of this freedom in the cases determined by law.

12. The guarantee of the rights of man and citizen requires a public force; this force then is instituted for the advantage of all and not for the personal benefit of those to whom it is entrusted.

13. For the maintenance of the public force and for the expenses of administration a general tax is indispensable; it ought to be equally apportioned among all the citizens according to their means.

14. All the citizens have the right to ascertain, by themselves or by their representatives, the necessity of the public tax, to consent to it freely, to follow the employment of it, and to determine the quota, the assessment, the collection, and the duration of it.

15. Society has a right to call for an account of his administration from every public agent.

16. Any society in which the guarantee of the rights is not secured, or the separation of powers not determined, has no constitution at all.

17. Property being a sacred and inviolable right, no one can be deprived of it, unless a legally established public necessity evidently demands it, under the condition of a just and prior indemnity.

DECREE ON CHURCH LANDS (NOVEMBER 2, 1789)

The National Assembly decrees, 1st, that all the ecclesiastical estates are at the disposal of the nation, on condition of providing in a suitable manner for the expense of worship, the maintenance of its ministers, and the relief of the poor, under the supervision and following the directions of the provinces; and, that in the provisions to be made, in order to provide for the maintenance of the ministers of religion, there can be assured for the endowment of each cure not less than 1,200 livres per annum, not including the dwelling and the gardens attached.

DECREE ABOLISHING THE NOBILITY (JUNE 19, 1790)

Hereditary nobility is forever abolished; in consequence the titles of prince, duke, count, marquis, viscount, baron, knight, noble, etc., shall neither be taken by anyone whomsoever nor given to anybody.

A citizen may take only the true name of his family; no one may wear liveries nor cause them to be worn, nor have armorial bearings.

CIVIL CONSTITUTION OF THE CLERGY

Title I

ARTICLE I. Each [of France's 83 new] departments shall form a single diocese. . .

. . . All other bishoprics in the eighty-three departments of the kingdom, which are not included by name in the present article, are, and forever shall be, abolished.

. . . No church or parish of France nor any French citizen may acknowledge upon any occasion, or upon any pretext whatsoever, the authority of an ordinary bishop or of an archbishop whose see shall be under the supremacy of a foreign power, nor that of his representatives residing in France or elsewhere; without prejudice, however, to the unity of the faith and the intercourse which shall be maintained with the visible head of the universal Church, as hereafter provided.

VI. A new arrangement and division of all the parishes of the kingdom shall be undertaken immediately in concert with the bishop and the district administration.

XX. All titles and offices other than those mentioned in the present constitution, dignities, canonries, prebends, half prebends, chapels, chaplainships, both in cathedral and collegiate churches, all regular and secular chapters for either sex, abbacies and priorships. . . for either sex. . . are from the day of this decree extinguished and abolished and shall never be reestablished in any form.

Title II

ARTICLE I. [**ELECTION OF CHURCH OFFICIALS**] Beginning with the day of publication of the present decree, there shall be but one mode of choosing bishops and parish priests, namely that of **election**.

II. All elections shall be by ballot and shall be decided by the absolute majority of the votes.

VI. The election of a bishop can only take place or be undertaken upon Sunday, in the principal church of the chief town of the department, at the close of the parish mass, at which all the electors are required to be present.

VII. In order to be eligible to a bishopric, one must have fulfilled for fifteen years at least the duties of the church ministry in the diocese, as a parish priest, officiating minister, or curate, or as superior, or as directing vicar of the seminary.

XIX. [**ELECTIONS NOT SUBJECT TO PAPAL CONFIRMATION**] The new bishop may not apply to the pope for any form of confirmation, but shall send notice of his election to the pope, as the visible head of the universal Church, as a testimony to the unity of faith and communion maintained with him.

XXI. [**BISHOPS MUST TAKE OATH SWEARING LOYALTY TO THE CONSTITUTION**] Before the ceremony of consecration begins, the bishop elect shall take a solemn oath, in the presence of the municipal officers, of the people, and of the clergy, to guard with care the faithful of his diocese who are confided to him, to be loyal to the nation, the law, and the king, and to support with all his power the constitution decreed by the National Assembly and accepted by the king.

XI. Bishoprics and cures shall be looked upon as vacant until those elected to fill them shall have taken the oath above mentioned.

Title III

ARTICLE I. [**CATHOLIC OFFICIALS TO BECOME EMPLOYEES OF THE STATE**] The ministers of religion, performing as they do the first and most important functions of society and forced to live continuously in the place where they discharge the offices to which they have been called by the confidence of the people, shall be supported by the nation.

II. [**SALARIES TO BE FIXED BY THE STATE**] Every bishop, priest, and officiating clergyman in a chapel of ease shall be furnished with a suitable dwelling, on condition, however, that the occupant shall make all the necessary current repairs. This shall not affect at present, in any way, those parishes where the priest now receives a money equivalent instead of his dwelling. The departments shall, moreover, have cognizance of suits arising in this connection, brought by the parishes and by the priests. Salaries shall be assigned to each, as indicated below.

III. The bishop of Paris shall receive fifty thousand livres; the bishops of the cities having a population of fifty thousand (p. 426) or more, twenty thousand livres; other bishops, twelve thousand livres.

V. The salaries of the parish priests shall be as follows: in Paris, six thousand livres; in cities having a population of fifty thousand or over, four thousand livres; in those having a population of less than fifty thousand and more than ten thousand, three thousand livres; in cities and towns of which the population is below ten thousand and more than three thousand, twenty-four hundred livres.

In all other cities, towns, and villages where the parish shall have a population between three thousand and twenty-five hundred, two thousand livres; in those between twenty-five hundred and two thousand, eighteen hundred livres; in those having a population of less than two thousand, and more than one thousand, the salary shall be fifteen hundred livres; in those having one thousand inhabitants and under, twelve hundred livres.

VII. The salaries *in money* of the ministers of religion shall be paid every three months, in advance, by the treasurer of the district.

XII. In view of the salary which is assured to them by the present constitution, the bishops, parish priests, and curates shall perform the Episcopal and priestly functions *gratis.*

Title IV

ARTICLE I. The law requiring the residence of ecclesiastics in the districts under their charge shall be strictly observed. All vested with an ecclesiastical office or function shall be subject to this, without distinction or exception.

II. No bishop shall absent himself from his diocese more than two weeks consecutively during the year, except in case of real necessity and with the consent of the directory of the department in which his see is situated.

III. In the same manner, the parish priests and the curates may not absent themselves from the place of their duties beyond the term fixed above, except for weighty reasons, and even in such cases the priests must obtain the permission both of their bishop and of the directory of their district, and the curates that of the parish priest.

VI. Bishops, parish priests, and curates may, as active citizens, be present at the primary and electoral assemblies; they may be chosen electors, or as deputies to the legislative body, or as members of the general council of the communes or of the administrative councils of their districts or departments.

CIVIL CONSTITUTION, SECTION D: OBLIGATORY OATH (NOVEMBER 27, 1790)

D1. (Section D provisions) The bishops and former archbishops and the *cures* kept in their positions shall be required, if they have not already done so, to take the oath for which they are liable . . . concerning the civil constitution of the clergy. In consequence they shall swear . . . to look with care after the faithful of their diocese or the parish which is intrusted to them, to be faithful to the nation, to the law and to the king, and to maintain with all their power the constitution decreed by the National Assembly and accepted by the king; to wit those who are actually in their diocese or parish within a week; those who are absent therefrom but are in France, within a month; and those who are abroad within two months. All to date from the publication of the present decree.

5. Those of the said bishops, former archbishops, *cures*, and other ecclesiastical public functionaries, who shall not have taken . . . the oath which is prescribed for them respectively, shall be reputed to have renounced their office and there shall be provision made for their replacement, as in case of vacancy by resignation.

CONSTITUTION OF 1791 (PROPOSED)

Introduction

The National Assembly, wishing to establish the French constitution upon the principles which it has just recognized and declared, abolishes irrevocably the institutions that have injured liberty and the equality of rights.

There is no longer nobility, nor peerage, nor hereditary distinctions, nor distinctions of orders, nor feudal regime, nor patrimonial jurisdictions, nor any titles, denominations, or prerogatives derived therefrom, nor any order of chivalry, nor any corporations or decorations which demanded proofs of nobility or that were grounded upon distinctions of birth, nor any superiority other than that of public officials in the exercise of their functions.

There is no longer either sale or inheritance of any public office.

There is no longer for any part of the nation nor for any individual any privilege or exception to the law that is common to all Frenchmen.

There are no longer corporations of professions, arts, and crafts.

The law no longer recognizes religious vows, nor any other obligation which may be contrary to natural rights or to the constitution.

Title I. Fundamental Provisions: Natural and Civil Rights

The constitution guarantees as natural and civil rights:

1. That all the citizens are eligible to offices and employments, without any other distinction than that of virtue and talent;
2. That all the taxes shall be apportioned among all the citizens in proportion to their means;

The constitution likewise guarantees as natural and civil rights:

Liberty to every man to move about, to remain, and to depart without liability to arrest or detention, except according to the forms determined by the constitution;

Liberty to every man to speak, to write, to print and publish his ideas without having his writings subjected to any censorship or inspection before their publication, and to follow the religious worship to which he is attached;

Liberty to the citizens to meet peaceably and without arms, in obedience to the police laws;

Liberty to address individually signed petitions to the constituted authorities.

The legislative power cannot make any law that attacks and impedes the exercise of the natural and civil rights contained in the present title and guaranteed by the constitution; but as liberty consists only in the power to do anything that is not injurious to the rights of others or to the public security, the law can establish penalties against acts which, in attacking the public security or the rights of others, may be injurious to society.

The constitution guarantees the inviolability of property or a just and prior indemnity for that of which a legally established public necessity may demand the sacrifice.

Property intended for the expenses of worship and for all services of public utility belongs to the nation and is at all times at its disposal.

There shall be created and organized a system of public instruction, common to all citizens, gratuitous as regards the parts of education indispensable for all men, and whose establishments shall be gradually distributed in accordance with the division of the kingdom.

There shall be established national fêtes to preserve the memory of the French revolution, to maintain fraternity among the citizens, and to attach them to the constitution, the fatherland, and the laws.

Title II. On Marriage

The law considers marriage as only a civil contract.

Title III. Sovereignty: Division of Powers

1. Sovereignty is one, indivisible, inalienable, and imprescriptible: it belongs to the nation: no section of the people nor any individual can attribute to himself the exercise thereof.

2. The nation, from which alone emanates all the powers, can exercise them only be delegation.

3. The legislative power is delegated to the National Assembly.

4. The government is monarchical: the executive power is delegated to the king, in order to be exercised under his authority by ministers and other responsible agents, in the manner which shall be determined hereinafter.

5. The judicial power is delegated to judges elected at states times by the people.

Chapt I: Legislature: National Legislative Assembly
The legislative body shall not be dissolved by the king.

It is composed of only one chamber.

It shall be formed every two years by new elections.

The elected members shall take an oath: "to maintain with all their power the constitution of the kingdom, decreed by the National Constituent Assembly, in the years 1789, 1790, and 1791; and not to propose nor to consent within the course of the legislature to anything which may injure it, and to be in everything faithful to the nation, the law, and the king.

The representatives of the nation are inviolable; they cannot be questioned, accused, nor tried at any time for what they have said, written, or done in the exercise of their functions as representatives.

CHAPTER II. OF THE ROYALTY

The person of the king is inviolable and sacred: his only title is King of the French/

There is no authority in France superior to that of the law; the king reigns only by it and it is only in the name of the law that he can demand obedience.

The king, upon his accession to the throne, shall take to the nation, in the presence of the legislative body, the oath: "to be faithful to the nation and the law, to employ all the power which is delegated to him to maintain the constitution decreed by the National Constituent Assembly in the years 1789, 1790, and 1791, and to cause the laws to be executed."

If the king puts himself at the head of an army and directs the forces thereof against the nation, or if he does not by a formal instrument place himself in opposition to any such enterprise which may be conducted in his name, he shall be considered to have abdicated the throne.

After the express or legal abdication, the king shall be in the class of citizens and can be accused and tried like them for acts subsequent to his abdication.

The individual estates which the king possess are irrevocably united to the domain of the nation.

The nation provides for the splendor of the throne by a civil list, determined by the legislative body.

The ministers of the king must have the budgets approved by the legislative body; and no minister can be prosecuted for any acts of his administration, without a decree from the legislative body.

CHAPTER III. OF THE EXERCISE OF LEGISLATIVE POWER

The constitution delegates exclusively to the legislative body the following powers and functions:

1. To propose and enact the laws; the king can only invite the legislative body to take the matter under consideration;

2. To fix public expenditures and taxes;

3. To determine the form of money;

4. To permit or forbid the introduction of foreign troops upon French soil;

5. War can only be declared by a decree of the legislative body.

6. The ratification of treaties of peace, alliance, and commerce belongs to the legislative body.

THE MONARCH'S RELATION TO LEGISLATION: THE ROYAL SANCTION

The decrees of the legislative body are presented to the king, who can refuse his consent to them.

In the case where the king refuses his consent, this refusal is only suspensive: When the two legislatures following that which shall have presented the decree shall have again presented the same decree in the same terms, the king shall be considered to have given the sanction.

The king is supreme head of general administration of the kingdom: the task of looking after the maintenance of public order and tranquility is confided to him.

The king is the supreme head of the army and navy.

The king appoints ambassadors, and confers the command of armies and fleets.

Appendix B: Rousseau's *First Discourse: On the Moral Effects of the Arts and Sciences*

Translated by G. D. H. Cole [1915]

[Note for the editors: This version of Jean-Jacques Rousseau's First Discourse *has been edited, reorganized, and slightly abridged for Reacting students. Some of the original footnotes have been omitted. Rousseau submitted this essay for a competition sponsored by the Academy of Dijon. The question proposed by the academy was: "Has the restoration of arts and sciences [a reference, surely, to the advance of music, plays, and literature, of whom, Voltaire was perhaps the exemplar] had a purifying effect upon morals?" The materials in brackets are by the editors and were not in the original.]*

PREFACE

The question before me is: "Whether the Restoration of the arts and sciences has had the effect of purifying or corrupting morals." Which side am I to take?

I feel the difficulty of treating this subject fittingly, before the tribunal which is to judge of what I advance. How can I presume to belittle the sciences before one of the most learned assemblies in Europe, to commend ignorance in a famous Academy, and reconcile my contempt for study with the respect due to the truly learned? I was aware of these inconsistencies, but not discouraged by them. It is not science, I said to myself, that I am attacking; it is virtue that I am defending, and that before virtuous men—and goodness is ever dearer to the good than learning to the learned. What then have I to fear? The sagacity of the assembly before which I am pleading? That, I acknowledge, is to be feared; but rather on account of faults of construction than of the views I hold . . . I have upheld the cause of truth to the best of my natural abilities, whatever my apparent success, there is one reward which cannot fail me. That reward I shall find in the bottom of my heart.

PART I

It is a noble and beautiful spectacle to see man raising himself, so to speak, from nothing by his own exertions; dissipating, by the light of reason, all the thick clouds in which he was by nature enveloped; mounting above himself; soaring in thought even to the celestial regions; like the sun, encompassing with giant strides the vast extent of the universe; and, what is still grander and more wonderful, going back into himself, there to study man and get to know his own nature, his duties and his end. All these miracles we have seen renewed within the last few generations.

Europe had relapsed into the barbarism of the earliest ages; the inhabitants of this part of the world, which is at present so highly enlightened, were plunged, some centuries ago, in a state still worse than ignorance. A scientific jargon, more despicable than mere ignorance, had usurped the name of knowledge, and opposed an almost invincible obstacle to its restoration. Things had come to such a pass, that it required a complete revolution to bring men back to common sense. This came at last from the quarter from which it was least to be expected. It was the stupid Mussulman [the Muslim peoples of North Africa and the Middle East], the eternal scourge of letters, who was the immediate cause of their revival among us. The fall of the throne of Constantine [the Turks captured Constantinople in 1453], brought to Italy the relics of ancient Greece [especially, the literature and art of Athens], and with these precious spoils France in turn was enriched. The sciences soon followed literature, and the art of thinking joined that of writing: an order which may seem strange, but is perhaps only too natural.

. . . The mind, as well as the body, has its needs: those of the body are the basis of society, those of the mind its ornaments. So long as government and law provide for the security and well-being of men in their common life, the arts, literature, and the sciences, less despotic though perhaps more powerful, fling garlands of flowers over the chains which weigh them down. They stifle in men's breasts that sense of original liberty, for which they seem to have been born; cause them to love their own slavery, and so make of them what is called a civilized people. Necessity raised up thrones; the arts and sciences have made them strong. Powers of the earth, cherish all talents and protect those who cultivate them. Civilized peoples, cultivate such pursuits: to them, happy slaves, you owe that delicacy and exquisiteness of taste, which is so much your boast, that sweetness of disposition and urbanity of manners which make intercourse so easy and agreeable among you- in a word, the appearance of all the virtues, without being in possession of one of them.

It was for this sort of accomplishment, which is by so much the more captivating, as it seems less affected, that Athens and Rome were so much distinguished in the boasted times of their splendour and magnificence: and it is doubtless in the same respect that our own age and nation will excel all periods and peoples. An air of philosophy without pedantry; an address at once natural and engaging, distant equally from Teutonic clumsiness and Italian pantomime; these are the effects of a taste acquired by liberal studies and improved by conversation with the world.

What happiness would it be for those who live among us, if our external appearance were always a true mirror of our hearts; if decorum were but virtue; if the maxims we professed were the rules of our conduct; and if real philosophy were inseparable from the title of a philosopher! But so many good qualities too seldom go together; virtue rarely appears in so much pomp and state. Richness of apparel may proclaim the man of fortune, and elegance the man of taste; but true health and manliness are known by different signs. It is under the homespun of the labourer, and not beneath the gilt and tinsel of the courtier, that we should look for strength and vigour of body. External ornaments are no less foreign to virtue, which is the strength and activity of the mind. The honest man is an athlete, who loves to wrestle stark naked; he scorns all those vile trappings, which prevent the exertion of his strength, and were, for the most part, invented only to conceal some deformity.

Before art had moulded our behavior [or, more precisely, our manners and customs], and taught our passions to speak an artificial language, our morals were rude but natural; and the different ways in which we behaved proclaimed at the first glance the difference of our dispositions. Human nature was not at bottom better then than now; but men found their security in the ease with which they could see through one another, and this advantage, of which we no longer feel the value, prevented their having many vices.

Nowadays, when more subtle study and a more refined taste have reduced the art of pleasing to a system, there prevails in modern manners a servile and deceptive conformity; so that one would think every mind had been cast in the same mould. Politeness requires this thing; decorum that; ceremony has its forms, and fashion its laws, and these we must always follow, never the promptings of our own nature. We no longer dare seem what we really are, but lie under a perpetual restraint; in the meantime the herd of men, which we call society, all act under the same circumstances exactly alike, unless very particular and powerful motives prevent them. Thus we never know with whom we have to deal; and even to know our friends we must wait for some critical and pressing occasion; that is, till it is too late; for it is on those very occasions that such knowledge is of use to us.

What a train of vices must attend this uncertainty! Sincere friendship, real esteem, and perfect confidence are banished from among men. Jealousy, suspicion, fear, coldness, reserve, hate, and fraud lie constantly concealed under that uniform and deceitful veil of politeness; that boasted candour and urbanity, for which we are indebted to the light and leading of this age. We shall no longer take in vain by our oaths the name of our Creator; but we shall insult Him with our blasphemies, and our scrupulous ears will take no offence. We have grown too modest to brag of our own deserts; but we do not scruple to decry those of others. We do not grossly outrage even our enemies, but artfully calumniate them. Our hatred of other nations diminishes, but patriotism dies with it. Ignorance is held in contempt; but a dangerous skepticism has succeeded it. Some vices indeed are condemned and others grown dishonorable; but we have still many that are honored with the names of virtues, and it is become necessary that we should either have, or at least pretend to have them. Let who will extol the moderation of our modern sages, I see nothing in it but a refinement of intemperance as unworthy of my commendation as their artificial simplicity.

Such is the purity to which our morals have attained; this is the virtue we have made our own. Let the arts and sciences claim the share they have had in this salutary work. I shall add but one reflection more; suppose an inhabitant of some distant country should endeavor to form an idea of European morals from the state of the sciences, the perfection of the arts, the propriety of our public entertainments, the politeness of our behavior, the affability of our conversation, our constant professions of benevolence, and from those tumultuous assemblies of people of all ranks, who seem, from morning till night, to have no other care than to oblige one another. Such a stranger, I maintain, would arrive at a totally false view of our morality.

Where there is no effect, it is idle to look for a cause: but here the effect is certain and the depravity actual; our minds have been corrupted in proportion as the arts and sciences have improved. Will it be said, that this is a misfortune peculiar to the present age? No, gentlemen, the evils resulting from our vain curiosity are as old as the world. The daily ebb and flow of the tides are not more regularly influenced by the moon than the morals of a people by the progress of the arts and sciences. [That the moon controlled the tides are influenced by the position of the mood was first gained wide acceptance in the 1700s; Galileo had argued—a century earlier—that the rotation of the earth created the tides.] As their light has risen above our horizon, virtue has taken flight, and the same phenomenon has been constantly observed in all times and places.

[What follows is a history lesson: ancient civilizations lose their ardor and decline once they embrace the "arts."]

Consider Egypt, the first school of mankind, that ancient country, famous for its fertility under a brazen sky; the spot from which Sesostris once set out to conquer the world. Egypt became the mother of philosophy and the fine arts; soon she was conquered by Cambyses, and then successively by the Greeks, the Romans, the Arabs, and finally the Turks.

Consider Greece, once peopled by heroes, who twice vanquished Asia. Letters, as yet in their infancy, had not corrupted the disposition of its inhabitants; but the progress of the sciences soon produced a dissoluteness of manners and the imposition of the Macedonian yoke: (King Philip of Macedonia conquered most of the Greek city states in 338 B.C.]: from which time Greece, always learned, always voluptuous, and always a slave, has experienced amid all its revolutions no more than a change of masters. Not all the eloquence of Demosthenes could breathe life into a body which luxury and the arts had once enervated.

It was not till the days of Ennius and Terence (ancient Roman poets in the second century, B.C.) that Rome, founded by a shepherd, and made illustrious by peasants, began to degenerate. But after the appearance of an Ovid, a Catullus, a Martial, and the rest of those numerous obscene authors, whose very names are enough to put modesty to the blush, Rome, once the shrine of virtue, became the theater of vice, a scorn among the nations, and an object of derision even to barbarians. . .

What shall I say of that metropolis of the Eastern Empire, which, by its situation, seemed destined to be the capital of the world; that refuge of the arts and sciences, when they were banished from the rest of Europe, more perhaps by wisdom than barbarism? The most profligate debaucheries, the most abandoned villainies, the most atrocious crimes, plots, murders, and assassinations form the warp and woof of the history of Constantinople. Such is the pure source from which have flowed to us the floods of knowledge on which the present age so prides itself.

[And even today—in the mid 1700s—a society is corrupted and weakened by its reliance on men of letters: the Confucian literati of China.]

But why bother searching the past for proofs of a truth, of which the present affords us ample evidence? There is in Asia a vast empire, where learning is held in honor, and leads to the highest dignities in the State. [This refers to China as run by Confucian literati.] If the sciences improved our morals, if they inspired us with courage and taught us to lay down our lives for the good of our country, the Chinese should be wise, free, and invincible. But, if there be no vice they do not practise, no crime with which they are not familiar; if the sagacity of their ministers, the supposed wisdom of their laws, and the multitude of inhabitants who people that vast empire, have alike failed to preserve them from the yoke of the rude and ignorant Tartars. [Rousseau errs here: the Tartars refers to the Mongols, an earlier dynasty; after the fall of the Ming dynasty in the mid 1600s, China was governed by the Manchus—not the Mongols—during the Qing dynasty]. Of what use were their men of science and literature? What advantage has that country reaped from the honors bestowed on its learned men? Can it be that of being peopled by a race of scoundrels and slaves?

Contrast with these instances the morals of those few nations which, being preserved from the contagion of useless knowledge, have by their virtues become happy in themselves and afforded an example to the rest of the world. . . [Many peoples] have preferred other activities to those of the mind. They were not ignorant that in other countries there were men who spent their time in disputing idly about the sovereign good, and about vice and virtue. They knew that these useless thinkers were lavish in their own praises, and stigmatized other nations contemptuously as barbarians. But they noted the morals of these people, and so learnt what to think of their learning.

[Here Rousseau prefers Spartan simplicity and virtue to Athenian arts and cleverness.]

Can it be forgotten that, in the very heart of Greece, there arose a city as famous for the happy ignorance of its inhabitants, as for the wisdom of its laws; a republic of demi-gods rather than of men, so greatly superior their virtues seemed to those of mere humanity? Sparta, eternal proof of the vanity of science, while the vices, under the conduct of the fine arts, were being introduced into Athens, even while its tyrant was carefully collecting together the works of the prince of poets, was driving from her walls artists and the arts, the learned and their learning!

[Rousseau then leads to the outcome: Sparta's defeat of Athens during the Peloponnesian War.]

The difference was seen in the outcome. Athens became the seat of politeness and taste, the country of orators and philosophers. The elegance of its buildings equalled that of its language; on every side might be seen marble and canvas, animated by the hands of the most skilled artists. From Athens we derive those astonishing performances, which will serve as models to every corrupt age.

The picture of Lacedaemon [Sparta] is not so highly colored. There, the neighboring nations used to say, "men were born virtuous, their native air seeming to inspire them with virtue." But its inhabitants have left us nothing but the memory of their heroic actions: monuments that should not count for less in our eyes than the most curious relics of Athenian marble.

[Rousseau invokes Socrates' criticisms of Athens, and of its arts and letters.]

It is true that, among the Athenians, there were some few wise men who withstood the general torrent, and preserved their integrity even in the company of the Muses. But hear the judgment which the principal, and most unhappy of them, passed on the artists and learned men of his day. "I have considered the poets," says he, "and I look upon them as people whose talents impose both on themselves and on others; they give themselves out for wise men, and are taken for such; but in reality they are anything sooner than that."

"From the poets," continues Socrates, "I turned to the artists. Nobody was more ignorant of the arts than myself; nobody was more fully persuaded that the artists were possessed of amazing knowledge. I soon discovered, however, that they were in as bad a way as the poets, and that both had fallen into the same misconception. Because the most skillful of them excel others in their particular jobs, they think themselves wiser than all the rest of mankind. This arrogance spoilt all their skill in my eyes, so that, putting myself in the place of the oracle, and asking myself whether I would rather be what I am or what they are, know what they know, or know that I know nothing, I very readily answered, for myself and the god, that I had rather remain as I am.

"None of us, neither the sophists, nor the poets, nor the orators, nor the artists, nor I, know what is the nature of the true, the good, or the beautiful. But there is this difference between us; that, though none of these people know anything, they all think they know something; whereas for my part, if I know nothing, I am at least in no doubt of my ignorance. So the superiority of wisdom, imputed to me by the oracle, is reduced merely to my being fully convinced that I am ignorant of what I do not know."

Thus we find Socrates, the wisest of men in the judgment of the gods, and the most learned of all the Athenians in the opinion of all Greece, speaking in praise of ignorance. Were he alive now, there is little reason to think that our modern scholars and artists would induce him to change his mind. No, gentlemen, that honest man would still persist in despising our vain sciences. He would lend no aid to swell the flood of books that flows from every quarter: he would leave to us, as he did to his disciples, only the example and memory of his virtues; that is the noblest method of instructing mankind.

Socrates had begun at Athens, and the elder Cato proceeded at Rome, to inveigh against those seductive and subtle Greeks, who corrupted the virtue and destroyed the courage of their fellow-citizens: culture, however, prevailed. Rome was filled with philosophers and orators, military discipline was neglected, agriculture was held in contempt, men formed sects, and forgot their country. To the sacred names of liberty, disinterestedness, and obedience to law, succeeded those of Epicurus, Zeno, and Arcesilaus. It was even a saying among their own philosophers that since learned men appeared among them, honest men had been in eclipse. Before that time the Romans were satisfied with the practice of virtue; they were undone when they began to study it. . .

What fatal splendour has succeeded the ancient Roman simplicity? What is this foreign language, this effeminacy of manners? What is the meaning of these statues, paintings, and buildings? Fools, what have you done? You, the lords of the earth, have made yourselves the slaves of the frivolous nations you have subdued. You are governed by rhetoricians, and it has been only to enrich architects, painters, sculptors, and stage-players that you have watered Greece and Asia with your blood. Even the spoils of Carthage are the prize of a flute-player. Romans! Romans! Make haste to demolish those amphitheaters, break to pieces those statues, burn those paintings; drive from among you those slaves who keep you in subjection, and whose fatal arts are corrupting your morals. Let other hands make themselves illustrious by such vain talents; the only talent worthy of Rome is that of conquering the world and making virtue its ruler.

[And now to early modern Europe: England and France:]

But let pass the distance of time and place, and let us see what has happened in our own time and country; or rather let us banish odious descriptions that might offend our delicacy, and spare ourselves the pains of repeating the same things under different names. It was not for nothing that I invoked the Manes of Fabricius; for what have I put into his mouth that might not have come with as much propriety from Louis the Twelfth or Henry the Fourth? It is true that in France Socrates would not have drunk the hemlock, but he would have drunk of a potion infinitely more bitter, of insult, mockery, and contempt a hundred times worse than death.

Thus it is that luxury, profligacy, and slavery have been, in all ages, the scourge of the efforts of our pride to emerge from that happy state of ignorance, in which the wisdom of providence had placed us. That thick veil with which it has covered all its operations seems to be a sufficient proof that it never designed us for such fruitless researches. But is there, indeed, one lesson it has taught us, by which we have rightly profited, or which we have neglected with impunity?

Let men learn for once that nature would have preserved them from science, as a mother snatches a dangerous weapon from the hands of her child. Let them know that all the secrets she hides are so many evils from which she protects them, and that the very difficulty they find in acquiring knowledge is not the least of her bounty towards them. Men are perverse; but they would have been far worse, if they had had the misfortune to be born learned.

How humiliating are these reflections to humanity, and how mortified by them our pride should be! What! It will be asked, is uprightness the child of ignorance? Is virtue inconsistent with learning? What consequences might not be drawn from such suppositions? But to reconcile these apparent contradictions, we need only examine closely the emptiness and vanity of those pompous titles, which are so liberally bestowed on human knowledge, and which so blind our judgment. Let us consider, therefore, the arts and sciences in themselves. Let us see what must result from their advancement, and let us not hesitate to admit the truth of all those points on which our arguments coincide with the inductions we can make from history.

PART TWO

[Knowledge—or arts and sciences—have emerged out of evil, and generated more of the same]:

An ancient tradition passed out of Egypt into Greece, that some god, who was an enemy to the repose of mankind, was the inventor of the sciences. What must the Egyptians, among whom the sciences first arose, have thought of them? And they beheld, near at hand, the sources from which they sprang. In fact, whether we turn to the annals of the world, or eke out with philosophical investigations the uncertain chronicles of history, we shall not find for human knowledge an origin answering to the idea we are pleased to entertain of it at present. Astronomy was born of superstition, eloquence of ambition, hatred, falsehood, and flattery; geometry of avarice; physics of an idle curiosity; and even moral philosophy of human pride. Thus the arts and sciences owe their birth to our vices; we should be less doubtful of their advantages, if they had sprung from our virtues.

Their evil origin is, indeed, but too plainly reproduced in their objects. What would become of the arts, were they not cherished by luxury? If men were not unjust, of what use were jurisprudence? What would become of history, if there were no tyrants, wars, or conspiracies? In a word who would pass his life in barren speculations, if everybody, attentive only to the obligations of humanity and the necessities of nature, spent his whole life in serving his country, obliging his friends, and relieving the unhappy? Are we then made to live and die on the brink of that well at the bottom of which Truth lies hid? This reflection alone is, in my opinion, enough to discourage at first setting out every man who seriously endeavors to instruct himself by the study of philosophy.

What a variety of dangers surrounds us! What a number of wrong paths present themselves in the investigation of the sciences! Through how many errors, more perilous than truth itself is useful, must we not pass to arrive at it? The disadvantages we lie under are evident; for falsehood is capable of an infinite variety of combinations; but the truth has only one manner of being. Besides, where is the man who sincerely desires to find it? Or even admitting his good will, by what characteristic marks is he sure of knowing it? Amid the infinite diversity of opinions where is the criterion by which we may certainly judge of it? Again, what is still more difficult, should we even be fortunate enough to discover it, who among us will know how to make right use of it?

If our sciences are futile in the objects they propose, they are no less dangerous in the effects they produce. Being the effect of idleness, they generate idleness in their turn; and an irreparable loss of time is the first prejudice which they must necessarily cause to society. To live without doing some good is a great evil as well in the political as in the moral world; and hence every useless citizen should be regarded as a pernicious person. Tell me then, illustrious philosophers, of whom we learn the ratios in which attraction acts in vacuo; and in the revolution of the planets, the relations of spaces traversed in equal times; by whom we are taught what curves have conjugate points, points of inflexion, and cusps; how the soul and body correspond, like two clocks, without actual communication; what planets may be inhabited; and what insects reproduce in an extraordinary manner. Answer me, I say, you from whom we receive all this sublime information, whether we should have been less numerous, worse governed, less formidable, less flourishing, or more perverse, supposing you had taught us none of all these fine things. Reconsider therefore the importance of your productions; and, since the labours of the most enlightened of our learned men and the best of our citizens are of so little utility, tell us what we ought to think of that numerous herd of obscure writers and useless litterateurs, who devour without any return the substance of the State.

Useless, do I say? Would God they were! Society would be more peaceful, and morals less corrupt. But these vain and futile declaimers go forth on all sides, armed with their fatal paradoxes, to sap the foundations of our faith, and nullify virtue. They smile contemptuously at such old names as patriotism and religion, and consecrate their talents and philosophy to the destruction and defamation of all that men hold sacred. Not that they bear any real hatred to virtue or dogma; they are the enemies of public opinion alone; to bring them to the foot of the altar, it would be enough to banish them to a land of atheists. What extravagancies will not the rage of singularity induce men to commit!

The waste of time is certainly a great evil; but still greater evils attend upon literature and the arts. One is luxury, produced like them by indolence and vanity. Luxury is seldom unattended by the arts and sciences; and they are always attended by luxury. I know that our philosophy, fertile in paradoxes, pretends, in contradiction to the experience of all ages, that luxury contributes to the splendour of States. But, without insisting on the necessity of sumptuary laws, can it be denied that rectitude of morals is essential to the duration of empires, and that luxury is diametrically opposed to such rectitude? Let it be admitted that luxury is a certain indication of wealth; that it even serves, if you will, to increase such wealth; what conclusion is to be drawn from this paradox, so worthy of the times? And what will become of virtue if riches are to be acquired at any cost? The politicians of the ancient world were always talking of morals and virtue; ours speak of nothing but commerce and money. One of them will tell you that in such a country a man is worth just as much as he will sell for at Algiers: another, pursuing the same mode of calculation, finds that in some countries a man is worth nothing, and in others still less than nothing; they value men as they do droves of oxen. According to them, a man is worth no more to the State than the amount he consumes; and thus a Sybarite would be worth at least thirty Lacedaemonians [Sparta]. Let these writers tell me, however, which of the two republics, Sybaris or Sparta, was subdued by a handful of peasants, and which became the terror of Asia.

What then is the precise point in dispute about luxury? It is to know which is most advantageous to empires, that their existence should be brilliant and momentary, or virtuous and lasting. I say brilliant, but with what lustre? A taste for ostentation never prevails in the same minds as a taste for honesty. No, it is impossible that understandings, degraded by a multitude of futile cares, should ever rise to what is truly great and noble; even if they had the strength, they would want the courage.

Every artist loves applause. The praise of his contemporaries is the most valuable part of his recompense. What then will he do to obtain it, if he have the misfortune to be born among a people, and at a time, when learning is in vogue, and the superficiality of youth is in a position to lead the fashion; when men have sacrificed their taste to those who tyrannize over their liberty, and one sex dare not approve anything but what is proportionate to the pusillanimity of the other; when the greatest masterpieces of dramatic poetry are condemned, and the noblest of musical productions neglected? This is what he will do. He will lower his genius to the level of the age, and will rather submit to compose mediocre works, that will be admired during his lifetime, than labour at sublime achievements which will not be admired till long after he is dead. Let the famous Voltaire tell us how many nervous and masculine beauties he has sacrificed to our false delicacy, and how much that is great and noble, that spirit of gallantry, which delights in what is frivolous and petty, has cost him.

It is thus that the dissolution of morals, the necessary consequence of luxury, brings with it in its turn the corruption of taste. Further, if by chance there be found among men of average ability, an individual with enough strength of mind to refuse to comply with the spirit of the age, and to debase himself by puerile productions, his lot will be hard. He will die in indigence and oblivion. This is not so much a prediction as a fact already confirmed by experience!

We cannot reflect on the morality of mankind without contemplating with pleasure the picture of the simplicity which prevailed in the earliest times. This image may be justly compared to a beautiful coast, adorned only by the hands of nature; towards which our eyes are constantly turned, and which we see receding with regret. While men were innocent and virtuous and loved to have the gods for witnesses of their actions, they dwelt together in the same huts; but when they became vicious, they grew tired of such inconvenient onlookers, and banished them to magnificent temples. Finally, they expelled their deities even from these, in order to dwell there themselves; or at least the temples of the gods were no longer more magnificent than the palaces of the citizens. This was the height of degeneracy; nor could vice ever be carried to greater lengths than when it was seen, supported, as it were, at the doors of the great, on columns of marble, and graven on Corinthian capitals. As the conveniences of life increase, as the arts are brought to perfection, and luxury spreads, true courage flags, the virtues disappear; and all this is the effect of the sciences and of those acts which are exercised in the privacy of men's dwellings.

When the Goths ravaged Greece, the libraries only escaped the flames owing to an opinion that was set on foot among them, that it was best to leave the enemy with a possession so calculated to divert their attention from military exercises, and keep them engaged in indolent and sedentary occupations. Charles the Eighth found himself master of Tuscany and the kingdom of Naples, almost without drawing sword; and all his court attributed this unexpected success to the fact that the princes and nobles of Italy applied themselves with greater earnestness to the cultivation of their understandings than to active and martial pursuits. In fact, says the sensible person who records these characteristics, experience plainly tells us that in military matters and all that resemble them application to the sciences tends rather to make men effeminate and cowardly than resolute and vigorous.

The Romans confessed that military virtue was extinguished among them, in proportion as they became connoisseurs in the arts of the painter, the engraver, and the goldsmith, and began to cultivate the fine arts. Indeed, as if this famous country was to be for ever an example to other nations, the rise of the Medici and the revival of letters has once more destroyed, this time perhaps for ever, the martial reputation which Italy seemed a few centuries ago to have recovered.

The ancient republics of Greece, with that wisdom which was so conspicuous in most of their institutions, forbade their citizens to pursue all those inactive and sedentary occupations, which by enervating and corrupting the body diminish also the vigour of the mind. With what courage, in fact, can it be thought that hunger and thirst, fatigues, dangers, and death, can be faced by men whom the smallest want overwhelms and the slightest difficulty repels? With what resolution can soldiers support the excessive toils of war, when they are entirely unaccustomed to them? With what spirits can they make forced marches under officers who have not even the strength to travel on horseback? It is no answer to cite the reputed valour of all the modern warriors who are so scientifically trained. I hear much of their bravery in a day's battle; but I am told nothing of how they support excessive fatigue, how they stand the severity of the seasons and the inclemency of the weather. A little sunshine or snow, or the want of a few superfluities, is enough to cripple and destroy one of our finest armies in a few days. Intrepid warriors! Permit me for once to tell you the truth, which you seldom hear. Of your bravery I am fully satisfied. I have no doubt that you would have triumphed with Hannibal at Cannae, and at Trasimene: that you would have passed the Rubicon with Caesar, and enabled him to enslave his country; but you never would have been able to cross the Alps with the former, or with the latter to subdue your own ancestors, the Gauls.

A war does not always depend on the events of battle: there is in generalship an art superior to that of gaining victories. A man may behave with great intrepidity under fire, and yet be a very bad officer. Even in the common soldier, a little more strength and vigour would perhaps be more useful than so much courage, which after all is no protection from death. And what does it matter to the State whether its troops perish by cold and fever, or by the sword of the enemy?

If the cultivation of the sciences is prejudicial to military qualities, it is still more so to moral qualities. Even from our infancy an absurd system of education serves to adorn our wit and corrupt our judgment. We see, on every side, huge institutions, where our youth are educated at great expense, and instructed in everything but their duty. Your children will be ignorant of their own language, when they can talk others which are not spoken anywhere. They will be able to compose verses which they can hardly understand; and, without being capable of distinguishing truth from error, they will possess the art of making them unrecognizable by specious arguments. But magnanimity, equity, temperance, humanity, and courage will be words of which they know not the meaning. The dear name of country will never strike on their ears; and if they ever hear speak of God, it will be less to fear than to be frightened of Him. I would as soon, said a wise man, that my pupil had spent his time in the tennis court as in this manner; for there his body at least would have got exercise. I well know that children ought to be kept employed, and that idleness is for them the danger most to be feared. But what should they be taught? This is undoubtedly an important question. Let them be taught what they are to practice when they come to be men; not what they ought to forget.

Our gardens are adorned with statues and our galleries with pictures. What would you imagine these masterpieces of art, thus exhibited to public admiration, represent? The great men who have defended their country, or the still greater men who have enriched it by their virtues? Far from it. They are the images of every perversion of heart and mind, carefully selected from ancient mythology, and presented to the early curiosity of our children, doubtless that they may have before their eyes the representations of vicious actions, even before they are able to read.

[Rousseau adds the element of "inequality" as another source of the ills of overly-mannered civilizations: this anticipates the theme of his second discourse "on the origins of inequality."]

Whence arise all those abuses, unless it be from that fatal inequality introduced among men by the difference of talents and the cheapening of virtue? This is the most evident effect of all our studies, and the most dangerous of all their consequences. The question is no longer whether a man is honest, but whether he is clever. We do not ask whether a book is useful, but whether it is well written. Rewards are lavished on wit and ingenuity, while virtue is left unhonored. There are a thousand prizes for fine discourses, and none for good actions. I should be glad, however, to know whether the honor attaching to the best discourse that ever wins the prize in this Academy is comparable with the merit of having founded the prize.

A wise man does not go in chase of fortune; but he is by no means insensible to glory, and when he sees it so ill distributed, his virtue, which might have been animated by a little emulation, and turned to the advantage of society, droops. and dies away in obscurity and indigence. It is for this reason that the agreeable arts must in time everywhere be preferred to the useful; and this truth has been but too much confirmed since the revival of the arts and sciences. We have physicists, geometricians, chemists, astronomers, poets, musicians, and painters in plenty; but we have no longer a citizen among us; or if there be found a few scattered over our abandoned countryside, they are left to perish there unnoticed and neglected. Such is the condition to which we are reduced, and such are our feelings towards those who give us our daily bread, and our children milk.

I confess, however, that the evil is not so great as it might have become. The eternal providence, in placing salutary simples beside noxious plants, and making poisonous animals contain their own antidote, has taught the sovereigns of the earth, who are its ministers, to imitate its wisdom. It is by following this example that the truly great monarch, to whose glory every age will add new lustre, drew from the very bosom of the arts and sciences the very fountains of a thousand lapses from rectitude, those famous societies, which, while they are depositaries of the dangerous trust of human knowledge, are yet the sacred guardians of morals, by the attention they pay to their maintenance among themselves in all their purity, and by the demands which they make on every member whom they admit.

These wise institutions, confirmed by his august successor and imitated by all the kings of Europe, will serve at least to restrain men of letters, who, all aspiring to the honor of being admitted into these Academies, will keep watch over themselves, and endeavor to make themselves worthy of such honor by useful performances and irreproachable morals. Those Academies also, which, in proposing prizes for literary merit, make choice of such subjects as are calculated to arouse the love of virtue in the hearts of citizens, prove that it prevails in themselves, and must give men the rare and real pleasure of finding learned societies devoting themselves to the enlightenment of mankind, not only by agreeable exercises of the intellect, but also by useful instructions.

An objection which may be made is, in fact, only an additional proof of my argument. So much precaution proves but too evidently the need for it. We never seek remedies for evils that do not exist. Why, indeed, must these bear all the marks of ordinary remedies, on account of their inefficacy? The numerous establishments in favour of the learned are only adapted to make men mistake the objects of the sciences, and turn men's attention to the cultivation of them. One would be inclined to think, from the precautions everywhere taken, that we are overstocked with husbandmen, and are afraid of a shortage of philosophers. I will not venture here to enter into a comparison between agriculture and philosophy, as they would not bear it. I shall only ask: What is philosophy? What is contained in the writings of the most celebrated philosophers? What are the lessons of these friends of wisdom. To hear them, should we not take them for so many mountebanks, exhibiting themselves in public, and crying out, Here, Here, come to me, I am the only true doctor? One of them teaches that there is no such thing as matter, but that everything exists only in representation. Another declares that there is no other substance than matter, and no other God than the world itself. A third tells you that there are no such things as virtue and vice, and that moral good and evil are chimeras; while a fourth informs you that men are only beasts of prey, and may conscientiously devour one another. Why, my great philosophers, do you not reserve these wise and profitable lessons for your friends and children? You would soon reap the benefit of them, nor should we be under the apprehension of our own becoming your disciples.

[Scholars, in pursuit of knowledge, lose sight of faith.]

Such are the wonderful men, whom their contemporaries held in the highest esteem during their lives, and to whom immortality has been attributed since their decease. Such are the wise maxims we have received from them, and which are transmitted, from age to age, to our descendants. Paganism, though given over to all the extravagances of human reason, has left nothing to compare with the shameful monuments which have been prepared by the art of printing, during the reign of the gospel. . . Go, famous writings, of which the ignorance and rusticity of our forefathers would have been incapable. Go to our descendants, along with those still more pernicious works which reek of the corrupted manners of the present age! Let them together convey to posterity a faithful history of the progress and advantages of our arts and sciences. If they are read, they will leave not a doubt about the question we are now discussing, and unless mankind should then be still more foolish than we, they will lift up their hands to Heaven and exclaim in bitterness of heart: "Almighty God! Thou who holdest in Thy hand the minds of men, deliver us from the fatal arts and sciences of our forefathers; give us back ignorance, innocence, and poverty, which alone can make us happy and are precious in Thy sight."

[Real genius needs no teachers; indeed, institutions of higher learning rarely advance it.]

But if the progress of the arts and sciences had added nothing to our real happiness; if it has corrupted our morals, and if that corruption has vitiated our taste, what are we to think of the herd of text-book authors, who have removed those impediments which nature purposely laid in the way to the Temple of the Muses, in order to guard its approach and try the powers of those who might be tempted to seek knowledge? What are we to think of those compilers who have indiscreetly broken open the door of the sciences, and introduced into their sanctuary a populace unworthy to approach it, when it was greatly to be wished that all who should be found incapable of making a considerable progress in the career of learning should have been repulsed at the entrance, and thereby cast upon those arts which are useful to society. A man who will be all his life a bad versifier, or a third-rate geometrician, might have made nevertheless an excellent clothier. Those whom nature intended for her disciples have not needed masters. Bacon, Descartes, and Newton, those teachers of mankind, had themselves no teachers. What guide indeed could have taken them so far as their sublime genius directed them? Ordinary masters would only have cramped their intelligence, by confining it within the narrow limits of their own capacity. It was from the obstacles they met with at first that they learned to exert themselves, and bestirred themselves to traverse the vast field which they covered. If it be proper to allow some men to apply themselves to the study of the arts and sciences, it is only those who feel themselves able to walk alone in their footsteps and to outstrip them. It belongs only to these few to raise monuments to the glory of the human understanding. But if we are desirous that nothing should be above their genius, nothing should be beyond their hopes. This is the only encouragement they require. . .

As for us, ordinary men, on whom Heaven has not been pleased to bestow such great talents; as we are not destined to reap such glory, let us remain in our obscurity. Let us not covet a reputation we should never attain, and which, in the present state of things, would never make up to us for the trouble it would have cost us, even if we were fully qualified to obtain it. Why should we build our happiness on the opinions of others, when we can find it in our own hearts? Let us leave to others the task of instructing mankind in their duty, and confine ourselves to the discharge of our own. We have no occasion for greater knowledge than this. Virtue! Sublime science of simple minds, are such industry and preparation needed if we are to know you? Are not your principles graven on every heart? Need we do more, to learn your laws, than examine ourselves and listen to the voice of conscience, when the passions are silent? This is the true philosophy, with which we must learn to be content, without envying the fame of those celebrated men, whose names are immortal in the republic of letters. Let us, instead of envying them, endeavor to make, between them and us, that honorable distinction which was formerly seen to exist between two great peoples, that the one knew how to speak, and the other how to act properly.

Appendix C: Burke's *Reflections on the Revolution in France*

[Editor's Note: Edmund Burke's reflections were originally letters to a young Frenchman, in Paris, who has expressed his admiration for the French revolution for doing away with the old system of France. Burke disagrees.]

Edmund Burke, *Reflections on the Revolution in France* (1790) [excerpts]

Dear Sir:

You are pleased to call again, and with some earnestness, for my thoughts on the late proceedings in France. I will not give you reason to imagine that I think my sentiments of such value as to wish myself to be solicited about them. They are of too little consequence to be very anxiously either communicated or withheld. My errors, if any, are my own. My reputation alone is to answer for them. . .

You see, Sir, that though I do most heartily wish that France may be animated by a spirit of rational liberty, and that I think you bound, in all honest policy, to provide a permanent body in which that spirit may reside, and an effectual organ by which it may act, it is my misfortune to entertain great doubts concerning several material points in your late transactions.

[WHY THE FRENCH ERR IN DESTROYING THE OLD SYSTEM AND ATTEMPTING TO BUILD A "NEW" SOCIETY FROM SCRATCH]

You [French people] might, if you pleased, have profited of our [British] example and have given to your recovered freedom [the King's concessions after the Fall of the Bastille] a correspondent dignity. Your privileges, though discontinued, were not lost to memory. Your constitution, it is true, whilst you were out of possession, suffered waste and dilapidation; but [the old system of government in France] possessed in some parts the walls and the basic foundations of a noble and venerable castle. You might have repaired those walls; you might have built on those old foundations. Your [ancient] constitution [the one that resulted in calling the Estates-General] was suspended before it was perfected, but you had the elements of a constitution very nearly as good as could be wished. In your old states you possessed that variety of parts corresponding with the various descriptions of which your community was happily composed; you had all that combination and all that opposition of interests; you had that action and counteraction which, in the natural and in the political world, from the reciprocal struggle of discordant powers, draws out the harmony of the universe. These opposed and conflicting interests which you considered as so great a blemish in your old and in our present constitution[1]

---

[1] "Our present constitution" refers to the system of government in England that emerged after the Glorious Revolution of 1688-1689 that placed restrictions on the monarchy and gradually shifted power from the monarchy to Parliament. The "opposed and conflicting interests" might be translated as "checks and balances"—a reference to the role of Parliament in restricting the power of the monarchy. But it also alludes to the United States Constitution, which had been approved

interpose a salutary check to all precipitate resolutions. They render deliberation a matter, not of choice, but of necessity; they make all change a subject of compromise, which naturally begets moderation; they produce temperaments preventing the sore evil of harsh, crude, unqualified reformations, and rendering all the headlong exertions of arbitrary power, in the few or in the many, for ever impracticable. Through that diversity of members and interests, general liberty had as many securities as there were separate views in the several orders, whilst, by pressing down the whole by the weight of a real monarchy, the separate parts would have been prevented from warping and starting from their allotted places.

You had all these advantages in your ancient states, but you chose to act as if you had never been molded into civil society and had everything to begin anew. You began ill, because you began by despising everything that belonged to you. You set up your trade without a capital. If the last generations of your country appeared without much luster in your eyes, you might have passed them by and derived your claims from a more early race of ancestors. Under a pious predilection for those ancestors, your imaginations would have realized in them a standard of virtue and wisdom beyond the vulgar practice of the hour; and you would have risen with the example to whose imitation you aspired. Respecting your forefathers, you would have been taught to respect yourselves. You would not have chosen to consider the French as a people of yesterday, as a nation of lowborn servile wretches until the emancipating year of 1789. In order to furnish, at the expense of your honor, an excuse to your apologists here for several enormities of yours, you would not have been content to be represented as a gang of Maroon slaves suddenly broke loose from the house of bondage, and therefore to be pardoned for your abuse of the liberty to which you were not accustomed and ill fitted. Would it not, my worthy friend, have been wiser to have you thought, what I, for one, always thought you, a generous and gallant nation, long misled to your disadvantage by your high and romantic sentiments of fidelity, honor, and loyalty; that events had been unfavorable to you, but that you were not enslaved through any illiberal or servile disposition; that in your most devoted submission you were actuated by a principle of public spirit, and that it was your country you worshiped in the person of your king? Had you made it to be understood that in the delusion of this amiable error you had gone further than your wise ancestors, that you were resolved to resume your ancient privileges, whilst you preserved the spirit of your ancient and your recent loyalty and honor; or if, diffident of yourselves and not clearly discerning the almost obliterated constitution of your ancestors, you had looked to your neighbors in this land who had kept alive the ancient principles and models of the old common law of Europe meliorated and adapted to its present state — by following wise examples you would have given new examples of wisdom to the world. You would have rendered the cause of liberty venerable in the eyes of every worthy mind in every nation. You would have shamed despotism from the earth by showing that freedom was not only reconcilable, but, as when well disciplined it is, auxiliary to law. You would have had an unoppressive but a productive revenue. You would have had a flourishing commerce to feed it. You would have had a free constitution, a potent monarchy, a disciplined army, a reformed and venerated clergy, a mitigated but spirited nobility to lead your virtue, not to overlay it; you would have had a liberal order of commons to emulate and to recruit that nobility; you would have had a protected, satisfied, laborious,

---

by the Constitutional Convention just three years earlier—in 1787—and was ratified by each of the states during the next three years. Yet "opposed and conflicting interests" was also a concept that Rousseau tended to regard as "factions," which inhibited the emergence of a collective, general will.

and obedient people, taught to seek and to recognize the happiness that is to be found by virtue in all conditions; in which consists the true moral equality of mankind, and not in that monstrous fiction which, by inspiring false ideas and vain expectations into men destined to travel in the obscure walk of laborious life, serves only to aggravate and embitter that real inequality which it never can remove, and which the order of civil life establishes as much for the benefit of those whom it must leave in a humble state as those whom it is able to exalt to a condition more splendid, but not more happy. You had a smooth and easy career of felicity and glory laid open to you, beyond anything recorded in the history of the world, but you have shown that difficulty is good for man.

[THE TRAGEDY THAT ENSUED AS A RESULT OF THE REVOLUTIONARIES' REPUDIATION OF THE FRENCH PAST]

Compute your gains: see what is got by those extravagant and presumptuous speculations which have taught your leaders [of the revolutionaries] to despise all their predecessors, and all their contemporaries, and even to despise themselves until the moment in which they become truly despicable. By following those false lights, France has bought undisguised calamities at a higher price than any nation has purchased the most unequivocal blessings! France has bought poverty by crime! France has not sacrificed her virtue to her interest, but she has abandoned her interest, that she might prostitute her virtue. All other nations have begun the fabric of a new government, or the reformation of an old, by establishing originally or by enforcing with greater exactness some rites or other of religion. All other people have laid the foundations of civil freedom in severer manners and a system of a more austere and masculine morality. France, when she let loose the reins of regal authority, doubled the license of a ferocious dissoluteness in manners and of an insolent irreligion in opinions and practice, and has extended through all ranks of life, as if she were communicating some privilege or laying open some secluded benefit, all the unhappy corruptions that usually were the disease of wealth and power. This is one of the new principles of equality in France.

France, by the perfidy of her leaders, has utterly disgraced the tone of lenient council in the cabinets of princes, and disarmed it of its most potent topics. She has sanctified the dark, suspicious maxims of tyrannous distrust, and taught kings to tremble at (what will hereafter be called) the delusive plausibilities of moral politicians. Sovereigns will consider those who advise them to place an unlimited confidence in their people as subverters of their thrones, as traitors who aim at their destruction by leading their easy good-nature, under specious pretenses, to admit combinations of bold and faithless men into a participation of their power. This alone (if there were nothing else) is an irreparable calamity to you and to mankind. Remember that your parliament of Paris [a kind of municipal legislature] told your king that, in calling the [Estates-General] together, he had nothing to fear but the prodigal excess of their zeal in providing for the support of the throne. [For such lies] these men should hide their heads. It is right that they should bear their part in the ruin which their counsel has brought on their sovereign and their country.

Such sanguine declarations tend to lull authority asleep; to encourage it rashly to engage in perilous adventures of untried policy; to neglect those provisions, preparations, and precautions which distinguish benevolence from imbecility, and without which no man can answer for the salutary effect of any abstract plan of government or of freedom. For want of these, they have seen the medicine of the state corrupted into its poison. They have seen the French rebel against a mild and lawful monarch [Louis XVI] with more fury, outrage, and insult than ever any people has been known to rise against the most illegal usurper or the most sanguinary tyrant. Their resistance was made to concession, their revolt was from protection, their blow was aimed at a hand holding out graces, favors, and immunities.

This was unnatural. The rest is in order. They have found their punishment in their success: laws overturned; tribunals subverted; industry without vigor; commerce expiring; the [tax] revenue unpaid, yet the people impoverished; a church pillaged, and a state not relieved; civil and military anarchy made the constitution of the kingdom; everything human and divine sacrificed to the idol of public credit, and national bankruptcy the consequence; and, to crown all, the paper securities of new, precarious, tottering power, the discredited paper securities of impoverished fraud and beggared rapine[2], held out as a currency for the support of an empire in lieu of the two great recognized species [gold and silver] that represent the lasting, conventional credit of mankind, which disappeared and hid themselves in the earth from whence they came, when the principle of property, whose creatures and representatives they are, was systematically subverted.

Were all these dreadful things necessary? Were they the inevitable results of the desperate struggle of determined patriots, compelled to wade through blood and tumult to the quiet shore of a tranquil and prosperous liberty? No! nothing like it. The fresh ruins of France, which shock our feelings wherever we can turn our eyes, are not the devastation of civil war; they are the sad but instructive monuments of rash and ignorant counsel in time of profound peace. They are the display of inconsiderate and presumptuous, because unresisted and irresistible, authority. The persons who have thus squandered away the precious treasure of their crimes, the persons who have made this prodigal and wild waste of public evils (the last stake reserved for the ultimate ransom of the state) have met in their progress with little or rather with no opposition at all. Their whole march was more like a triumphal procession than the progress of a war. Their pioneers have gone before them and demolished and laid everything level at their feet. Not one drop of their blood have they shed in the cause of the country they have ruined. They have made no sacrifices to their projects of greater consequence than their shoebuckles, whilst they were imprisoning their king, murdering their fellow citizens, and bathing in tears and plunging in poverty and distress thousands of worthy men and worthy families. Their cruelty has not even been the base result of fear. It has been the effect of their sense of perfect safety, in authorizing treasons, robberies, rapes, assassinations, slaughters, and burnings throughout their harassed land. But the cause of all was plain from the beginning.

---

[2] "Discredited paper securities of impoverished fraud and beggared rapine" refers to the *Assignats,* the paper notes that the National Assembly legalized as currency, supplementing gold and silver coins and notes redeemable in specie. The *Assignats* were valuable insofar as they were funded by the sale of land that the National Assembly had confiscated from the Catholic Church. This confiscation is what Burke means by "beggared rapine": the National Assembly, destitute of funds to run the government, sought to steal it from the Catholic Church, or so Burke suggests.

[WHO WAS RESPONSIBLE FOR THIS CALAMITY? THE COMPOSITION OF THE NATIONAL ASSEMBLY WILL UNDERMINE FRANCE]

This unforced choice, this fond election of evil, would appear perfectly unaccountable if we did not consider the composition of the National Assembly. I do not mean its formal constitution, which, as it now stands, is exceptionable enough, but the materials of which, in a great measure, it is composed, which is of ten thousand times greater consequence than all the formalities in the world. If we were to know nothing of this assembly but by its title and function, no colors could paint to the imagination anything more venerable. In that light the mind of an inquirer, subdued by such an awful image as that of the virtue and wisdom of a whole people collected into a focus, would pause and hesitate in condemning things even of the very worst aspect. Instead of blamable, they would appear only mysterious. But no name, no power, no function, no artificial institution whatsoever can make the men of whom any system of authority is composed any other than God, and nature, and education, and their habits of life have made them. Capacities beyond these the people have not to give. Virtue and wisdom may be the objects of their choice, but their choice confers neither the one nor the other on those upon whom they lay their ordaining hands. They have not the engagement of nature, they have not the promise of revelation, for any such powers.

After I had read over the list of the persons and descriptions elected into the *Tiers Etat* [Third Estate], nothing which they afterwards did could appear astonishing. Among them, indeed, I saw some of known rank, some of shining talents; but of any practical experience in the state, not one man was to be found. The best were only men of theory. But whatever the distinguished few may have been, it is the substance and mass of the body which constitutes its character and must finally determine its direction. In all bodies, those who will lead must also, in a considerable degree, follow. They must conform their propositions to the taste, talent, and disposition of those whom they wish to conduct; therefore, if an assembly is viciously or feebly composed in a very great part of it, nothing but such a supreme degree of virtue as very rarely appears in the world, and for that reason cannot enter into calculation, will prevent the men of talent disseminated through it from becoming only the expert instruments of absurd projects! If, what is the more likely event, instead of that unusual degree of virtue, they should be actuated by sinister ambition and a lust of meretricious glory, then the feeble part of the assembly, to whom at first they conform, becomes in its turn the dupe and instrument of their designs. In this political traffic, the leaders will be obliged to bow to the ignorance of their followers, and the followers to become subservient to the worst designs of their leaders.

…In the calling of the States-General of France, the first thing that struck me was a great departure from the ancient course. I found the representation for the Third Estate composed of six hundred persons. They were equal in number to the representatives of both the other orders. If the orders were to act separately, the number would not, beyond the consideration of the expense, be of much moment. But when it became apparent that the three orders were to be melted down into one, the policy and necessary effect of this numerous representation became obvious. A very small desertion from either of the other two orders must throw the power of both into the hands of the third. In fact, the whole power of the state was soon resolved into that body. Its due composition became therefore of infinitely the greater importance.

[WHY LAWYERS ARE NOT SUITED TO GOVERN]

Judge, Sir, of my surprise when I found that a very great proportion of the assembly (a majority, I believe, of the members who attended) was composed of practitioners in the law. It was composed, not of distinguished magistrates, who had given pledges to their country of their science, prudence, and integrity; not of leading advocates, the glory of the bar; not of renowned professors in universities; — but for the far greater part, as it must in such a number, of the inferior, unlearned, mechanical, merely instrumental members of the profession. There were distinguished exceptions, but the general composition was of obscure provincial advocates, of stewards of petty local jurisdictions, country attornies, notaries, and the whole train of the ministers of municipal litigation, the fomenters and conductors of the petty war of village vexation. From the moment I read the list, I saw distinctly, and very nearly as it has happened, all that was to follow.

…Whenever the supreme authority is vested in a body so composed, it must evidently produce the consequences of supreme authority placed in the hands of men not taught habitually to respect themselves, who had no previous fortune in character at stake, who could not be expected to bear with moderation, or to conduct with discretion, a power which they themselves, more than any others, must be surprised to find in their hands. Who could flatter himself that these men, suddenly and, as it were, by enchantment snatched from the humblest rank of subordination, would not be intoxicated with their unprepared greatness? Who could conceive that men who are habitually meddling, daring, subtle, active, of litigious dispositions and unquiet minds would easily fall back into their old condition of obscure contention and laborious, low, unprofitable chicane? Who could doubt but that, at any expense to the state, of which they understood nothing, they must pursue their private interests, which they understand but too well? It was not an event depending on chance or contingency. It was inevitable; it was necessary; it was planted in the nature of things. They must join (if their capacity did not permit them to lead) in any project which could procure to them a litigious constitution; which could lay open to them those innumerable lucrative jobs which follow in the train of all great convulsions and revolutions in the state, and particularly in all great and violent permutations of property. Was it to be expected that they would attend to the stability of property, whose existence had always depended upon whatever rendered property questionable, ambiguous, and insecure? Their objects would be enlarged with their elevation, but their disposition and habits, and mode of accomplishing their designs, must remain the same.

Well! but these men were to be tempered and restrained by other descriptions, of more sober and more enlarged understandings. Were they then to be awed by the supereminent authority and awful dignity of a handful of country clowns who have seats in that assembly, some of whom are said not to be able to read and write, and by not a greater number of traders who, though somewhat more instructed and more conspicuous in the order of society, had never known anything beyond their counting house? No! Both these descriptions were more formed to be overborne and swayed by the intrigues and artifices of lawyers than to become their counterpoise. With such a dangerous disproportion, the whole must needs be governed by them. To the faculty of law was joined a pretty considerable proportion of the faculty of medicine. This faculty had not, any more than that of the law, possessed in France its just estimation. Its professors, therefore, must have the qualities of men not habituated to sentiments of dignity. But supposing they had ranked as they ought to do, and as with us they do actually, the sides of sickbeds are not the academies for forming statesmen and legislators. Then came the dealers in stocks and funds, who must be eager, at any expense, to change their ideal paper wealth for the more solid substance of land. To these were joined men of other descriptions, from whom as little knowledge of, or attention to, the interests of a great state was to be expected, and as little regard to the stability of any institution; men formed to be instruments, not controls. Such in general was the composition of the Tiers Etat [the Third Estate] in the National Assembly, in which was scarcely to be perceived the slightest traces of what we call the natural landed interest of the country.

We know that the British House of Commons, without shutting its doors to any merit in any class, is, by the sure operation of adequate causes, filled with everything illustrious in rank, in descent, in hereditary and in acquired opulence, in cultivated talents, in military, civil, naval, and politic distinction that the country can afford. But supposing, what hardly can be supposed as a case, that the House of Commons should be composed in the same manner with the Tiers Etat [the Third Estate] in France, would this dominion of chicane be borne with patience or even conceived without horror? God forbid I should insinuate anything derogatory to that profession which is another priesthood, administering the rights of sacred justice. But whilst I revere men in the functions which belong to them, and would do as much as one man can do to prevent their exclusion from any, I cannot, to flatter them, give the lie to nature. They are good and useful in the composition; they must be mischievous if they preponderate so as virtually to become the whole. Their very excellence in their peculiar functions may be far from a qualification for others. It cannot escape observation that when men are too much confined to professional and faculty habits and, as it were, inveterate in the recurrent employment of that narrow circle, they are rather disabled than qualified for whatever depends on the knowledge of mankind, on experience in mixed affairs, on a comprehensive, connected view of the various, complicated, external and internal interests which go to the formation of that multifarious thing called a state.

After all, if the House of Commons were to have a wholly professional and faculty composition, what is the power of the House of Commons, circumscribed and shut in by the immovable barriers of laws, usages, positive rules of doctrine and practice, counterpoised by the House of Lords, and every moment of its existence at the discretion of the crown to continue, prorogue, or dissolve us? The power of the House of Commons, direct or indirect, is indeed great; and long may it be able to preserve its greatness and the spirit belonging to true greatness at the full; and it will do so as long as it can keep the breakers of law in India from becoming the makers of law for England. The power, however, of the House of Commons, when least diminished, is as a drop of water in the ocean, compared to that residing in a settled majority of your National Assembly. That assembly, since the destruction of the orders, has no fundamental law, no strict convention, no respected usage to restrain it. Instead of finding themselves obliged to conform to a fixed constitution, they have a power to make a constitution which shall conform to their designs. Nothing in heaven or upon earth can serve as a control on them. What ought to be the heads, the hearts, the dispositions that are qualified or that dare, not only to make laws under a fixed constitution, but at one heat to strike out a totally new constitution for a great kingdom, and in every part of it, from the monarch on the throne to the vestry of a parish? But — "fools rush in where angels fear to tread". In such a state of unbounded power for undefined and undefinable purposes, the evil of a moral and almost physical inaptitude of the man to the function must be the greatest we can conceive to happen in the management of human affairs.

[WHY THE CLERGY, AS REPRESENTED IN THE THIRD ESTATE, ARE UNSUITED TO GOVERN]

Having considered the composition of the Third Estate as it stood in its original frame, I took a view of the representatives of the clergy. There, too, it appeared that full as little regard was had to the general security of property or to the aptitude of the deputies for the public purposes, in the principles of their election. That election was so contrived as to send a very large proportion of mere country curates to the great and arduous work of new-modeling a state: men who never had seen the state so much as in a picture — men who knew nothing of the world beyond the bounds of an obscure village; who, immersed in hopeless poverty, could regard all property, whether secular or ecclesiastical, with no other eye than that of envy; among whom must be many who, for the smallest hope of the meanest dividend in plunder, would readily join in any attempts upon a body of wealth in which they could hardly look to have any share except in a general scramble. Instead of balancing the power of the active chicaners in the other assembly, these curates must necessarily become the active coadjutors, or at best the passive instruments, of those by whom they had been habitually guided in their petty village concerns. They, too, could hardly be the most conscientious of their kind who, presuming upon their incompetent understanding, could intrigue for a trust which led them from their natural relation to their flocks and their natural spheres of action to undertake the regeneration of kingdoms. This preponderating weight, being added to the force of the body of chicane in the Tiers Etat, completed that momentum of ignorance, rashness, presumption, and lust of plunder, which nothing has been able to resist.

To observing men it must have appeared from the beginning that the majority of the Third Estate, in conjunction with such a deputation from the clergy as I have described, whilst it pursued the destruction of the nobility, would inevitably become subservient to the worst designs of individuals in that class. In the spoil and humiliation of their own order these individuals would possess a sure fund for the pay of their new followers. To squander away the objects which made the happiness of their fellows would be to them no sacrifice at all. Turbulent, discontented men of quality, in proportion as they are puffed up with personal pride and arrogance, generally despise their own order. One of the first symptoms they discover of a selfish and mischievous ambition is a profligate disregard of a dignity which they partake with others. To be attached to the subdivision, to love the little platoon we belong to in society, is the first principle (the germ as it were) of public affections. It is the first link in the series by which we proceed toward a love to our country and to mankind. The interest of that portion of social arrangement is a trust in the hands of all those who compose it; and as none but bad men would justify it in abuse, none but traitors would barter it away for their own personal advantage.

[THE QUALIFICATIONS NECESSARY FOR GOVERNMENT]

...Believe me, Sir, those who attempt to level, never equalize. In all societies, consisting of various descriptions of citizens, some description must be uppermost. The levelers, therefore, only change and pervert the natural order of things; they load the edifice of society by setting up in the air what the solidity of the structure requires to be on the ground. The association of tailors and carpenters, of which the republic (of Paris, for instance) is composed, cannot be equal to the situation into which by the worst of usurpations — an usurpation on the prerogatives of nature — you attempt to force them.

The Chancellor of France, at the opening of the states, said, in a tone of oratorical flourish, that all occupations were honorable. If he meant only that no honest employment was disgraceful, he would not have gone beyond the truth. But in asserting that anything is honorable, we imply some distinction in its favor. The occupation of a hairdresser or of a working tallow-chandler cannot be a matter of honor to any person — to say nothing of a number of other more servile employments. Such descriptions of men ought not to suffer oppression from the state; but the state suffers oppression if such as they, either individually or collectively, are permitted to rule. In this you think you are combating prejudice, but you are at war with nature.

…I do not, my dear Sir, conceive you to be of that sophistical, captious spirit, or of that uncandid dullness, as to require, for every general observation or sentiment, an explicit detail of the correctives and exceptions which reason will presume to be included in all the general propositions which come from reasonable men. You do not imagine that I wish to confine power, authority, and distinction to blood and names and titles. No, Sir. There is no qualification for government but virtue and wisdom, actual or presumptive. Wherever they are actually found, they have, in whatever state, condition, profession, or trade, the passport of Heaven to human place and honor. Woe to the country which would madly and impiously reject the service of the talents and virtues, civil, military, or religious, that are given to grace and to serve it, and would condemn to obscurity everything formed to diffuse luster and glory around a state. Woe to that country, too, that, passing into the opposite extreme, considers a low education, a mean contracted view of things, a sordid, mercenary occupation as a preferable title to command.

Everything ought to be open, but not indifferently, to every man. No rotation; no appointment by lot; no mode of election operating in the spirit of sortition or rotation can be generally good in a government conversant in extensive objects. Because they have no tendency, direct or indirect, to select the man with a view to the duty or to accommodate the one to the other. I do not hesitate to say that the road to eminence and power, from obscure condition, ought not to be made too easy, nor a thing too much of course. If rare merit be the rarest of all rare things, it ought to pass through some sort of probation. The temple of honor ought to be seated on an eminence. If it be opened through virtue, let it be remembered, too, that virtue is never tried but by some difficulty and some struggle.

[WHY INHERITANCE OF PROPERTY IS JUSTIFIED—AND WHY THE FRENCH REVOLUTIONARIES ERR IN CONFISCATING IT FROM NOBLEMEN AND THE CHURCH]

…The power of perpetuating our property in our families is one of the most valuable and interesting circumstances belonging to it, and that which tends the most to the perpetuation of society itself. It makes our weakness subservient to our virtue, it grafts benevolence even upon avarice. The possessors of family wealth, and of the distinction which attends hereditary possession (as most concerned in it), are the natural securities for this transmission. With us the House of Peers is formed upon this principle. It is wholly composed of hereditary property and hereditary distinction, and made, therefore, the third of the legislature and, in the last event, the sole judge of all property in all its subdivisions. The House of Commons, too, though not necessarily, yet in fact, is always so composed, in the far greater part. Let those large proprietors be what they will — and they have their chance of being amongst the best — they are, at the very worst, the ballast in the vessel of the commonwealth. For though hereditary wealth and the rank which goes with it are too much idolized by creeping sycophants and the blind, abject admirers of power, they are too rashly slighted in shallow speculations of the petulant, assuming, short-sighted coxcombs of philosophy. Some decent, regulated preeminence, some preference (not exclusive appropriation) given to birth is neither unnatural, nor unjust, nor impolitic.

[THE DIFFERENCE BETWEEN THE REAL AND PRETENDED RIGHTS OF MAN]

…Far am I from denying in theory, full as far is my heart from withholding in practice (if I were of power to give or to withhold) the real rights of men. In denying their false claims of right, I do not mean to injure those which are real, and are such as their pretended rights would totally destroy. If civil society be made for the advantage of man, all the advantages for which it is made become his right. It is an institution of beneficence; and law itself is only beneficence acting by a rule. Men have a right to live by that rule; they have a right to do justice, as between their fellows, whether their fellows are in public function or in ordinary occupation. They have a right to the fruits of their industry and to the means of making their industry fruitful. They have a right to the acquisitions of their parents, to the nourishment and improvement of their offspring, to instruction in life, and to consolation in death. Whatever each man can separately do, without trespassing upon others, he has a right to do for himself; and he has a right to a fair portion of all which society, with all its combinations of skill and force, can do in his favor. In this partnership all men have equal rights, but not to equal things. He that has but five shillings in the partnership has as good a right to it as he that has five hundred pounds has to his larger proportion. But he has not a right to an equal dividend in the product of the joint stock; and as to the share of power, authority, and direction which each individual ought to have in the management of the state, that I must deny to be amongst the direct original rights of man in civil society; for I have in my contemplation the civil social man, and no other. It is a thing to be settled by convention.

If civil society be the offspring of convention, that convention must be its law. That convention must limit and modify all the descriptions of constitution which are formed under it. Every sort of legislative, judicial, or executory power are its creatures. They can have no being in any other state of things; and how can any man claim under the conventions of civil society rights which do not so much as suppose its existence — rights which are absolutely repugnant to it? One of the first motives to civil society, and which becomes one of its fundamental rules, is that no man should be judge in his own cause. By this each person has at once divested himself of the first fundamental right of uncovenanted man, that is, to judge for himself and to assert his own cause. He abdicates all right to be his own governor. He inclusively, in a great measure, abandons the right of self-defense, the first law of nature. Men cannot enjoy the rights of an uncivil and of a civil state together. That he may obtain justice, he gives up his right of determining what it is in points the most essential to him. That he may secure some liberty, he makes a surrender in trust of the whole of it.

[GOVERNMENT MUST EXERCISE RESTRAINT OVER MEN'S PASSIONS; NATURAL RIGHTS PHILOSOPHY FAILS TO RECOGNIZE THIS]

Government is not made in virtue of natural rights, which may and do exist in total independence of it, and exist in much greater clearness and in a much greater degree of abstract perfection; but their abstract perfection is their practical defect. By having a right to everything they want everything. Government is a contrivance of human wisdom to provide for human wants. Men have a right that these wants should be provided for by this wisdom. Among these wants is to be reckoned the want, out of civil society, of a sufficient restraint upon their passions. Society requires not only that the passions of individuals should be subjected, but that even in the mass and body, as well as in the individuals, the inclinations of men should frequently be thwarted, their will controlled, and their passions brought into subjection. This can only be done by a power out of themselves, and not, in the exercise of its function, subject to that will and to those passions which it is its office to bridle and subdue. In this sense the restraints on men, as well as their liberties, are to be reckoned among their rights. But as the liberties and the restrictions vary with times and circumstances and admit to infinite modifications, they cannot be settled upon any abstract rule; and nothing is so foolish as to discuss them upon that principle.

The moment you take away anything from the full rights of men, each to govern himself, and suffer any artificial, positive limitation upon those rights, from that moment the whole organization of government becomes a consideration of convenience. This it is which makes the constitution of a state and the due distribution of its powers a matter of the most delicate and complicated skill. It requires a deep knowledge of human nature and human necessities, and of the things which facilitate or obstruct the various ends which are to be pursued by the mechanism of civil institutions. The state is to have recruits to its strength, and remedies to its distempers. What is the use of discussing a man's abstract right to food or medicine? The question is upon the method of procuring and administering them. In that deliberation I shall always advise to call in the aid of the farmer and the physician rather than the professor of metaphysics.

[WHY GOVERNMENT MUST BE CONSTRUCTED ON HISTORICAL FOUNDATIONS AND NOT INVENTED FROM SCRATCH]

The science of constructing a commonwealth, or renovating it, or reforming it, is, like every other experimental science, not to be taught a priori. Nor is it a short experience that can instruct us in that practical science, because the real effects of moral causes are not always immediate; but that which in the first instance is prejudicial may be excellent in its remoter operation, and its excellence may arise even from the ill effects it produces in the beginning. The reverse also happens: and very plausible schemes, with very pleasing commencements, have often shameful and lamentable conclusions. In states there are often some obscure and almost latent causes, things which appear at first view of little moment, on which a very great part of its prosperity or adversity may most essentially depend. The science of government being therefore so practical in itself and intended for such practical purposes — a matter which requires experience, and even more experience than any person can gain in his whole life, however sagacious and observing he may be — it is with infinite caution that any man ought to venture upon pulling down an edifice which has answered in any tolerable degree for ages the common purposes of society, or on building it up again without having models and patterns of approved utility before his eyes.

The nature of man is intricate; the objects of society are of the greatest possible complexity; and, therefore, no simple disposition or direction of power can be suitable either to man's nature or to the quality of his affairs. When I hear the simplicity of contrivance aimed at and boasted of in any new political constitutions, I am at no loss to decide that the artificers are grossly ignorant of their trade or totally negligent of their duty.

...The pretended rights of these theorists are all extremes; and in proportion as they are metaphysically true, they are morally and politically false. The rights of men are in a sort of middle, incapable of definition, but not impossible to be discerned. The rights of men in governments are their advantages; and these are often in balances between differences of good, in compromises sometimes between good and evil, and sometimes between evil and evil. Political reason is a computing principle: adding, subtracting, multiplying, and dividing, morally and not metaphysically or mathematically, true moral denominations.

By these theorists the right of the people is almost always sophistically confounded with their power. The body of the community, whenever it can come to act, can meet with no effectual resistance; but till power and right are the same, the whole body of them has no right inconsistent with virtue, and the first of all virtues, prudence. Men have no right to what is not reasonable and to what is not for their benefit; for though a pleasant writer said, *liceat perire poetis* [Horace: "Let poets have the right to perish if they so desire"] when one of them, in cold blood, is said to have leaped into the flames of a volcanic revolution . . .

[WHY THE ARREST OF KING LOUIS UNDERMINED THE AUTHORITY OF THE NATIONAL ASSEMBLY AND TURNED IT INTO A FARCE]

...The arrest of the King, my dear Sir, was not the triumph of France. I must believe that, as a nation, it overwhelmed you with shame and horror. I must believe that the National Assembly find themselves in a state of the greatest humiliation in not being able to punish the authors of this triumph or the actors in it, and that they are in a situation in which any inquiry they may make upon the subject must be destitute even of the appearance of liberty or impartiality. The apology of that assembly is found in their situation; but when we approve what they must bear, it is in us the degenerate choice of a vitiated mind.

With a compelled appearance of deliberation, they vote under the dominion of a stern necessity. They sit in the heart, as it were, of a foreign republic: they have their residence in a city whose constitution has emanated neither from the charter of their king nor from their legislative power. There they are surrounded by an army not raised either by the authority of their crown or by their command, and which, if they should order to dissolve itself, would instantly dissolve them. There they sit, after a gang of assassins had driven away some hundreds of the members, whilst those who held the same moderate principles, with more patience or better hope, continued every day exposed to outrageous insults and murderous threats. There a majority, sometimes real, sometimes pretended, captive itself, compels a captive king to issue as royal edicts, at third hand, the polluted nonsense of their most licentious and giddy coffeehouses. It is notorious that all their measures are decided before they are debated. It is beyond doubt that, under the terror of the bayonet and the lamp-post and the torch to their houses, they are obliged to adopt all the crude and desperate measures suggested by clubs composed of a monstrous medley of all conditions, tongues, and nations. Among these are found persons, in comparison of whom Catiline [a disreputable Roman patrician, whose failed revolution led to his death at the hands of the Roman army] would be thought scrupulous and Cethegus [a Roman orator] a man of sobriety and moderation. Nor is it in these clubs alone that the public measures are deformed into monsters.

They undergo a previous distortion in academies, intended as so many seminaries for these clubs, which are set up in all the places of public resort. In these meetings of all sorts every counsel, in proportion as it is daring and violent and perfidious, is taken for the mark of superior genius. Humanity and compassion are ridiculed as the fruits of superstition and ignorance. Tenderness to individuals is considered as treason to the public. Liberty is always to be estimated perfect, as property is rendered insecure. Amidst assassination, massacre, and confiscation, perpetrated or meditated, they are forming plans for the good order of future society. Embracing in their arms the carcasses of base criminals and promoting their relations on the title of their offences, they drive hundreds of virtuous persons to the same end, by forcing them to subsist by beggary or by crime.

The Assembly, their organ, acts before them the farce of deliberation with as little decency as liberty. They act like the comedians of a fair before a riotous audience; they act amidst the tumultuous cries of a mixed mob of ferocious men, and of women lost to shame, who, according to their insolent fancies, direct, control, applaud, explode them, and sometimes mix and take their seats amongst them, domineering over them with a strange mixture of servile petulance and proud, presumptuous authority. As they have inverted order in all things, the gallery is in the place of the house. This assembly, which overthrows kings and kingdoms, has not even the physiognomy and aspect of a grave legislative body. . . They have a power given to them, like that of the evil principle, to subvert and destroy, but none to construct, except such machines as may be fitted for further subversion and further destruction.

Who is it that admires, and from the heart is attached to, national representative assemblies, but must turn with horror and disgust from such a profane burlesque, and abominable perversion of that sacred institute? Lovers of monarchy, lovers of republics must alike abhor it. The members of your assembly must themselves groan under the tyranny of which they have all the shame, none of the direction, and little of the profit. I am sure many of the members who compose even the majority of that body must feel as I do... Miserable king! miserable assembly! How must that assembly be silently scandalized with those of their members who could call a day which seemed to blot the sun out of heaven "un beau jour!" [a beautiful day]. How must they be inwardly indignant at hearing others who thought fit to declare to them "that the vessel of the state would fly forward in her course toward regeneration with more speed than ever", from the stiff gale of treason and murder which preceded our preacher's triumph! What must they have felt whilst, with outward patience and inward indignation, they heard, of the slaughter of innocent gentlemen in their houses, that "the blood spilled was not the most pure!" What must they have felt, when they were besieged by complaints of disorders which shook their country to its foundations, at being compelled coolly to tell the complainants that they were under the protection of the law, and that they would address the king (the captive king) to cause the laws to be enforced for their protection; when the enslaved ministers of that captive king had formally notified to them that there were neither law nor authority nor power left to protect? What must they have felt at being obliged, as a felicitation on the present new year, to request their captive king to forget the stormy period of the last, on account of the great good which he was likely to produce to his people; to the complete attainment of which good they adjourned the practical demonstrations of their loyalty, assuring him of their obedience when he should no longer possess any authority to command?

[WHY THE KING'S ARREST MAY CAUSE MONARCHS TO BECOME TYRANTS]

This mixed system of opinion and sentiment had its origin in the ancient chivalry; and the principle, though varied in its appearance by the varying state of human affairs, subsisted and influenced through a long succession of generations even to the time we live in. If it should ever be totally extinguished, the loss I fear will be great. It is this which has given its character to modern Europe. It is this which has distinguished it under all its forms of government, and distinguished it to its advantage, from the states of Asia and possibly from those states which flourished in the most brilliant periods of the antique world. It was this which, without confounding ranks, had produced a noble equality and handed it down through all the gradations of social life. It was this opinion which mitigated kings into companions and raised private men to be fellows with kings. Without force or opposition, it subdued the fierceness of pride and power, it obliged sovereigns to submit to the soft collar of social esteem, compelled stern authority to submit to elegance, and gave a domination, vanquisher of laws, to be subdued by manners.

But now all is to be changed. All the pleasing illusions which made power gentle and obedience liberal, which harmonized the different shades of life, and which, by a bland assimilation, incorporated into politics the sentiments which beautify and soften private society, are to be dissolved by this new conquering empire of light and reason. All the decent drapery of life is to be rudely torn off. All the super-added ideas, furnished from the wardrobe of a moral imagination, which the heart owns and the understanding ratifies as necessary to cover the defects of our naked, shivering nature, and to raise it to dignity in our own estimation, are to be exploded as a ridiculous, absurd, and antiquated fashion.

On this scheme of things, a king is but a man, a queen is but a woman; a woman is but an animal, and an animal not of the highest order. All homage paid to the sex in general as such, and without distinct views, is to be regarded as romance and folly. Regicide, and parricide, and sacrilege are but fictions of superstition, corrupting jurisprudence by destroying its simplicity. The murder of a king, or a queen, or a bishop, or a father are only common homicide; and if the people are by any chance or in any way gainers by it, a sort of homicide much the most pardonable, and into which we ought not to make too severe a scrutiny.

On the scheme of this barbarous philosophy, which is the offspring of cold hearts and muddy understandings, and which is as void of solid wisdom as it is destitute of all taste and elegance, laws are to be supported only by their own terrors and by the concern which each individual may find in them from his own private speculations or can spare to them from his own private interests. In the groves of their academy, at the end of every vista, you see nothing but the gallows. Nothing is left which engages the affections on the part of the commonwealth. On the principles of this mechanic philosophy, our institutions can never be embodied, if I may use the expression, in persons, so as to create in us love, veneration, admiration, or attachment. But that sort of reason which banishes the affections is incapable of filling their place. These public affections, combined with manners, are required sometimes as supplements, sometimes as correctives, always as aids to law. The precept given by a wise man, as well as a great critic, for the construction of poems is equally true as to states: — Non satis est pulchra esse poemata, dulcia sunto. [It is not enough that poems be beautiful; they should also be tender.] There ought to be a system of manners in every nation which a well-informed mind would be disposed to relish. To make us love our country, our country ought to be lovely.

But power, of some kind or other, will survive the shock in which manners and opinions perish; and it will find other and worse means for its support. The usurpation which, in order to subvert ancient institutions, has destroyed ancient principles will hold power by arts similar to those by which it has acquired it. When the old feudal and chivalrous spirit of fealty, which, by freeing kings from fear, freed both kings and subjects from the precautions of tyranny, shall be extinct in the minds of men, plots and assassinations will be anticipated by preventive murder and preventive confiscation, and that long roll of grim and bloody maxims which form the political code of all power not standing on its own honor and the honor of those who are to obey it.
Kings will be tyrants from policy when subjects are rebels from principle.

When ancient opinions and rules of life are taken away, the loss cannot possibly be estimated. From that moment we have no compass to govern us; nor can we know distinctly to what port we steer. Europe, undoubtedly, taken in a mass, was in a flourishing condition the day on which your revolution was completed. How much of that prosperous state was owing to the spirit of our old manners and opinions is not easy to say; but as such causes cannot be indifferent in their operation, we must presume that on the whole their operation was beneficial.

[WHY DESTROYING THE ANCIENT ORDER WILL DESTROY LIBERTY IN FRANCE AND PEACE IN EUROPE]

We are but too apt to consider things in the state in which we find them, without sufficiently adverting to the causes by which they have been produced and possibly may be upheld. Nothing is more certain than that our manners, our civilization, and all the good things which are connected with manners and with civilization have, in this European world of ours, depended for ages upon two principles and were, indeed, the result of both combined: I mean the spirit of a gentleman and the spirit of religion. The nobility and the clergy, the one by profession, the other by patronage, kept learning in existence, even in the midst of arms and confusions, and whilst governments were rather in their causes than formed. Learning paid back what it received to nobility and to priesthood, and paid it with usury, by enlarging their ideas and by furnishing their minds. Happy if they had all continued to know their indissoluble union and their proper place! Happy if learning, not debauched by ambition, had been satisfied to continue the instructor, and not aspired to be the master! Along with its natural protectors and guardians, learning will be cast into the mire and trodden down under the hoofs of a swinish multitude.

...I wish you may not be going fast, and by the shortest cut, to that horrible and disgustful situation. Already there appears a poverty of conception, a coarseness, and a vulgarity in all the proceedings of the Assembly and of all their instructors. Their liberty is not liberal. Their science is presumptuous ignorance. Their humanity is savage and brutal.

... France has always more or less influenced manners in England; and when your fountain is choked up and polluted, the stream will not run long, or not run clear, with us or perhaps with any nation. This gives all Europe, in my opinion, but too close and connected a concern in what is done in France. Excuse me, therefore, if I have dwelt too long on the atrocious spectacle of the 6th of October, 1789, or have given too much scope to the reflections which have arisen in my mind on occasion of the most important of all revolutions, which may be dated from that day — I mean a revolution in sentiments, manners, and moral opinions. As things now stand, with everything respectable destroyed without us, and an attempt to destroy within us every principle of respect, one is almost forced to apologize for harboring the common feelings of men.

[WHY THE KING'S IMPRISONMENT IS UNJUST]

...But [Reverend Price, an Englishman who praised the French Revolution and condemned the French monarchy] exults in this "leading in triumph", because truly Louis the Sixteenth was "an arbitrary monarch"; that is, in other words, neither more nor less than because he was Louis the Sixteenth, and because he had the misfortune to be born king of France, with the prerogatives of which a long line of ancestors and a long acquiescence of the people, without any act of his, had put him in possession. A misfortune it has indeed turned out to him that he was born king of France. But misfortune is not crime, nor is indiscretion always the greatest guilt. I shall never think that a prince the acts of whose whole reign was a series of concessions to his subjects, who was willing to relax his authority, to remit his prerogatives, to call his people to a share of freedom not known, perhaps not desired, by their ancestors — such a prince, though he should be subjected to the common frailties attached to men and to princes, though he should have once thought it necessary to provide force against the desperate designs manifestly carrying on against his person and the remnants of his authority — though all this should be taken into consideration, I shall be led with great difficulty to think he deserves the cruel and insulting triumph of Paris and of Dr. Price. I tremble for the cause of liberty from such an example to kings. I tremble for the cause of humanity in the unpunished outrages of the most wicked of mankind. But there are some people of that low and degenerate fashion of mind, that they look up with a sort of complacent awe and admiration to kings who know to keep firm in their seat, to hold a strict hand over their subjects, to assert their prerogative, and, by the awakened vigilance of a severe despotism, to guard against the very first approaches to freedom. Against such as these they never elevate their voice. Deserters from principle, listed with fortune, they never see any good in suffering virtue, nor any crime in prosperous usurpation.

If it could have been made clear to me that the king and queen of France (those I mean who were such before the triumph) were inexorable and cruel tyrants, that they had formed a deliberate scheme for massacring the National Assembly (I think I have seen something like the latter insinuated in certain publications), I should think their captivity just. If this be true, much more ought to have been done, but done, in my opinion, in another manner. The punishment of real tyrants is a noble and awful act of justice; and it has with truth been said to be consolatory to the human mind. But if I were to punish a wicked king, I should regard the dignity in avenging the crime. Justice is grave and decorous, and in its punishments rather seems to submit to a necessity than to make a choice. Had Nero [Roman emperor 54-68 CE], or Agrippina [wife of Roman emperor Claudio, 49-54 CE], or Louis the Eleventh [King of France 1461-83], or Charles the Ninth [King of France 1560 74] been the subject; if Charles the Twelfth [1697-1718] of Sweden, after the murder of Patkul, or his predecessor Christina, after the murder of Monaldeschi, had fallen into your hands, Sir, or into mine, I am sure our conduct would have been different.

If the French king, or king of the French (or by whatever name he is known in the new vocabulary of your constitution), has in his own person and that of his queen really deserved these unavowed, but unavenged, murderous attempts and those frequent indignities more cruel than murder, such a person would ill deserve even that subordinate executory trust which I understand is to be placed in him, nor is he fit to be called chief in a nation which he has outraged and oppressed. A worse choice for such an office in a new commonwealth than that of a deposed tyrant could not possibly be made. But to degrade and insult a man as the worst of criminals and afterwards to trust him in your highest concerns as a faithful, honest, and zealous servant is not consistent to reasoning, nor prudent in policy, nor safe in practice. Those who could make such an appointment must be guilty of a more flagrant breach of trust than any they have yet committed against the people. As this is the only crime in which your leading politicians could have acted inconsistently, I conclude that there is no sort of ground for these horrid insinuations. I think no better of all the other calumnies.

[WHY THE PROPONENTS OF THE ENLIGHTENMENT OVERESTIMATE THEIR OWN CLEVERNESS]

…You see, Sir, that in this enlightened age I am bold enough to confess that we are generally men of untaught feelings, that, instead of casting away all our old prejudices, we cherish them to a very considerable degree, and, to take more shame to ourselves, we cherish them because they are prejudices; and the longer they have lasted and the more generally they have prevailed, the more we cherish them. We are afraid to put men to live and trade each on his own private stock of reason, because we suspect that this stock in each man is small, and that the individuals would do better to avail themselves of the general bank and capital of nations and of ages. Many of our men of speculation, instead of exploding general prejudices, employ their sagacity to discover the latent wisdom which prevails in them. If they find what they seek, and they seldom fail, they think it more wise to continue the prejudice, with the reason involved, than to cast away the coat of prejudice and to leave nothing but the naked reason; because prejudice, with its reason, has a motive to give action to that reason, and an affection which will give it permanence. Prejudice is of ready application in the emergency; it previously engages the mind in a steady course of wisdom and virtue and does not leave the man hesitating in the moment of decision skeptical, puzzled, and unresolved. Prejudice renders a man's virtue his habit, and not a series of unconnected acts. Through just prejudice, his duty becomes a part of his nature.

Your literary men and your politicians, and so do the whole clan of the enlightened among us, essentially differ in these points. They have no respect for the wisdom of others, but they pay it off by a very full measure of confidence in their own. With them it is a sufficient motive to destroy an old scheme of things because it is an old one. As to the new, they are in no sort of fear with regard to the duration of a building run up in haste, because duration is no object to those who think little or nothing has been done before their time, and who place all their hopes in discovery. They conceive, very systematically, that all things which give perpetuity are mischievous, and therefore they are at inexpiable war with all establishments. They think that government may vary like modes of dress, and with as little ill effect; that there needs no principle of attachment, except a sense of present convenience, to any constitution of the state. They always speak as if they were of opinion that there is a singular species of compact between them and their magistrates which binds the magistrate, but which has nothing reciprocal in it, but that the majesty of the people has a right to dissolve it without any reason but its will. Their attachment to their country itself is only so far as it agrees with some of their fleeting projects; it begins and ends with that scheme of polity which falls in with their momentary opinion.

These doctrines, or rather sentiments, seem prevalent with your new statesmen. But they are wholly different from those on which we have always acted in this country.

...Formerly, your affairs were your own concern only. We felt for them as men, but we kept aloof from them because we were not citizens of France. But when we see the model held up to ourselves, we must feel as Englishmen, and feeling, we must provide as Englishmen. Your affairs, in spite of us, are made a part of our interest, so far at least as to keep at a distance your panacea, or your plague. If it be a panacea, we do not want it. We know the consequences of unnecessary physic. If it be a plague, it is such a plague that the precautions of the most severe quarantine ought to be established against it.

[WHY RELIGION MUST BE THE BASIS OF CIVIL SOCIETY]

...We know, and what is better, we feel inwardly, that religion is the basis of civil society and the source of all good and of all comfort. In England we are so convinced of this, that there is no rust of superstition with which the accumulated absurdity of the human mind might have crusted it over in the course of ages, that ninety-nine in a hundred of the people of England would not prefer to impiety. We shall never be such fools as to call in an enemy to the substance of any system to remove its corruptions, to supply its defects, or to perfect its construction. If our religious tenets should ever want a further elucidation, we shall not call on atheism to explain them. We shall not light up our temple from that unhallowed fire. It will be illuminated with other lights. It will be perfumed with other incense than the infectious stuff which is imported by the smugglers of adulterated metaphysics. If our ecclesiastical establishment should want a revision, it is not avarice or rapacity, public or private, that we shall employ for the audit, or receipt, or application of its consecrated revenue. Violently condemning neither the Greek nor the Armenian, nor, since heats are subsided, the Roman system of religion, we prefer the Protestant, not because we think it has less of the Christian religion in it, but because, in our judgment, it has more. We are Protestants, not from indifference, but from zeal.

We know, and it is our pride to know, that man is by his constitution a religious animal; that atheism is against, not only our reason, but our instincts; and that it cannot prevail long. But if, in the moment of riot and in a drunken delirium from the hot spirit drawn out of the alembic of hell, which in France is now so furiously boiling, we should uncover our nakedness by throwing off that Christian religion which has hitherto been our boast and comfort, and one great source of civilization amongst us and amongst many other nations, we are apprehensive (being well aware that the mind will not endure a void) that some uncouth, pernicious, and degrading superstition might take place of it.

For that reason, before we take from our establishment the natural, human means of estimation and give it up to contempt, as you have done, and in doing it have incurred the penalties you well deserve to suffer, we desire that some other may be presented to us in the place of it. We shall then form our judgment.

On these ideas, instead of quarrelling with establishments, as some do who have made a philosophy and a religion of their hostility to such institutions, we cleave closely to them. We are resolved to keep an established church, an established monarchy, an established aristocracy, and an established democracy, each in the degree it exists, and in no greater. I shall show you presently how much of each of these we possess.

It has been the misfortune (not, as these gentlemen think it, the glory) of this age that everything is to be discussed as if the constitution of our country were to be always a subject rather of altercation than enjoyment. For this reason, as well as for the satisfaction of those among you (if any such you have among you) who may wish to profit of examples, I venture to trouble you with a few thoughts upon each of these establishments. I do not think they were unwise in ancient Rome who, when they wished to new-model their laws, set commissioners to examine the best constituted republics within their reach.

First, I beg leave to speak of our church establishment, which is the first of our prejudices, not a prejudice destitute of reason, but involving in it profound and extensive wisdom. I speak of it first. It is first and last and midst in our minds. For, taking ground on that religious system of which we are now in possession, we continue to act on the early received and uniformly continued sense of mankind. That sense not only, like a wise architect, hath built up the august fabric of states, but, like a provident proprietor, to preserve the structure from profanation and ruin, as a sacred temple purged from all the impurities of fraud and violence and injustice and tyranny, hath solemnly and forever consecrated the commonwealth and all that officiate in it. This consecration is made that all who administer the government of men, in which they stand in the person of God himself, should have high and worthy notions of their function and destination, that their hope should be full of immortality, that they should not look to the paltry pelf of the moment nor to the temporary and transient praise of the vulgar, but to a solid, permanent existence in the permanent part of their nature, and to a permanent fame and glory in the example they leave as a rich inheritance to the world.

Such sublime principles ought to be infused into persons of exalted situations, and religious establishments provided that may continually revive and enforce them. Every sort of moral, every sort of civil, every sort of politic institution, aiding the rational and natural ties that connect the human understanding and affections to the divine, are not more than necessary in order to build up that wonderful structure Man, whose prerogative it is to be in a great degree a creature of his own making, and who, when made as he ought to be made, is destined to hold no trivial place in the creation. But whenever man is put over men, as the better nature ought ever to preside, in that case more particularly, he should as nearly as possible be approximated to his perfection.

[RELIGION IS AN ESSENTIAL PROP TO GOVERNMENT]

The consecration of the state by a state religious establishment is necessary, also, to operate with a wholesome awe upon free citizens, because, in order to secure their freedom, they must enjoy some determinate portion of power. To them, therefore, a religion connected with the state, and with their duty toward it, becomes even more necessary than in such societies where the people, by the terms of their subjection, are confined to private sentiments and the management of their own family concerns. All persons possessing any portion of power ought to be strongly and awfully impressed with an idea that they act in trust, and that they are to account for their conduct in that trust to the one great Master, Author, and Founder of society.

This principle ought even to be more strongly impressed upon the minds of those who compose the collective sovereignty than upon those of single princes. Without instruments, these princes can do nothing. Whoever uses instruments, in finding helps, finds also impediments. Their power is, therefore, by no means complete, nor are they safe in extreme abuse. Such persons, however elevated by flattery, arrogance, and self-opinion, must be sensible that, whether covered or not by positive law, in some way or other they are accountable even here for the abuse of their trust. If they are not cut off by a rebellion of their people, they may be strangled by the very janissaries kept for their security against all other rebellion. Thus we have seen the king of France sold by his soldiers for an increase of pay. But where popular authority is absolute and unrestrained, the people have an infinitely greater, because a far better founded, confidence in their own power. They are themselves, in a great measure, their own instruments. They are nearer to their objects. Besides, they are less under responsibility to one of the greatest controlling powers on the earth, the sense of fame and estimation. The share of infamy that is likely to fall to the lot of each individual in public acts is small indeed, the operation of opinion being in the inverse ratio to the number of those who abuse power. Their own approbation of their own acts has to them the appearance of a public judgment in their favor. A perfect democracy is, therefore, the most shameless thing in the world. As it is the most shameless, it is also the most fearless. No man apprehends in his person that he can be made subject to punishment. Certainly the people at large never ought, for as all punishments are for example toward the conservation of the people at large, the people at large can never become the subject of punishment by any human hand. It is therefore of infinite importance that they should not be suffered to imagine that their will, any more than that of kings, is the standard of right and wrong. They ought to be persuaded that they are full as little entitled, and far less qualified with safety to themselves, to use any arbitrary power whatsoever; that therefore they are not, under a false show of liberty, but in truth to exercise an unnatural, inverted domination, tyrannically to exact from those who officiate in the state not an entire devotion to their interest, which is their right, but an abject submission to their occasional will, extinguishing thereby in all those who serve them all moral principle, all sense of dignity, all use of judgment, and all consistency of character; whilst by the very same process they give themselves up a proper, a suitable, but a most contemptible prey to the servile ambition of popular sycophants or courtly flatterers.

When the people have emptied themselves of all the lust of selfish will, which without religion it is utterly impossible they ever should, when they are conscious that they exercise, and exercise perhaps in a higher link of the order of delegation, the power, which to be legitimate must be according to that eternal, immutable law in which will and reason are the same, they will be more careful how they place power in base and incapable hands. In their nomination to office, they will not appoint to the exercise of authority as to a pitiful job, but as to a holy function, not according to their sordid, selfish interest, nor to their wanton caprice, nor to their arbitrary will, but they will confer that power (which any man may well tremble to give or to receive) on those only in whom they may discern that predominant proportion of active virtue and wisdom, taken together and fitted to the charge, such as in the great and inevitable mixed mass of human imperfections and infirmities is to be found.

When they are habitually convinced that no evil can be acceptable, either in the act or the permission, to him whose essence is good, they will be better able to extirpate out of the minds of all magistrates, civil, ecclesiastical, or military, anything that bears the least resemblance to a proud and lawless domination.

…To avoid, therefore, the evils of inconstancy and versatility, ten thousand times worse than those of obstinacy and the blindest prejudice, we have consecrated the state, that no man should approach to look into its defects or corruptions but with due caution, that he should never dream of beginning its reformation by its subversion, that he should approach to the faults of the state as to the wounds of a father, with pious awe and trembling solicitude. By this wise prejudice we are taught to look with horror on those children of their country who are prompt rashly to hack that aged parent in pieces and put him into the kettle of magicians, in hopes that by their poisonous weeds and wild incantations they may regenerate the paternal constitution and renovate their father's life.

[HOW FRANCE DESTROYS ITS SOCIAL CONTRACT WHEN IT ATTEMPTS TO RECONSTRUCT ITS COMPOSITION]

Society is indeed a contract. Subordinate contracts for objects of mere occasional interest may be dissolved at pleasure — but the state ought not to be considered as nothing better than a partnership agreement in a trade of pepper and coffee, calico, or tobacco, or some other such low concern, to be taken up for a little temporary interest, and to be dissolved by the fancy of the parties. It is to be looked on with other reverence, because it is not a partnership in things subservient only to the gross animal existence of a temporary and perishable nature. It is a partnership in all science; a partnership in all art; a partnership in every virtue and in all perfection. As the ends of such a partnership cannot be obtained in many generations, it becomes a partnership not only between those who are living, but between those who are living, those who are dead, and those who are to be born. Each contract of each particular state is but a clause in the great primeval contract of eternal society, linking the lower with the higher natures, connecting the visible and invisible world, according to a fixed compact sanctioned by the inviolable oath which holds all physical and all moral natures, each in their appointed place. This law is not subject to the will of those who by an obligation above them, and infinitely superior, are bound to submit their will to that law. The municipal corporations of that universal kingdom are not morally at liberty at their pleasure, and on their speculations of a contingent improvement, wholly to separate and tear asunder the bands of their subordinate community and to dissolve it into an unsocial, uncivil, unconnected chaos of elementary principles. It is the first and supreme necessity only, a necessity that is not chosen but chooses, a necessity paramount to deliberation, that admits no discussion and demands no evidence, which alone can justify a resort to anarchy. This necessity is no exception to the rule, because this necessity itself is a part, too, of that moral and physical disposition of things to which man must be obedient by consent or force; but if that which is only submission to necessity should be made the object of choice, the law is broken, nature is disobeyed, and the rebellious are outlawed, cast forth, and exiled from this world of reason, and order, and peace, and virtue, and fruitful penitence, into the antagonist world of madness, discord, vice, confusion, and unavailing sorrow.

... [God] who gave our nature to be perfected by our virtue willed also the necessary means of its perfection. He willed therefore the state — He willed its connection with the source and original archetype of all perfection. They who are convinced of this His will, which is the law of laws and the sovereign of sovereigns, cannot think it reprehensible that this our corporate fealty and homage, that this our recognition of a seigniory paramount, I had almost said this oblation of the state itself as a worthy offering on the high altar of universal praise, should be performed as all public, solemn acts are performed, in buildings, in music, in decoration, in speech, in the dignity of persons, according to the customs of mankind taught by their nature; that is, with modest splendor and unassuming state, with mild majesty and sober pomp. For those purposes they think some part of the wealth of the country is as usefully employed as it can be in fomenting the luxury of individuals. It is the public ornament. It is the public consolation. It nourishes the public hope. The poorest man finds his own importance and dignity in it, whilst the wealth and pride of individuals at every moment makes the man of humble rank and fortune sensible of his inferiority and degrades and vilifies his condition. It is for the man in humble life, and to raise his nature and to put him in mind of a state in which the privileges of opulence will cease, when he will be equal by nature, and may be more than equal by virtue, that this portion of the general wealth of his country is employed and sanctified.

[WHY THE CONFISCATION OF PROPERTY IS UNJUST]

... I hope we shall never be so totally lost to all sense of the duties imposed upon us by the law of social union as, upon any pretext of public service, to confiscate the goods of a single unoffending citizen. Who but a tyrant (a name expressive of everything which can vitiate and degrade human nature) could think of seizing on the property of men unaccused, unheard, untried, by whole descriptions, by hundreds and thousands together? Who that had not lost every trace of humanity could think of casting down men of exalted rank and sacred function, some of them of an age to call at once for reverence and compassion, of casting them down from the highest situation in the commonwealth, wherein they were maintained by their own landed property, to a state of indigence, depression, and contempt?

The confiscators truly have made some allowance to their victims from the scraps and fragments of their own tables from which they have been so harshly driven, and which have been so bountifully spread for a feast to the harpies of usury. But to drive men from independence to live on alms is itself great cruelty. That which might be a tolerable condition to men in one state of life, and not habituated to other things, may, when all these circumstances are altered, be a dreadful revolution, and one to which a virtuous mind would feel pain in condemning any guilt except that which would demand the life of the offender. But to many minds this punishment of degradation and infamy is worse than death. Undoubtedly it is an infinite aggravation of this cruel suffering that the persons who were taught a double prejudice in favor of religion, by education and by the place they held in the administration of its functions, are to receive the remnants of their property as alms from the profane and impious hands of those who had plundered them of all the rest; to receive (if they are at all to receive), not from the charitable contributions of the faithful but from the insolent tenderness of known and avowed atheism, the maintenance of religion measured out to them on the standard of the contempt in which it is held, and for the purpose of rendering those who receive the allowance vile and of no estimation in the eyes of mankind.

But this act of seizure of property, it seems, is a judgment in law, and not a confiscation. They have, it seems, found out in the academies of the Palais Royal and the Jacobins that certain men had no right to the possessions which they held under law, usage, the decisions of courts, and the accumulated prescription of a thousand years. They say that ecclesiastics are fictitious persons, creatures of the state, whom at pleasure they may destroy, and of course limit and modify in every particular; that the goods they possess are not properly theirs but belong to the state which created the fiction; and we are therefore not to trouble ourselves with what they may suffer in their natural feelings and natural persons on account of what is done toward them in this their constructive character. Of what import is it under what names you injure men and deprive them of the just emoluments of a profession, in which they were not only permitted but encouraged by the state to engage, and upon the supposed certainty of which emoluments they had formed the plan of their lives, contracted debts, and led multitudes to an entire dependence upon them?

You do not imagine, Sir, that I am going to compliment this miserable distinction of persons with any long discussion. The arguments of tyranny are as contemptible as its force is dreadful. Had not your confiscators, by their early crimes, obtained a power which secures indemnity to all the crimes of which they have since been guilty or that they can commit, it is not the syllogism of the logician, but the lash of the executioner, that would have refuted a sophistry which becomes an accomplice of theft and murder. The sophistic tyrants of Paris are loud in their declamations against the departed regal tyrants, who in former ages have vexed the world. They are thus bold, because they are safe from the dungeons and iron cages of their old masters. Shall we be more tender of the tyrants of our own time, when we see them acting worse tragedies under our eyes? Shall we not use the same liberty that they do, when we can use it with the same safety — when to speak honest truth only requires a contempt of the opinions of those whose actions we abhor?

[WHY THE BOURGEOISIE RESENT AND ATTACK THE NOBILITY]

...The monied property [the Bourgeoisie] was long looked on with rather an evil eye by the people. They saw it connected with their distresses, and aggravating them. It was no less envied by the old landed interests [the Nobles], partly for the same reasons that rendered it obnoxious to the people, but much more so as it eclipsed, by the splendor of an ostentatious luxury, the unendowed pedigrees and naked titles of several among the nobility. Even when the nobility which represented the more permanent landed interest united themselves by marriage (which sometimes was the case) with the other description, the wealth which saved the family from ruin was supposed to contaminate and degrade it. Thus the enmities and heartburnings of these parties were increased even by the usual means by which discord is made to cease and quarrels are turned into friendship. In the meantime, the pride of the wealthy men, not noble or newly noble, increased with its cause. They felt with resentment an inferiority, the grounds of which they did not acknowledge. There was no measure to which they were not willing to lend themselves in order to be revenged of the outrages of this rival pride and to exalt their wealth to what they considered as its natural rank and estimation. They struck at the nobility through the crown and the church. They attacked them particularly on the side on which they thought them the most vulnerable, that is, the possessions of the church, which, through the patronage of the crown, generally devolved upon the nobility.

...As [the new monied class, also known as the Bourgeoisie] appear principal leaders in all the late transactions, their junction and politics will serve to account, not upon any principles of law or of policy, but as a cause, for the general fury with which all the landed property of ecclesiastical corporations has been attacked; and the great care which, contrary to their pretended principles, has been taken of a monied interest originating from the authority of the crown. All the envy against wealth and power was artificially directed against other descriptions of riches. On what other principle than that which I have stated can we account for an appearance so extraordinary and unnatural as that of the ecclesiastical possessions, which had stood so many successions of ages and shocks of civil violences, and were girded at once by justice and by prejudice, being applied to the payment of debts comparatively recent, invidious, and contracted by a decried and subverted government?

[THE NATIONAL ASSEMBLY, IN STEALING CHURCH LAND, HAS BEHAVED WITH UNPRECEDENTED BARBARITY]

...What had the clergy to do with [the incurring and payment of the national debt]? What had they to do with any public engagement further than the extent of their own debt? To that, to be sure, their estates were bound to the last acre. Nothing can lead more to the true spirit of the Assembly, which sits for public confiscation, with its new equity and its new morality, than an attention to their proceeding with regard to this debt of the clergy. The body of confiscators, true to that monied interest for which they were false to every other, have found the clergy competent to incur a legal debt. Of course, they declared them legally entitled to the property which their power of incurring the debt and mortgaging the estate implied, recognizing the rights of those persecuted citizens in the very act in which they were thus grossly violated.

Few barbarous conquerors have ever made so terrible a revolution in property. None of the heads of the Roman factions, when they established *crudelem illam hastam* ["that cruel spear," a reference to the Roman practice of sticking a spear into the ground to indicate property seized in battle] in all their auctions of rapine, have ever set up to sale the goods of the conquered citizen to such an enormous amount. It must be allowed in favor of those tyrants of antiquity that what was done by them could hardly be said to be done in cold blood. Their passions were inflamed, their tempers soured, their understandings confused with the spirit of revenge, with the innumerable reciprocated and recent inflictions and retaliations of blood and rapine. They were driven beyond all bounds of moderation by the apprehension of the return of power, with the return of property, to the families of those they had injured beyond all hope of forgiveness.

[WHY THE LEADERS OF THE REVOLUTION HAVE FAILED]

…When all the frauds, impostures, violences, rapines, burnings, murders, confiscations, compulsory paper currencies, and every description of tyranny and cruelty employed to bring about and to uphold this Revolution have their natural effect, that is, to shock the moral sentiments of all virtuous and sober minds, the abettors of this philosophic system immediately strain their throats in a declamation against the old monarchical government of France. When they have rendered that deposed power sufficiently black, they then proceed in argument as if all those who disapprove of their new abuses must of course be partisans of the old, that those who reprobate their crude and violent schemes of liberty ought to be treated as advocates for servitude. I admit that their necessities do compel them to this base and contemptible fraud. Nothing can reconcile men to their proceedings and projects but the supposition that there is no third option between them and some tyranny as odious as can be furnished by the records of history, or by the invention of poets. This prattling of theirs hardly deserves the name of sophistry. It is nothing but plain impudence. Have these gentlemen never heard, in the whole circle of the worlds of theory and practice, of anything between the despotism of the monarch and the despotism of the multitude? Have they never heard of a monarchy directed by laws, controlled and balanced by the great hereditary wealth and hereditary dignity of a nation, and both again controlled by a judicious check from the reason and feeling of the people at large acting by a suitable and permanent organ? Is it then impossible that a man may be found who, without criminal ill intention or pitiable absurdity, shall prefer such a mixed and tempered government to either of the extremes, and who may repute that nation to be destitute of all wisdom and of all virtue which, having in its choice to obtain such a government with ease, or rather to confirm it when actually possessed, thought proper to commit a thousand crimes and to subject their country to a thousand evils in order to avoid it? Is it then a truth so universally acknowledged that a pure democracy is the only tolerable form into which human society can be thrown, that a man is not permitted to hesitate about its merits without the suspicion of being a friend to tyranny, that is, of being a foe to mankind?

[WHY THE NATIONAL ASSEMBLY WILL BECOME A TYRANNY]

I do not know under what description to class the present ruling authority in France. It affects to be a pure democracy, though I think it in a direct train of becoming shortly a mischievous and ignoble oligarchy. But for the present I admit it to be a contrivance of the nature and effect of what it pretends to. I reprobate no form of government merely upon abstract principles. There may be situations in which the purely democratic form will become necessary. There may be some (very few, and very particularly circumstanced) where it would be clearly desirable. This I do not take to be the case of France or of any other great country. Until now, we have seen no examples of considerable democracies. The ancients were better acquainted with them. Not being wholly unread in the authors who had seen the most of those constitutions, and who best understood them, I cannot help concurring with their opinion that an absolute democracy, no more than absolute monarchy, is to be reckoned among the legitimate forms of government. They think it rather the corruption and degeneracy than the sound constitution of a republic. If I recollect rightly, Aristotle observes that a democracy has many striking points of resemblance with a tyranny. Of this I am certain, that in a democracy the majority of the citizens is capable of exercising the most cruel oppressions upon the minority whenever strong divisions prevail in that kind of polity, as they often must; and that oppression of the minority will extend to far greater numbers and will be carried on with much greater fury than can almost ever be apprehended from the dominion of a single scepter. In such a popular persecution, individual sufferers are in a much more deplorable condition than in any other. Under a cruel prince they have the balmy compassion of mankind to assuage the smart of their wounds; they have the plaudits of the people to animate their generous constancy under their sufferings; but those who are subjected to wrong under multitudes are deprived of all external consolation. They seem deserted by mankind, overpowered by a conspiracy of their whole species.

But admitting democracy not to have that inevitable tendency to party tyranny, which I suppose it to have, and admitting it to possess as much good in it when unmixed as I am sure it possesses when compounded with other forms, does monarchy, on its part, contain nothing at all to recommend it? I do not often quote Bolingbroke, nor have his works in general left any permanent impression on my mind. He is a presumptuous and a superficial writer. But he has one observation which, in my opinion, is not without depth and solidity. He says that he prefers a monarchy to other governments because you can better ingraft any description of republic on a monarchy than anything of monarchy upon the republican forms. I think him perfectly in the right. The fact is so historically, and it agrees well with the speculation.

I know how easy a topic it is to dwell on the faults of departed greatness. By a revolution in the state, the fawning sycophant of yesterday is converted into the austere critic of the present hour. But steady, independent minds, when they have an object of so serious a concern to mankind as government under their contemplation, will disdain to assume the part of satirists and declaimers. They will judge of human institutions as they do of human characters. They will sort out the good from the evil, which is mixed in mortal institutions, as it is in mortal men.

[THE FRENCH MONARCHY, THOUGH FLAWED, WAS NOT IRREPARABLE]

Your government in France, though usually, and I think justly, reputed the best of the unqualified or ill-qualified monarchies, was still full of abuses. These abuses accumulated in a length of time, as they must accumulate in every monarchy not under the constant inspection of a popular representative. I am no stranger to the faults and defects of the subverted government of France, and I think I am not inclined by nature or policy to make a panegyric upon anything which is a just and natural object of censure. But the question is not now of the vices of that monarchy, but of its existence. Is it, then, true that the French government was such as to be incapable or undeserving of reform, so that it was of absolute necessity that the whole fabric should be at once pulled down and the area cleared for the erection of a theoretic, experimental edifice in its place? All France was of a different opinion in the beginning of the year 1789. The instructions to the representatives to the States-General, from every district in that kingdom, were filled with projects for the reformation of that government without the remotest suggestion of a design to destroy it. Had such a design been even insinuated, I believe there would have been but one voice, and that voice for rejecting it with scorn and horror. Men have been sometimes led by degrees, sometimes hurried, into things of which, if they could have seen the whole together, they never would have permitted the most remote approach.

When those instructions were given, there was no question but that abuses existed, and that they demanded a reform; nor is there now. In the interval between the instructions and the revolution things changed their shape; and in consequence of that change, the true question at present is, Whether those who would have reformed or those who have destroyed are in the right?

To hear some men speak of the late monarchy of France, you would imagine that they were talking of Persia bleeding under the ferocious sword of Tahmas Kouli Khan, or at least describing the barbarous anarchic despotism of Turkey, where the finest countries in the most genial climates in the world are wasted by peace more than any countries have been worried by war, where arts are unknown, where manufactures languish, where science is extinguished, where agriculture decays, where the human race itself melts away and perishes under the eye of the observer. Was this the case of France? I have no way of determining the question but by reference to facts. Facts do not support this resemblance. Along with much evil there is some good in monarchy itself, and some corrective to its evil from religion, from laws, from manners, from opinions the French monarchy must have received, which rendered it (though by no means a free, and therefore by no means a good, constitution) a despotism rather in appearance than in reality.

[THE FRENCH NOBILITY DID NOT IN THE MAIN MISTREAT THE PEASANT CLASS]

…As to their behavior to the inferior classes, they appeared to me to comport themselves toward them with good nature and with something more nearly approaching to familiarity than is generally practiced with us in the intercourse between the higher and lower ranks of life. To strike any person, even in the most abject condition, was a thing in a manner unknown and would be highly disgraceful. Instances of other ill-treatment of the humble part of the community were rare; and as to attacks made upon the property or the personal liberty of the commons, I never heard of any whatsoever from them; nor, whilst the laws were in vigor under the ancient government, would such tyranny in subjects have been permitted. As men of landed estates, I had no fault to find with their conduct, though much to reprehend and much to wish changed in many of the old tenures. Where the letting of their land was by rent, I could not discover that their agreements with their farmers were oppressive; nor when they were in partnership with the farmer, as often was the case, have I heard that they had taken the lion's share. The proportions seemed not inequitable. There might be exceptions, but certainly they were exceptions only. I have no reason to believe that in these respects the landed noblesse of France were worse than the landed gentry of this country, certainly in no respect more vexatious than the landholders, not noble, of their own nation. In cities the nobility had no manner of power, in the country very little. You know, Sir, that much of the civil government, and the police in the most essential parts, was not in the hands of that nobility which presents itself first to our consideration. The revenue, the system and collection of which were the most grievous parts of the French government, was not administered by the men of the sword, nor were they answerable for the vices of its principle or the vexations, where any such existed, in its management.

Denying, as I am well warranted to do, that the nobility had any considerable share in the oppression of the people in cases in which real oppression existed, I am ready to admit that they were not without considerable faults and errors. A foolish imitation of the worst part of the manners of England, which impaired their natural character without substituting in its place what, perhaps, they meant to copy, has certainly rendered them worse than formerly they were. Habitual dissoluteness of manners, continued beyond the pardonable period of life, was more common amongst them than it is with us; and it reigned with the less hope of remedy, though possibly with something of less mischief by being covered with more exterior decorum. They countenanced too much that licentious philosophy which has helped to bring on their ruin [a reference to the *solons* of Paris where the *philosophes* held forth.] There was another error amongst them more fatal. Those of the commons who approached to or exceeded many of the nobility in point of wealth were not fully admitted to the rank and estimation which wealth, in reason and good policy, ought to bestow in every country, though I think not equally with that of other nobility. The two kinds of aristocracy were too punctiliously kept asunder, less so, however, than in Germany and some other nations.

This separation, as I have already taken the liberty of suggesting to you, I conceive to be one principal cause of the destruction of the old nobility. The military, particularly, was too exclusively reserved for men of family. But, after all, this was an error of opinion, which a conflicting opinion would have rectified. A permanent assembly in which the commons had their share of power would soon abolish whatever was too invidious and insulting in these distinctions, and even the faults in the morals of the nobility would have been probably corrected by the greater varieties of occupation and pursuit to which a constitution by orders would have given rise.

All this violent cry against the nobility I take to be a mere work of art. To be honored and even privileged by the laws, opinions, and inveterate usages of our country, growing out of the prejudice of ages, has nothing to provoke horror and indignation in any man. Even to be too tenacious of those privileges is not absolutely a crime. The strong struggle in every individual to preserve possession of what he has found to belong to him and to distinguish him is one of the securities against injustice and despotism implanted in our nature. It operates as an instinct to secure property and to preserve communities in a settled state. What is there to shock in this? Nobility is a graceful ornament to the civil order. It is the Corinthian capital of polished society. *Omnes boni nobilitati semper favemus* [Cicéro: Those who are good regard the nobility favorably.] was the saying of a wise and good man. It is indeed one sign of a liberal and benevolent mind to incline to it with some sort of partial propensity. He feels no ennobling principle in his own heart who wishes to level all the artificial institutions which have been adopted for giving a body to opinion, and permanence to fugitive esteem. It is a sour, malignant, envious disposition, without taste for the reality or for any image or representation of virtue, that sees with joy the unmerited fall of what had long flourished in splendor and in honor. I do not like to see anything destroyed, any void produced in society, any ruin on the face of the land. It was, therefore, with no disappointment or dissatisfaction that my inquiries and observations did not present to me any incorrigible vices in the noblesse of France, or any abuse which could not be removed by a reform very short of abolition. Your noblesse did not deserve punishment; but to degrade is to punish.

[WHY THE PEOPLE OF FRANCE SHOULD LOOK TO HISTORY FOR WISDOM]

…We do not draw the moral lessons we might from history. On the contrary, without care it may be used to vitiate our minds and to destroy our happiness. In history a great volume is unrolled for our instruction, drawing the materials of future wisdom from the past errors and infirmities of mankind. It may, in the perversion, serve for a magazine furnishing offensive and defensive weapons for parties in church and state, and supplying the means of keeping alive or reviving dissensions and animosities, and adding fuel to civil fury. History consists for the greater part of the miseries brought upon the world by pride, ambition, avarice, revenge, lust, sedition, hypocrisy, ungoverned zeal, and all the train of disorderly appetites which shake the public with the same— troublesome storms that toss the private state, and render life unsweet.

These vices are the causes of those storms. Religion, morals, laws, prerogatives, privileges, liberties, rights of men are the pretexts. The pretexts are always found in some specious appearance of a real good. You would not secure men from tyranny and sedition by rooting out of the mind the principles to which these fraudulent pretexts apply? If you did, you would root out everything that is valuable in the human breast. As these are the pretexts, so the ordinary actors and instruments in great public evils are kings, priests, magistrates, senates, parliaments, national assemblies, judges, and captains. You would not cure the evil by resolving that there should be no more monarchs, nor ministers of state, nor of the gospel; no interpreters of law; no general officers; no public councils. You might change the names. The things in some shape must remain. A certain quantum of power must always exist in the community in some hands and under some appellation. Wise men will apply their remedies to vices, not to names; to the causes of evil which are permanent, not to the occasional organs by which they act, and the transitory modes in which they appear. Otherwise you will be wise historically, a fool in practice. Seldom have two ages the same fashion in their pretexts and the same modes of mischief. Wickedness is a little more inventive. Whilst you are discussing fashion, the fashion is gone by. The very same vice assumes a new body. The spirit transmigrates, and, far from losing its principle of life by the change of its appearance, it is renovated in its new organs with a fresh vigor of a juvenile activity. It walks abroad, it continues its ravages, whilst you are gibbeting the carcass or demolishing the tomb. You are terrifying yourselves with ghosts and apparitions, whilst your house is the haunt of robbers. It is thus with all those who, attending only to the shell and husk of history, think they are waging war with intolerance, pride, and cruelty, whilst, under color of abhorring the ill principles of antiquated parties, they are authorizing and feeding the same odious vices in different factions, and perhaps in worse.

[WHY THE CLERGY IS INNOCENT OF GUILT]

If your clergy, or any clergy, should show themselves vicious beyond the fair bounds allowed to human infirmity, and to those professional faults which can hardly be separated from professional virtues, though their vices never can countenance the exercise of oppression, I do admit that they would naturally have the effect of abating very much of our indignation against the tyrants who exceed measure and justice in their punishment. I can allow in clergymen, through all their divisions, some tenaciousness of their own opinion, some overflowings of zeal for its propagation, some predilection to their own state and office, some attachment to the interests of their own corps, some preference to those who listen with docility to their doctrines, beyond those who scorn and deride them. I allow all this, because I am a man who has to deal with men, and who would not, through a violence of toleration, run into the greatest of all intolerance. I must bear with infirmities until they fester into crimes.

Undoubtedly, the natural progress of the passions, from frailty to vice, ought to be prevented by a watchful eye and a firm hand. But is it true that the body of your clergy had passed those limits of a just allowance? From the general style of your late publications of all sorts one would be led to believe that your clergy in France were a sort of monsters, a horrible composition of superstition, ignorance, sloth, fraud, avarice, and tyranny. But is this true? I sit true that the lapse of time, the cessation of conflicting interests, the woeful experience of the evils resulting from party rage have had no sort of influence gradually to meliorate their minds? Is it true that they were daily renewing invasions on the civil power, troubling the domestic quiet of their country, and rendering the operations of its government feeble and precarious? Is it true that the clergy of our times have pressed down the laity with an iron hand and were in all places lighting up the fires of a savage persecution? Did they by every fraud endeavor to increase their estates? Did they use to exceed the due demands on estates that were their own? Or, rigidly screwing up right into wrong, did they convert a legal claim into a vexatious extortion? When not possessed of power, were they filled with the vices of those who envy it? Were they inflamed with a violent, litigious spirit of controversy? Goaded on with the ambition of intellectual sovereignty, were they ready to fly in the face of all magistracy, to fire churches, to massacre the priests of other descriptions, to pull down altars, and to make their way over the ruins of subverted governments to an empire of doctrine, sometimes flattering, sometimes forcing the consciences of men from the jurisdiction of public institutions into a submission of their personal authority, beginning with a claim of liberty and ending with an abuse of power?

…If there was in France, as in other countries there visibly is, a great abatement rather than any increase of these vices, instead of loading the present clergy with the crimes of other men and the odious character of other times, in common equity they ought to be praised, encouraged, and supported in their departure from a spirit which disgraced their predecessors, and for having assumed a temper of mind and manners more suitable to their sacred function.

…[T]he present ruling power has shown a disposition only to plunder the church. It has punished all prelates, which is to favor the vicious, at least in point of reputation. It has made a degrading pensionary establishment to which no man of liberal ideas or liberal condition will destine his children. It must settle into the lowest classes of the people… The new lawgivers have not ascertained anything whatsoever concerning [the newly elected bishops'] qualifications relative either to doctrine or to morals, no more than they have done with regard to the subordinate clergy; nor does it appear but that both the higher and the lower may, at their discretion, practice or preach any mode of religion or irreligion that they please. I do not yet see what the jurisdiction of bishops over their subordinates is to be, or whether they are to have any jurisdiction at all.

In short, Sir, it seems to me that this new ecclesiastical establishment is intended only to be temporary and preparatory to the utter abolition, under any of its forms, of the Christian religion, whenever the minds of men are prepared for this last stroke against it, by the accomplishment of the plan for bringing its ministers into universal contempt. They who will not believe that the philosophical fanatics who guide in these matters have long entertained such a design are utterly ignorant of their character and proceedings. These enthusiasts do not scruple to avow their opinion that a state can subsist without any religion better than with one, and that they are able to supply the place of any good which may be in it by a project of their own — namely, by a sort of education they have imagined, founded in a knowledge of the physical wants of men, progressively carried to an enlightened self-interest which, when well understood, they tell us, will identify with an interest more enlarged and public. The scheme of this education has been long known. Of late they distinguish it (as they have got an entirely new nomenclature of technical terms) by the name of a Civic Education.

[THE USURPATION OF AUTHORITY BY THE POWER-HUNGRY MEN OF THE NATIONAL ASSEMBLY]

… I can never consider this Assembly as anything else than a voluntary association of men who have availed themselves of circumstances to seize upon the power of the state. They have not the sanction and authority of the character under which they first met. They have assumed another of a very different nature and have completely altered and inverted all the relations in which they originally stood. They do not hold the authority they exercise under any constitutional law of the state. They have departed from the instructions of the people by whom they were sent, which instructions, as the Assembly did not act in virtue of any ancient usage or settled law, were the sole source of their authority. The most considerable of their acts have not been done by great majorities; and in this sort of near divisions, which carry only the constructive authority of the whole, strangers will consider reasons as well as resolutions.

If they had set up this new experimental government as a necessary substitute for an expelled tyranny, mankind would anticipate the time of prescription which, through long usage, mellows into legality governments that were violent in their commencement. All those who have affections which lead them to the conservation of civil order would recognize, even in its cradle, the child as legitimate which has been produced from those principles of cogent expediency to which all just governments owe their birth, and on which they justify their continuance. But they will be late and reluctant in giving any sort of countenance to the operations of a power which has derived its birth from no law and no necessity, but which, on the contrary, has had its origin in those vices and sinister practices by which the social union is often disturbed and sometimes destroyed. This Assembly has hardly a year's prescription. We have their own word for it that they have made a revolution. To make a revolution is a measure which requires an apology. To make a revolution is to subvert the ancient state of our country; and no common reasons are called for to justify so violent a proceeding. The sense of mankind authorizes us to examine into the mode of acquiring new power, and to criticize on the use that is made of it, with less awe and reverence than that which is usually conceded to a settled and recognized authority.

In obtaining and securing their power the Assembly proceeds upon principles the most opposite to those which appear to direct them in the use of it. An observation on this difference will let us into the true spirit of their conduct. Everything which they have done, or continue to do. in order to obtain and keep their power is by the most common arts. They proceed exactly as their ancestors of ambition have done before them. — Trace them through all their artifices, frauds, and violences, you can find nothing at all that is new. They follow precedents and examples with the punctilious exactness of a pleader. They never depart an iota from the authentic formulas of tyranny and usurpation. But in all the regulations relative to the public good, the spirit has been the very reverse of this. There they commit the whole to the mercy of untried speculations; they abandon the dearest interests of the public to those loose theories to which none of them would choose to trust the slightest of his private concerns. They make this difference, because in their desire of obtaining and securing power they are thoroughly in earnest; there they travel in the beaten road. The public interests, because about them they have no real solicitude, they abandon wholly to chance; I say to chance, because their schemes have nothing in experience to prove their tendency beneficial.

We must always see with a pity not unmixed with respect the errors of those who are timid and doubtful of themselves with regard to points wherein the happiness of mankind is concerned. But in these gentlemen there is nothing of the tender, parental solicitude which fears to cut up the infant for the sake of an experiment. In the vastness of their promises and the confidence of their predictions, they far outdo all the boasting of empirics. The arrogance of their pretensions in a manner provokes and challenges us to an inquiry into their foundation.

[THE FORMATION OF AN EXECUTIVE POWER REMOVED FROM KINGSHIP]

Let us now turn our eyes to what they have done toward the formation of an executive power. For this they have chosen a degraded king. This their first executive officer is to be a machine without any sort of deliberative discretion in any one act of his function. At best he is but a channel to convey to the National Assembly such matter as it may import that body to know. If he had been made the exclusive channel, the power would not have been without its importance, though infinitely perilous to those who would choose to exercise it. But public intelligence and statement of facts may pass to the Assembly with equal authenticity through any other conveyance. As to the means, therefore, of giving a direction to measures by the statement of an authorized reporter, this office of intelligence is as nothing.

To consider the French scheme of an executive officer, in its two natural divisions of civil and political. — In the first, it must be observed that, according to the new constitution, the higher parts of judicature, in either of its lines, are not in the king. The king of France is not the fountain of justice. The judges, neither the original nor the appellate, are of his nomination. He neither proposes the candidates, nor has a negative on the choice. He is not even the public prosecutor. He serves only as a notary to authenticate the choice made of the judges in the several districts. By his officers he is to execute their sentence. When we look into the true nature of his authority, he appears to be nothing more than a chief of bum bailiffs, sergeants at mace, catchpoles, jailers, and hangmen. It is impossible to place anything called royalty in a more degrading point of view.

A thousand times better had it been for the dignity of this unhappy prince that he had nothing at all to do with the administration of justice, deprived as he is of all that is venerable and all that is consolatory in that function, without power of originating any process, without a power of suspension, mitigation, or pardon. Everything in justice that is vile and odious is thrown upon him. It was not for nothing that the Assembly has been at such pains to remove the stigma from certain offices when they are resolved to place the person who had lately been their king in a situation but one degree above the executioner, and in an office nearly of the same quality. It is not in nature that, situated as the king of the French now is, he can respect himself or can be respected by others.

View this new executive officer on the side of his political capacity, as he acts under the orders of the National Assembly. To execute laws is a royal office; to execute orders is not to be a king. However, a political executive magistracy, though merely such, is a great trust. It is a trust indeed that has much depending upon its faithful and diligent performance, both in the person presiding in it and in all its subordinates. Means of performing this duty ought to be given by regulation; and dispositions toward it ought to be infused by the circumstances attendant on the trust. It ought to be environed with dignity, authority, and consideration, and it ought to lead to glory. The office of execution is an office of exertion. It is not from impotence we are to expect the tasks of power. What sort of person is a king to command executory service, who has no means whatsoever to reward it? Not in a permanent office; not in a grant of land; no, not in a pension of fifty pounds a year; not in the vainest and most trivial title. In France, the king is no more the fountain of honor than he is the fountain of justice. All rewards, all distinctions are in other hands. Those who serve the king can be actuated by no natural motive but fear — by a fear of everything except their master. His functions of internal coercion are as odious as those which he exercises in the department of justice. If relief is to be given to any municipality, the Assembly gives it. If troops are to be sent to reduce them to obedience to the Assembly, the king is to execute the order; and upon every occasion he is to be spattered over with the blood of his people. He has no negative; yet his name and authority is used to enforce every harsh decree. Nay, he must concur in the butchery of those who shall attempt to free him from his imprisonment or show the slightest attachment to his person or to his ancient authority.

[THE INABILITY OF ANY KING TO ACT WITHIN THE CONFINES OF THE NEW FRENCH STATE]

Executive magistracy ought to be constituted in such a manner that those who compose it should be disposed to love and to venerate those whom they are bound to obey. A purposed neglect or, what is worse, a literal but perverse and malignant obedience must be the ruin of the wisest counsels. In vain will the law attempt to anticipate or to follow such studied neglects and fraudulent attentions. To make them act zealously is not in the competence of law. Kings, even such as are truly kings, may and ought to bear the freedom of subjects that are obnoxious to them. They may, too, without derogating from themselves, bear even the authority of such persons if it promotes their service... I think it impossible that any king, when he has recovered his first terrors, can cordially infuse vivacity and vigor into measures which he knows to be dictated by those who, he must be persuaded, are in the highest degree ill affected to his person. Will any ministers who serve such a king (or whatever he may be called) with but a decent appearance of respect cordially obey the orders of those whom but the other day in his name they had committed to the Bastille? Will they obey the orders of those whom, whilst they were exercising despotic justice upon them, they conceived they were treating with lenity, and from whom, in a prison, they thought they had provided an asylum? If you expect such obedience amongst your other innovations and regenerations, you ought to make a revolution in nature and provide a new constitution for the human mind. Otherwise, your supreme government cannot harmonize with its executory system. There are cases in which we cannot take up with names and abstractions. You may call half a dozen leading individuals, whom we have reason to fear and hate, the nation. It makes no other difference than to make us fear and hate them the more. If it had been thought justifiable and expedient to make such a revolution by such means, and through such persons, as you have made yours, it would have been more wise to have completed the business of the fifth and sixth of October [when King Louis XVI and Marie Antoinette were arrested]. The new executive officer would then owe his situation to those who are his creators as well as his masters; and he might be bound in interest, in the society of crime, and (if in crimes there could be virtues) in gratitude to serve those who had promoted him to a place of great lucre and great sensual indulgence, and of something more; for more he must have received from those who certainly would not have limited an aggrandized creature, as they have done a submitting antagonist.

A king circumstanced as the present, if he is totally stupefied by his misfortunes so as to think it not the necessity but the premium and privilege of life to eat and sleep, without any regard to glory, can never be fit for the office. If he feels as men commonly feel, he must be sensible that an office so circumstanced is one in which he can obtain no fame or reputation. He has no generous interest that can excite him to action. At best, his conduct will be passive and defensive.

To inferior people such an office might be matter of honor. But to be raised to it, and to descend to it, are different things and suggest different sentiments. Does he really name the ministers? They will have a sympathy with him. Are they forced upon him? The whole business between them and the nominal king will be mutual counteraction. In all other countries, the office of ministers of state is of the highest dignity. In France it is full of peril, and incapable of glory. Rivals, however, they will have in their nothingness, whilst shallow ambition exists in the world, or the desire of a miserable salary is an incentive to short-sighted avarice. Those competitors of the ministers are enabled by your constitution to attack them in their vital parts, whilst they have not the means of repelling their charges in any other than the degrading character of culprits. The ministers of state in France are the only persons in that country who are incapable of a share in the national councils. What ministers! What councils! What a nation! — But they are responsible. It is a poor service that is to be had from responsibility. The elevation of mind to be derived from fear will never make a nation glorious. Responsibility prevents crimes. It makes all attempts against the laws dangerous. But for a principle of active and zealous service, none but idiots could think of it. Is the conduct of a war to be trusted to a man who may abhor its principle, who, in every step he may take to render it successful, confirms the power of those by whom he is oppressed? Will foreign states seriously treat with him who has no prerogative of peace or war? No, not so much as in a single vote by himself or his ministers, or by any one whom he can possibly influence. A state of contempt is not a state for a prince; better get rid of him at once.

[WHY FRANCE NEEDS AN ARMY IN ORDER TO PACIFY AND COERCE ITS PEOPLE]

Everything depends upon the army in such a government as yours, for you have industriously destroyed all the opinions and prejudices and, as far as in you lay, all the instincts which support government. Therefore, the moment any difference arises between your National Assembly and any part of the nation, you must have recourse to force. Nothing else is left to you, or rather you have left nothing else to yourselves. You see, by the report of your war minister, that the distribution of the army is in a great measure made with a view of internal coercion. You must rule by an army; and you have infused into that army by which you rule, as well as into the whole body of the nation, principles which after a time must disable you in the use you resolve to make of it. The king is to call out troops to act against his people, when the world has been told, and the assertion is still ringing in our ears, that troops ought not to fire on citizens. The colonies assert to themselves an independent constitution and a free trade. They must be constrained by troops. In what chapter of your code of the rights of men are they able to read that it is a part of the rights of men to have their commerce monopolized and restrained for the benefit of others? As the colonists rise on you, the Negroes rise on them. Troops again — massacre, torture, hanging! These are your rights of men! These are the fruits of metaphysic declarations wantonly made, and shamefully retracted! It was but the other day that the farmers of land in one of your provinces refused to pay some sort of rents to the lord of the soil. In consequence of this, you decree that the country people shall pay all rents and dues, except those which as grievances you have abolished; and if they refuse, then you order the king to march troops against them. You lay down metaphysic propositions which infer universal consequences, and then you attempt to limit logic by despotism. The leaders of the present system tell them of their rights, as men, to take fortresses, to murder guards, to seize on kings without the least appearance of authority even from the Assembly, whilst, as the sovereign legislative body, that Assembly was sitting in the name of the nation — and yet these leaders presume to order out the troops which have acted in these very disorders, to coerce those who shall judge on the principles, and follow the examples, which have been guaranteed by their own approbation.

[WHY THE FRENCH PEASANTS USE REVOLUTIONARY RHETORIC AGAINST THE REVOLUTION]

The leaders teach the people to abhor and reject all feudality as the barbarism of tyranny, and they tell them afterwards how much of that barbarous tyranny they are to bear with patience. As they are prodigal of light with regard to grievances, so the people find them sparing in the extreme with regard to redress. They know that not only certain quitrents and personal duties, which you have permitted them to redeem (but have furnished no money for the redemption), are as nothing to those burdens for which you have made no provision at all. They know that almost the whole system of landed property in its origin is feudal; that it is the distribution of the possessions of the original proprietors, made by a barbarous conqueror to his barbarous instruments; and that the most grievous effects of the conquest are the land rents of every kind, as without question they are.

The peasants, in all probability, are the descendants of these ancient proprietors, Romans or Gauls. But if they fail, in any degree, in the titles which they make on the principles of antiquaries and lawyers, they retreat into the citadel of the rights of men. There they find that men are equal; and the earth, the kind and equal mother of all, ought not to be monopolized to foster the pride and luxury of any men, who by nature are no better than themselves, and who, if they do not labor for their bread, are worse. They find that by the laws of nature the occupant and subduer of the soil is the true proprietor; that there is no prescription against nature; and that the agreements (where any there are) which have been made with the landlords, during the time of slavery, are only the effect of duress and force; and that when the people reentered into the rights of men, those agreements were made as void as everything else which had been settled under the prevalence of the old feudal and aristocratic tyranny. They will tell you that they see no difference between an idler with a hat and a national cockade and an idler in a cowl or in a rochet... As to the title by succession, they will tell you that the succession of those who have cultivated the soil is the true pedigree of property, and not rotten parchments and silly substitutions; that the lords have enjoyed their usurpation too long; and that if they allow to these lay monks any charitable pension, they ought to be thankful to the bounty of the true proprietor, who is so generous toward a false claimant to his goods.

When the peasants give you back that coin of sophistic reason on which you have set your image and superscription, you cry it down as base money and tell them you will pay for the future with French guards, and dragoons, and hussars. You hold up, to chastise them, the second-hand authority of a king, who is only the instrument of destroying, without any power of protecting either the people or his own person. Through him it seems you will make yourselves obeyed. They answer: You have taught us that there are no gentlemen, and which of your principles teach us to bow to kings whom we have not elected? We know without your teaching that lands were given for the support of feudal dignities, feudal titles, and feudal offices. When you took down the cause as a grievance, why should the more grievous effect remain? As there are now no hereditary honors, and no distinguished families, why are we taxed to maintain what you tell us ought not to exist? You have sent down our old aristocratic landlords in no other character, and with no other title, but that of exactors under your authority. Have you endeavored to make these your rent-gatherers respectable to us? No. You have sent them to us with their arms reversed, their shields broken, their impresses defaced; and so displumed, degraded, and metamorphosed, such unfeathered two-legged things, that we no longer know them. They are strangers to us. They do not even go by the names of our ancient lords. Physically they may be the same men, though we are not quite sure of that, on your new philosophic doctrines of personal identity. In all other respects they are totally changed. We do not see why we have not as good a right to refuse them their rents as you have to abrogate all their honors, titles, and distinctions. This we have never commissioned you to do; and it is one instance, among many indeed, of your assumption of undelegated power. We see the burghers of Paris, through their clubs, their mobs, and their national guards, directing you at their pleasure and giving that as law to you which, under your authority, is transmitted as law to us. Through you these burghers dispose of the lives and fortunes of us all. Why should not you attend as much to the desires of the laborious husbandman with regard to our rent, by which we are affected in the most serious manner, as you do to the demands of these insolent burghers, relative to distinctions and titles of honor, by which neither they nor we are affected at all? But we find you pay more regard to their fancies than to our necessities. Is it among the rights of man to pay tribute to his equals? Before this measure of yours, we might have thought we were not perfectly equal. We might have entertained some old, habitual, unmeaning prepossession in favor of those landlords; but we cannot conceive with what other view than that of destroying all respect to them, you could have made the law that degrades them. You have forbidden us to treat them with any of the old formalities of respect, and now you send troops to saber and to bayonet us into a submission to fear and force, which you did not suffer us to yield to the mild authority of opinion.

...The people of Lyons, it seems, have refused lately to pay taxes. Why should they not? What lawful authority is there left to exact them? The king imposed some of them. The old states, methodized by orders, settled the more ancient. They may say to the Assembly: who are you, that are not our kings, nor the states we have elected, nor sit on the principles on which we have elected you? And who are we, that when we see the gabelles, which you have ordered to be paid, wholly shaken off, when we see the act of disobedience afterwards ratified by yourselves — who are we, that we are not to judge what taxes we ought or ought not to pay, and are not to avail ourselves of the same powers, the validity of which you have approved in others? To this the answer is, We will send troops. The last reason of kings is always the first with your Assembly. This military aid may serve for a time, whilst the impression of the increase of pay remains, and the vanity of being umpires in all disputes is flattered. But this weapon will snap short, unfaithful to the hand that employs it. The Assembly keep a school where, systematically, and with unremitting perseverance, they teach principles and form regulations destructive to all spirit of subordination, civil and military — and then they expect that they shall hold in obedience an anarchic people by an anarchic army.

[WHY THE FRENCH, UNDER REVOLUTION, ARE NOT FREE]

…The effects of the incapacity shown by the popular leaders in all the great members of the commonwealth are to be covered with the "all-atoning name" of liberty. In some people I see great liberty indeed; in many, if not in the most, an oppressive, degrading servitude. But what is liberty without wisdom and without virtue? It is the greatest of all possible evils; for it is folly, vice, and madness, without tuition or restraint. Those who know what virtuous liberty is cannot bear to see it disgraced by incapable heads on account of their having high-sounding words in their mouths. Grand, swelling sentiments of liberty I am sure I do not despise. They warm the heart; they enlarge and liberalize our minds; they animate our courage in a time of conflict. Old as I am, I read the fine raptures of Lucan [1st century Roman poet] and Corneille [17th century French playwright] with pleasure. Neither do I wholly condemn the little arts and devices of popularity. They facilitate the carrying of many points of moment; they keep the people together; they refresh the mind in its exertions; and they diffuse occasional gaiety over the severe brow of moral freedom. Every politician ought to sacrifice to the graces, and to join compliance with reason. But in such an undertaking as that in France, all these subsidiary sentiments and artifices are of little avail. To make a government requires no great prudence. Settle the seat of power, teach obedience, and the work is done. To give freedom is still more easy. It is not necessary to guide; it only requires to let go the rein. But to form a free government, that is, to temper together these opposite elements of liberty and restraint in one consistent work, requires much thought, deep reflection, a sagacious, powerful, and combining mind. This I do not find in those who take the lead in the National Assembly. Perhaps they are not so miserably deficient as they appear. I rather believe it. It would put them below the common level of human understanding. But when the leaders choose to make themselves bidders at an auction of popularity, their talents, in the construction of the state, will be of no service. They will become flatterers instead of legislators, the instruments, not the guides, of the people. If any of them should happen to propose a scheme of liberty, soberly limited and defined with proper qualifications, he will be immediately outbid by his competitors who will produce something more splendidly popular. Suspicions will be raised of his fidelity to his cause. Moderation will be stigmatized as the virtue of cowards, and compromise as the prudence of traitors, until, in hopes of preserving the credit which may enable him to temper and moderate, on some occasions, the popular leader is obliged to become active in propagating doctrines and establishing powers that will afterwards defeat any sober purpose at which he ultimately might have aimed.

But am I so unreasonable as to see nothing at all that deserves commendation in the indefatigable labors of this Assembly? I do not deny that, among an infinite number of acts of violence and folly, some good may have been done. They who destroy everything certainly will remove some grievance. They who make everything new have a chance that they may establish something beneficial. To give them credit for what they have done in virtue of the authority they have usurped, or which can excuse them in the crimes by which that authority has been acquired, it must appear that the same things could not have been accomplished without producing such a revolution. Most assuredly they might, because almost every one of the regulations made by them which is not very equivocal was either in the cession of the king, voluntarily made at the meeting of the states, or in the concurrent instructions to the orders. Some usages have been abolished on just grounds, but they were such that if they had stood as they were to all eternity, they would little detract from the happiness and prosperity of any state. The improvements of the National Assembly are superficial, their errors fundamental.

…I have little to recommend my opinions but long observation and much impartiality. They come from one who has been no tool of power, no flatterer of greatness; and who in his last acts does not wish to belie the tenor of his life. They come from one almost the whole of whose public exertion has been a struggle for the liberty of others; from one in whose breast no anger, durable or vehement, has ever been kindled but by what he considered as tyranny; and who snatches from his share in the endeavors which are used by good men to discredit opulent oppression the hours he has employed on your affairs; and who in so doing persuades himself he has not departed from his usual office; they come from one who desires honors, distinctions, and emoluments but little, and who expects them not at all; who has no contempt for fame, and no fear of obloquy; who shuns contention, though he will hazard an opinion; from one who wishes to preserve consistency, but who would preserve consistency by varying his means to secure the unity of his end, and, when the equipoise of the vessel in which he sails may be endangered by overloading it upon one side, is desirous of carrying the small weight of his reasons to that which may preserve its equipoise.

Appendix D: Gershoy, *The French Revolution & Napoleon*

[The essay that follows is a narrative account of the French Revolution beginning with the convening of the Estates-General in the spring of 1789. The game booklet elsewhere outlines the events that led up to this situation; if students seek further clarification of the deeper historical context, they should consult any of the texts mentioned in the bibliography. The account here ends—somewhat abruptly—after the departure of the King from Paris in June of 1791. But that, of course is when the game begins.]

Gershoy, Leo. *The French Revolution and Napoleon*, 1ˢᵗ Ed. (Englewood Cliffs, 1964), pp. 107-191

THE DESTRUCTION OF THE OLD REGIME

The Establishment of the National Assembly. Everywhere except in Paris the elections were over in April; and by May 1, 1789, almost all deputies were at Versailles. There were approximately seventeen hundred of them, including the alternates for all the orders. In a variety of petty ways the deputies of the Third Estate were made to feel their inferiority. Their somber and outlandish costumes of black cloth contrasted dismally with the splendid attire worn by the clergy and the nobles. At the formal and highly stilted reception for all the deputies (May 2), the king kept the commoners waiting for hours and then, while the high officials of the court stared at them with condescending curiosity, received them coldly. The formal mass in state which opened the Estates-General on May 4 furnished another occasion for humiliation, but the commoners took what comfort they could from the enthusiastic cheers of the townspeople of Versailles. After a long, almost interminable, day they retired to await the real opening of the Estates-General on the morrow. Their hopes were still fervent, though their spirits had been depressed by the chill of the royal reception.

Their disappointment in the king was not abated by what occurred on May 5, but changed from irritation to suspicion. To begin, the royal family delayed proceedings for hours; then the king appeared supposedly to announce the royal program. He read a short speech which was received well enough, though it could scarcely have had less content. The keeper of the royal seals followed with a longer address, which intimated that the crown did not object to the vote by head on financial matters, but opposed such a procedure for the discussion of political reform. Necker, on whom the commoners pinned their hopes, spoke last and at great length, leaving a spokesman to conclude his address. The king seemed impressed, probably less by the speech than by the applause of the commoners, which implied strongly that it might be unwise to dismiss powerful ministers, as the court faction desired. Necker spoke almost entirely about financial administration and the deficit, explaining that a few reforms and a program of economy would restore financial stability. He avoided the question of constitutional reforms and made hedging allusions to the question of the vote, intimating, however, that on certain matters it would be desirable to vote by order. When Necker's mouthpiece had finished, the master of ceremonies requested all the deputies to show their credentials.

The commoners, as their many commentaries reveal, were aghast at the proceedings. They had come to the capital to serve as true legislators of the nation; now the king and his principal minister served warning that the old order would be maintained, that no opportunity would be given them to "create" a constitution for France, to regenerate the administration and society. Spontaneously, they resolved to resist the policy of the court. They showed their independence by refusing to present their credentials, and the verification was accordingly postponed until the following day. Each order was assigned to separate rooms in the Salle des Menus Plaisirs.

The events of that day disclosed attitudes and tempers that boded ill for the future. Necker revealed his basic unimaginative mediocrity by failing to grasp the significance of the occasion. He had it in his power to guide the movement for reform under the aegis of the king. But his eye was dimmed to the future; it had grown weary contemplating the figures of receipts and expenditures. He had the soul of a bank clerk; the flame of the statesman did not burn in him. Had Louis XVI been as firm in character as he was benevolent in intention, he might have risen to the heights demanded of a leader. He was not craven, but he was readily influenced by those about him, too open to suggestions; and the suggestions emanating from his court counselors advised him to maintain the *status quo,* to keep the commoners in their place. The commoners were nettled, and in their impatience with the leaders on whom they had counted, but who had failed them, they sought new leaders in their own ranks. Unlike the privileged orders, they refused to verify their credentials separately.

One leader they found in Mirabeau, that *déclassé* noble of imposing ugliness whom frequent imprisonment, crushing debts, and innumerable scandalous adventures had not suppressed. His own order had rejected him, but such was his wide reputation for liberalism that the Third Estate of Aix-en-Provence had elected him to the Estates-General. Thanks to his many amanuenses and his own vigorous and capable gifts he had amassed an extraordinarily rich store of information and experience on problems of state. Experienced, of supple intellect, sure in his political faith of a constitutional monarchy, daring in his acts, and brilliant in oratory, Mirabeau rose rapidly to the leadership of the commoners. When the deputies of the Third Estate, or the Commons as they preferred to call themselves, resolved not to organize a separate body, nor to recognize the verification of the credentials of the deputies save in a common assembly, they adopted a policy that required political finesse and courage. These qualities they found in Mirabeau. With the sure sense of a political realist he directed the united commoners against the weaker of the privileged orders. "Send delegates to the clergy, gentlemen," he cried. "Do not send any to the nobles, for the nobles give orders and the clergy will negotiate."

After five weeks of unseemly bickering over the crucial matter of the organization of the Estates-General the commoners ended their inactivity. Upon the initiative of Abbé Sieyes, who had only recently taken his seat with them, and in defiance of the king's express command for the separate verification of credentials, they began to verify not as deputies of the Third Estate, but as representatives of the nation (June 12). During the next few days some of the parish priests came over, and on June 17 the commoners and their adherents among the ecclesiastics, declared themselves the *National Assembly* of France and proceeded to act as the representative body of the nation.

Their declaration was the first act of the Revolution; indeed, their declaration contained the whole theory and achievement of the Revolution. In a few deliberate and coldly logical phrases they set aside the entire theory and practice of a government and society based upon *privileged* orders and asserted the *democratic* theory of numbers and of popular sovereignty. "The denomination of National Assembly is the only one which is suitable for the Assembly in the present condition of things; because the members who compose it are the only representatives lawfully and publicly known and verified; because they are sent directly by almost the totality of the nation; because, lastly, the representation being one and indivisible, none of the deputies in whatever class or order he may be chosen, has the right to exercise his functions apart from the present Assembly." The commoners represented "at least ninety-six per cent of the nation"; therefore they constituted the National Assembly. The Assembly took pains to reassure the creditors of the state that the debt would be paid, ordered the provisional collection of the existing taxes, declared that new taxes were not valid without its consent, and denied the king the right to veto its future resolutions. Two days later, June 19, Mirabeau's expectations were realized, for by a small majority the clergy voted to join the Commons in the National Assembly and in that way gave endorsement to the illegal and revolutionary act of June 17. At once the court party, led by the queen and the count of Artois, the younger of the two brothers of Louis XVI, urged the harried monarch to take repressive measures; while Necker, equally insistent, outlined a program of reforms. Louis XVI half acquiesced in Necker's view, but at the same time he had decided to annul the measures of the Commons. Despite Necker's objections he made plans to hold a "royal session" of the Estates-General on June 22, on which occasion he intended to announce the policy of the court on the manner of voting and the question of reforms and thus settle the constitutional dispute which had made impossible the solution of the nation's problems.

The "Royal Session" of June 23. On the morning of June 20 the deputies of the Commons found the doors of their Assembly room closed to them, supposedly to allow necessary repairs within the hall for the holding of a special royal session two days later. It was a two minutes' walk to the near-by indoor tennis court, a bare little building with only a floor space and galleries for spectators. There the determined deputies betook themselves, resolved not to yield. Discussion began at once; several deputies were in favor of going to Paris, but from this decision Mounier dissuaded them. He boldly proposed that they should all take an oath "never to separate and to reassemble wherever circumstances demanded until the constitution of the realm was established and affirmed upon a solid basis." In the midst of great enthusiasm, Bailly, the astronomer and savant, who was the presiding officer of the Assembly, read the oath, and the deputies swore it after him. The "Tennis Court Oath" was a dramatic and stirring declaration, not, to be sure the beginning of the Revolution, for that had already begun, but an emphatic and courageous reaffirmation of the resolution passed three days earlier.

The immediate future of France lay with Louis XVI. He could have summoned the troops against the rebellious deputies, but such a course would have been catastrophic to France. He determined to intimidate the commoners with *threats* of force. He rejected Necker's conciliatory plan and postponed the royal session to June 23. Meantime a majority of the clergy and a bare sprinkling of noblemen joined the deputies of the Third Estate in the hall of the National Assembly. The Assembly was now composed of the majority of orders as well as of deputies.

Louis XVI was ready with his program on June 23. Before the royal session opened the commoners received a taste of what was to come. In spite of a heavy rain they were kept waiting for an hour before they were admitted, by a rear entrance, to the Salle des Menus

Plaisirs. Spectators were excluded and a detachment of troops surrounded the hall. Necker's seat was empty, which gave rise to the rumor that he had resigned, though in fact his resignation in protest over the king's policy did not come until after the session. The speech delivered by the king gave point to the obvious preparations that had been made to intimidate the deputies of the Third Estate. He spoke coldly, with majestic haughtiness ignoring the resolutions of June 17 and June 20. It was his royal wish to have "the ancient distinction of the three orders of the state maintained in its entirety." Subject to his approval, certain stipulated matters might be discussed in common, but constitutional questions were to be discussed separately. Having stated his policy on the disputed points, the monarch outlined the royal program of reform and indicated how far he was ready to go. All property rights without exception (signifying ecclesiastical and feudal property) were to be respected; and no change was to be made in the organization of the army. On the other hand the king promised wide and important financial powers to the Estates-General, agreed to the abolition of the most obnoxious feudal and fiscal abuses, and promised equality of taxation to his subjects. He signified his readiness to grant the basic rights of personal liberty to all citizens and ordered the establishment of provincial estates throughout the realm.

Submitted to the Estates-General on May 5, the king's program would undoubtedly have served as a basis for discussion. On June 23 it was outmoded since the Commons not only had gone beyond the royal program, but had taken a solemn oath to do that which the king forbade; namely, to draw up a new constitution. Consequently, his final words, an unveiled threat to dismiss the Estates-General and carry out his plans alone, if the commoners would not cooperate with him, and his command for the immediate separation of the three orders thrust the decision squarely upon the deputies of the Third Estate. The nobles and most of the clergy followed Louis XVI as he left the hall, but the commoners defied him and his threats. When the master of ceremonies repeated the royal command to Bailly, the thundering voice of Mirabeau filled the hall: "Go and tell those who sent you that we are here by the will of the people, and that we will go only if we are driven at the point of the bayonet."[1] Sieyes in his cold, imperturbable fashion proposed that the Assembly pass a resolution that it adhered to all its previous declarations. The resolution was passed. On Mirabeau's plea the Assembly voted that whoever attacked the inviolability of a deputy (arrested him for what he said in the Assembly) was guilty of a treasonable act punishable by death. Now the decision lay with Louis XVI, rather than with the commoners. He could choose between crushing the rebels or yielding. For the present he chose to yield and gave an order for the withdrawal of the royal bodyguard that had invested the hall.

The Appeal to the Troops. For a few days the king acted as though he had sincerely accepted the *fait accompli.* He prevailed upon the court faction to make its peace with Necker, who withdrew his resignation and remained in office. Within the following three days the deputies of the privileged orders again began to join the commoners, and by the 26th of June a majority of the clerics and a large minority of the nobles had taken their seats in the National Assembly. On the 27th, Louis XVI recognized realities by ordering the rest of the clergy and nobles to join the deputies of the Third Estate in the National

---

[1] Mirabeau's exact words are in dispute. Although there is no question of his intervention on this occasion, it is not unlikely that its importance has been exaggerated. For the accounts given by Mirabeau himself, the contemporary press, and the memoirs of the other deputies, consult Fling, *Source Book of the French Revolution,* pp. 123-148; and A. Brette, "La Seance royale du 23 juin," in *La Revolution française,* vol. XXII.

Assembly. The struggle was over. The Estates-General was no more; the union of the three classes in a genuine representative assembly of the nation was complete. In these new circumstances the Assembly settled down to its task of regenerating the government and society of France, On July 8, it appointed a committee on constitutional procedure, and on the morrow it assumed the name by which it was subsequently known, the National Constituent Assembly. With the loyal support of the king it would give France the new constitution that the nation desired.

Louis XVI's surrender to the rebellious commoners was more apparent than real. Yielding again to the conservative court faction, he determined to use force against the Assembly and restore the ancient order. He secretly called upon the soldiery, summoning to his aid seventeen regiments, totaling twenty thousand men, most of whom were Swiss and German mercenaries, ostensibly to protect life and property against the threatening crowds that gathered in Paris. The menace of the Parisian mob was only a pretext, for, turbulent as the populace was, it contemplated no outbreak against the government. The foreign mercenary troops were called because the regular troops of the government could not be relied upon to support repression. The French Guard, the most disciplined body of soldiers in France, was in mutiny, refusing to use arms against the demonstrators and shouting, "We are the soldiers of the nation! Long live the Third Estate!" The royal plan was ingenious. If the deputies permitted the troops to surround Versailles and Paris, the dissolution of the Assembly would be comparatively simple; if on the other hand they should protest, the king could denounce their action as an incitation to mob violence in Paris and direct the troops all the more legitimately against them. By the beginning of July the preparations for the royal coup d'état against the Assembly were well under way.

The troops, summoned from the frontiers and the provincial cities of the interior, began to arrive early in July. They were stationed before the royal palace at Versailles and along the road between Versailles and Paris. A smaller detachment was encamped in the Champ-de-Mars at Paris. The news of their coming threw the populace of Paris into consternation. All sorts of disquieting rumors circulated, predicting the arrest of prominent deputies and the dissolution of the Assembly. The peace was disturbed not only by redoubtable rumors but by bands of beggars and criminals who flocked into Paris from the country and other cities, driven there by hunger and the hope of plunder. Paris, at its quietest, was a turbulent city, prone to mob violence and sporadic outbreaks against the constituted authorities. Now its narrow crooked streets surged with excited and suspicious crowds of men and women. There were desperate figures among them, men who were contemptuous of the police and ready for any action that would bring them food and shelter; and there were patriotic enthusiasts, eager reformers, and fiery demagogues whose spirits had been inflamed by revolutionary journalism and the gripping events of the past few months. To such men came the news that the king had summoned his troops against the Assembly and Paris.

In the disorder the municipal authorities were powerless, so long as the French Guard fraternized with the newcomers to Paris and the unemployed masses of the city. On July 8, the Assembly adopted a motion made by Mirabeau and sent a delegation to the king, protesting against the concentration of troops and demanding the formation of a bourgeois guard to preserve order. Among the members of the delegation was a young lawyer from Arras, a certain Maximilien Robespierre, whose name was to loom large across the pages of the Revolution. The king's reply was a disingenuous proposal that the Assembly hold its meeting at some other city (farther from Paris), if the deputies feared the presence of troops which he had summoned to maintain order. But the Assembly refused to move and renewed its protests. On July 9, Louis showed his hand. He dismissed Necker and other liberal ministers, whose presence at the royal council thwarted the plans of the court faction, and ordered Necker to leave the country without further delay. He then formed a new ministry, composed of pronounced conservatives, Foulon, Breteuil, and Marshal de Broglie. His act was a formal challenge to the revolutionists, for there could no longer be any question of his ultimate intentions.

The destiny of the Revolution lay in the hands of the Parisians; and in Paris the center of revolutionary agitation was the Palais Royal. The police could not patrol it because it belonged to the duke of Orléans. Around the inner gardens, which were more than two hundred yards in length and a hundred in width, ran a vast framework of edifices housing sumptuous cafés, luxurious shops, bookstores and innumerable gambling dens. The space before the street level of the buildings, which was sheltered against sun and rain, furnished a covered gallery-promenade for the throngs of curiosity seekers, patriotic agitators, unemployed, and lawless vagrants from the rural districts who swarmed all over the enclosed gardens. There the Parisian crowds had brought the "soldier patriots" (the French Guard) when they liberated the soldiers of this mutinous regiment. There the French Guard and thousands of petty bourgeois sat around the cafe tables or trod the paths that ran through the gardens, discussing revolutionary politics and commenting noisily on the latest news from Versailles. There too, on the 12th of July, came the first report of the dismissal of Necker, confirming the disquieting rumors of the past week. The excitement in the Palais Royal became feverish when one of the fiery revolutionary journalists of Paris, Camille Desmoulins, leaped upon a table and passionately denounced the impending massacre of patriots. "There is not a moment to lose," he exclaimed, "we have only one course of action—to rush to arms . . ." The crowd rushed out, paraded the streets, Camille at the head, wearing green cockades (the color of Necker's liveries) and carrying the busts of Necker and the duke of Orléans in triumph before them. Later in the day the marchers clashed with a regiment of foreign cavalry, the Royal-German, at the Tuileries Gardens. The demonstrators sustained only insignificant physical injuries but suffered an emotional shock sufficient to provoke them to search for weapons and ammunition. From shop to shop the swelling crowd scurried in quest of arms, its ranks increased by many lawless recruits and by the French Guard, who hastily quit their barracks to join the rioters. Besenval, the commander of the royal troops, was extremely loath to use force against the demonstrators, and kept his men well within the limits of the Champ-de-Mars. The mob was unchecked all through the night of July 12, breaking into shops and pilfering, arms by preference but anything else that was available.

At this juncture the electors of Paris intervened to protect life and property against the lawless rioters, as well as to prevent the massacre of patriots which they imagined the mercenary royal troops were contemplating. After the election of the deputies of the Third Estate had ended, the electors returned to their homes; but they reorganized later in the sixty electoral districts of the city and petitioned the Assembly to form a civic guard to maintain order. On the 13th the electors assumed control of the situation and improvised a provisional municipal government. They named Fles-selles, the provost of the merchants, chairman, and ordered the formation of a "civic militia," or bourgeois guard, to maintain order in the city. Within a few hours the volunteer force, which included nobles, financiers, merchants, and even priests, was organized. It patrolled the city, with the help of the French Guard preserving comparative order during the day and far into the night of July 13.

The Fall of the Bastille. In the early morning of July 14, while the tocsin at the Hôtel de Ville summoned the volunteers to their task, the mob was roaming restlessly about the city, desperately intent upon getting arms. The news came that there were plenty at the Hôtel des Invalides and at the Bastille. Part of the mob stormed the Invalides and carried out great quantities of muskets and shot, while another group made its way to the eastern part of the city and surrounded the Bastille. The citizen guard of volunteers had also gathered before its walls during the forenoon, equally anxious to procure arms.

Originally a fortress outside the city walls, the gray rock of the Bastille with its walls ten feet thick and its towers more than ninety feet high then lay in the heart of the workingmen's section and was used as a state prison. Many horrifying stories were told about it, tales of vaults and dungeons deep in the earth, of prisoners doomed for years to maddening darkness, of cruel tortures and agonizing deaths. The stories were largely false, but the Parisians believed them; and in the eyes of all liberty-loving people in Europe the Bastille was the hateful symbol of despotism and oppression.
The governor of the Bastille, De Launay, was not unprepared for the mob. His garrison was ready, and the cannon were in place. Two drawbridges and the outer and inner courts separated the fortress from the milling crowd without. It seemed safe against attack. For hours the attack did not come, though the crowd in the streets before the Bastille grew thicker and more menacing. When it came, the attack was a terrible accident. De Launay had just rejected a petition demanding arms for the volunteer civic militia; but he had also given assurances that the cannon would not be used against the crowd unless he were attacked. To allow the deputation to leave, the drawbridge over the moat had been lowered, and a feverish throng poured over it until they stood under the very walls of the fortress. The drawbridge was then raised behind them, and from within the Bastille shots were fired upon the unarmed people.

Then the siege began. Despite the fury of the assailants, who dragged cannon through the streets of Paris, despite the valor of the experienced French Guard who directed operations, the Bastille might have held out for many hours. But the garrison grew mutinous and De Launay lowered the drawbridge of the fortress admitting the mob. The officers of the French Guard had granted De Launay and his men an honorable capitulation, but the promise could not be kept, for the besiegers were not to be restrained. Maddened by the losses in their own ranks and infuriated by what they regarded the governor's treachery in luring them into the inner court, they fell upon De Launay and the Swiss garrison and killed them. The sickening slaughter and the mutilation of the bodies were the deeds of an unleashed mob that was beyond the control of justice and mercy; but they were the deeds of a people whom an oppressive government had rendered callous to cruel violence and brutality. The verdict of posterity strongly condemns their actions, but many of their contemporaries everywhere in France and Europe rejoiced that they had stormed the stronghold of repression.

The royal plot against the Assembly had completely miscarried. Though the anxious Parisians still expected a movement of the troops, Louis XVI conceded the victory of the people. On the 15th he came before the Assembly to report that he had ordered the royal troops to leave Versailles, and on the following day he recalled Necker to the ministry. His advisers urged him to flee, from France, but he had more courage than they. He recognized the new municipal .government of Paris, and he went in person to give his sanction to its proceedings. With him went a deputation from the National Assembly and a detachment of the citizen militia of Paris, now renamed the National Guard. He recognized Bailly as the mayor of Paris and Lafayette as commander of the National

Guard. In testimony of his good faith he put on his hat the red, white, and blue cockade which Bailly gave him. By this gesture he accepted the events that had occurred, for if the white of the tricolor was the color of the Bourbons, the blue and the red were the colors of Paris.

Louis XVI might accept the Revolution, but the count of Artois, some of the court nobles, and other partisans of the Old Regime fled their country, disgusted and indignant over what they deemed the monarch's cowardice. Theirs was the first emigration, the precursor of others. July 14, 1789, ended the royal offensive against the Revolution. The English ambassador wrote to London that France was now a free country and its king a constitutional monarch. Louis XVI retained his throne, but henceforth he was secretly on the defensive, his authority and his security troubled by each new wave of popular emotion. The people led, and he followed; they led at first through the organ of the Assembly and later through more brutal and direct intervention.

The "Great Fear." The fall of the Bastille was not the spark that ignited the provinces of France, for the provinces were already aflame before the news reached the peasantry. The anxious quiet that had followed the spring disturbances of 1789 was shattered, *first,* not by the dramatic events of July 14, but by actual famine and the fear that all was not going well at Versailles and Paris. In the absence of definite news the peasants took their fears for realities, fear of the "aristocrats" at Versailles, and fear of the "brigands" whom the nobles were suspected of sending into the rural districts to butcher the peasantry. Early in July, as soon as the spring harvest began to ripen, starving farm hands began to pillage the fields. Those whose crops were menaced feared that the worst had come, that the "aristos" had struck. Maddened by their fears, they struck back at their hereditary oppressors, the feudal lords and the stewards of the seigneur. Even before the news of the fall of the Bastille could reach them, the peasants of Franche-Comté in the east of France were in full rebellion against their feudal lords. On July 27, 1789, Arthur Young wrote, "For what the country knows to the contrary, their deputies are in the Bastille, instead of the Bastille being razed; so the mobs plunder, burn and destroy in complete ignorance."

When the news of the Bastille finally did come, the peasants redoubled their attacks, and by the end of July and the beginning of August anarchy reigned in the provinces of western and eastern France. The fear that possessed the peasants—the "Great Fear," as their terror has been called—may not have been entirely spontaneous, but one need not accept the puerile explanation made by royalist historians that this amazing psychological phenomenon was inspired by "conspirators," by the duke of Orléans, or Mirabeau, or other Freemasons. It was a many-sided phenomenon that fed on its own strength until it ultimately consumed itself. Different peasant groups feared different things: some, that royalists were planning to starve them by raising the price of grain; others, that the city dwellers were marching upon the fields to cut down the harvest, or that brigands were coming to slay them; others still, that the country nobles were plotting with the court aristocracy, or perhaps with émigré nobles, to massacre them. The news that the Bastille had fallen only accentuated the panic and the anarchy by making the fears more credible and encouraging the violence of the peasants.

The rural police were powerless to curb the anarchy, and the king could not count upon the troops of the regular army. Not until the "Great Fear" had run its course could the newly formed National Guard gain control of the situation. The first mad wave of fear gradually spent itself, when the peasants realized that there were no brigands, and that those whom they suspected of coming to attack them were their fellow peasants, similarly armed against a nonexistent foe. The fear subsided, but the violence persisted. Vagrants and desperate criminals, unemployed workers from neighboring towns, and landless farm hands sacked granaries, cut down the harvest in fields, and terrorized the countryside. Whether landed or landless, the peasants turned instinctively upon their hated oppressors.

In many cases the lords of the manor gladly surrendered the manor rolls containing the record of the peasants' feudal dues; but where the chatêlain lacked the grace or sense to give them up voluntarily, the peasants used violence. If a particularly hated steward was massacred, or even if the manor house itself went up in flames, what mattered it to the peasants so long as the flames consumed the records? To a certain extent Jaurés's opinion that the peasant movement was "the violent abolition of the entire feudal system" is justified, for the peasant felt that he had been relieved of a crushing burden. His harvest was now his own (if it was not plundered), and no one dared ask him to pay his feudal dues. The proprietors of feudal land were not the sole victims of the "Great Fear," for the artisans in the towns also rose against their old oppressors, harsh judges, corrupt civil officials, money lenders, and grasping merchants. The Revolution was becoming a war of the classes.

In the meantime the provincial municipalities were responding to the stimulus of events in Paris. The townsmen had carefully followed the course of events in Paris, receiving detailed, if not always impartial, reports from their representatives in the Assembly. In certain cities, like Lyons, the bourgeoisie had not waited for the news of July 14 to form a new municipal government. Somewhat later elsewhere, but substantially in the same manner in all cities, large or small, at Bordeaux and Marseilles, at Nimes, Valence, and Tours, the citizens ousted the old oligarchic municipal administrations and elected new revolutionary councils or else combined the old government with a new council. In general their first action was to follow the example of the new government in Paris and organize local divisions of the National Guard. Indeed, these new municipalities and the local National Guard, which soon formed regional federations for mutual protection, were the most important consequences of the capture of the Bastille by the propertyless mob of Paris.

Before long the guardsmen were directed against the peasant rioters. The anarchy in the country frightened the stout burghers in the towns. It was one thing to destroy the local bastille, which symbolized the despotic tyranny of the upper classes, but an entirely different matter to attack property itself. The bourgeois, who possessed considerable landed property in the country, and prosperous peasant proprietors now feared that their own possessions might be seized by the pillagers. The municipalities had troops at their disposal, and they prepared to use them—to maintain order and enforce the rights of property. First they made sure of the loyalty of the National Guard. The soldiers took an oath of fidelity to the nation (rather than to the king) and the officers swore never to use their men against citizens "*except at the requisition of the civil and municipal authorities.*" Thus the citizen soldiers were turned against the riotous peasantry. The undisciplined violence of the latter was no match for the disciplined violence of the former. The victims of the struggles between rioters and the forces of law and order fell by hundreds. The war of the classes had become a grim reality, at least in the country districts.

The August Fourth Decrees. The Constituent Assembly was busily discussing the draft of a Declaration of Rights when the terrifying news from the provinces interrupted its constitutional debates. Assuredly, the deputies could not condone the terrorism that the unemployed in the cities practiced toward the bourgeois merchants. On the other hand, the reforming deputies could not defend the claims of the feudal nobility against the peasants and remain true to their principles of civil equality. Yet feudal property was also private property, and not a few commoners derived feudal rents from their landed estates. A committee, drawn up to consider the question, made a report recommending measures of repression, without relief or even discussion of the peasants' claims. Fortunately, there were liberal nobles in the Assembly who had a keener sense of realities than the best legal minds among the bourgeois deputies. They realized that, if the Assembly adopted the report of the committee, prolonged class war would follow between the landholding classes on the one hand and the propertyless peasantry on the other—a war in which the feudal nobles would pay the costs. Better, they reasoned, to renounce with good grace what was irretrievably lost and salvage whatever was possible.

Accordingly, in the discussion at the Breton Club,[2] which had already furnished the deputies of the Commons a central meeting place outside of the assembly hall, on the evening before the report of the committee, the duke of Aiguillon, one of the greatest landowners of France, declared that on the following day, August 4, he would propose in the Assembly that all feudal rents and rights should be surrendered at once. His proposal was less generous than it sounded, for he renounced only the personal rights outright and demanded a monetary compensation for the rights pertaining to the land. There is no question that the nobility were legally entitled to an indemnity. Yet Aiguillon's proposal was both more generous and wiser than the report of the committee.

On the 4th, after the deputies had listened in consternation to the horrible facts reported by the investigating committee, Aiguillon made ready to take the floor, but the viscount de Noailles, the impoverished cadet of an illustrious family, rose first and made the proposal that Aiguillon would have made. Though Noailles had nothing of his own to give up, Aiguillon heartily seconded the motion in a touching description of the peasants' condition. "The people are trying to shake off a yoke which has been over their heads for centuries," he said, "and we must confess that this insurrection, illegal as it is (for all violent aggression is), can find its legitimate excuse in the grievances of which it is the victim." The motion carried, after a brief discussion, and a frenzy of sacrifice overwhelmed the Assembly.

In an indescribable and sustained movement of interested and disinterested self-sacrifice, deputy after deputy arose to renounce his special rights and privileges on the altar of his country: the nobles, their hunting, fishing, and pigeon rights, and their detested judicial rights over their tenants as well; the clergy, their tithes; the wealthy bourgeois, their individual exemptions; the cities and provinces, their antique customs and privileges. During that long night of August 4 France of the Old Regime came to an end, and a new France was born with the dawn. Henceforth all Frenchmen would be citizens, subject to one law, paying the same taxes, and eligible to all offices. In their joy the deputies decided to proclaim Louis XVI "the Restorer of French liberty."

A cynical explanation of the night of August 4 denies all motives of generosity to the deputies. Contemporaries, as well as later historians, have endeavored to prove that the

---

[2] The Breton Club was, as its name signifies, an association composed originally of deputies from Brittany; but many deputies from other provinces soon joined it.

deputies surrendered what was already lost and, surrendering, sought to be well paid for their gesture.[3] Yet, calculated as the renunciations undoubtedly were, the enthusiastic spirit displayed was genuine. The deputies of the privileged orders found in Aiguillon's proposal a formula to calm the peasantry, end the disorders, and save their own rights at the cost of their privileges. The infectious enthusiasm for self-sacrifice that swept the Assembly made them renounce more than they had intended, but the difference was one of degree rather than of kind.

A week later, the definite decree concerning the abolition of these abuses and privileges was passed and presented to Louis XVI for his sanction. The modification of the original version was conservative; "reactionary," in Mathiez's opinion. The hunting and fishing rights of the nobility disappeared. Serfdom and all dues which represented it were abolished without indemnity, but all *real* or land dues were to be redeemed in a manner that would be prescribed later. Ecclesiastical tithes were abolished outright without indemnity, but it was deemed necessary, by prescribing a mode of money payments for subinfeudated tithes[4] and certain feudal rights, to safeguard the financial interests of the lay owners of those tithes as well as of the poorer nobles. Until the subinfeudated tithes and the feudal rights had been redeemed, ruled the final decree, they were to be paid. Other church dues were also abolished on the understanding that the state would consider other ways of   maintaining the clergy and providing for the expenses of worship. The payment of annates to the papacy was forbidden. All positions in the church, the administration, and the army were thrown open to the citizens. The administration of justice was to be free, and the sale of offices prohibited. A new system of justice was promised. The interests of workingmen in the towns were neglected, for the guilds were perpetuated. On the whole the August decrees outlined a comprehensive program of social, economic, and religious reforms. To realize this program was the task of the deputies. In theory they had destroyed the regime of privilege and instituted a regime of social and civic equality, but in theory only, for the beneficiaries of the regime which was ended obstructed the work of reconstruction, while those who received no benefits or insufficient benefits under the new program clamored for still more sweeping reforms.

THE ORGANIZATION OF REVOLUTIONARY FORCES

The Second Appeal to the Troops. While the provinces remained turbulent, comparative quiet descended upon Paris and Versailles. The National Constituent Assembly resumed its interrupted debates on the Declaration of Rights,[5] which was voted on August 27, despite the sharp discussion as to whether it should precede or follow the constitution. It was the death certificate of the Old Regime, but it contained the promise of a new life for France. Based upon the commonplaces of eighteenth century philosophy and universal in its application, it represented a thorough indictment of the old order and a statement of the general principles upon which the new was to be built. The division of the deputies into loose groups, or political parties, became more distinct in the course of the debates

---

[3] The *Memoires* of Barère show that the more foresighted nobles realized the value of making the gesture of voluntary renunciation before their hand was forced by the commoners. Cf. *Memoires de Barère*, I, 269.

[4] Subinfeudated tithes were those which had been farmed out to the highest bidders. They represented a private financial investment.

[5] The full title of the measure is the Declaration of the Rights of Man and of the Citizen. For the discussion of the Declaration, *cf.* pp. 142-148.

on the constitution. This was a new feature in French political life—the divergence of political parties, conservatives on the Right (that is, on the right of the presiding officer's table), moderates in the Center, and progressives and radicals on the Left. The sharpest discussion concerned the future relations of the executive and legislative divisions of the constitutional government which the deputies of the Constituent Assembly would establish by their labors. The first constitutional committee proposed that a bicameral legislature be established, that the right of absolute veto over the deliberations of the two chambers be given to the king, as well as the right to dissolve the legislature. On this question the Left split up temporarily into two large groups: the Anglophiles, whose leading spokesman in the Assembly was Jean-Joseph Mounier, of the committee, and the Patriots, whose leaders were Lafayette and Barnave. The first group supported the committee's proposal, for their ideal of government was the English parliamentary system. They hesitated to give too much power to untried representatives, fearing for the political stability of the state and fearing also that the pressure of the discontented people might force those inexperienced deputies to take discriminatory measures against private property. The other group, the Patriots, opposed the recommendations of the committee on the ground that it gave excessive and dangerous powers to the monarch and the aristocracy of birth. Above all they feared the absolute veto, and their fears seemed substantiated when it became known that the king had criticized the August decrees and was withholding his sanction of them. Popular agitators exaggerated his action and led the impressionable and suspicious populace of Paris to feel that the absolute veto was a veritable bogy.

When the constitutional proposals came to a vote, the motion for the upper house was rejected on September 10 by an enormous majority of some 800 votes; and the deputies voted to establish a unicameral legislature. On the following day the Assembly voted the king a suspensive and not an absolute veto[6] which gave him the right to suspend the execution of the laws, though not to refuse them outright. The motives of the different groups furnish an explanation of the voting. The parish priests and the lesser provincial nobles voted against the upper house and the absolute veto because they shared the misgivings of the Patriots. They were not minded to perpetuate the power of the great prelates and the court nobility. The extreme Right opposed the first conservative recommendation of the committee because it seemed likely to succeed. By voting it down, and supporting the proposal which they judged thoroughly unworkable, the more extreme conservatives hoped to bring on new disorders which in turn might lead to a reaction and give them an opportunity to regain their lost prerogatives. Mirabeau, who had at first supported the committee's proposals, reversed his position and voted for the suspensive veto, hoping that his support would gain him a position in the ministry. In reality, there was no difference between a suspensive and an absolute veto, for the suspensive veto delayed a law so long as to be practically equivalent to an absolute veto; but the point was certainly not appreciated outside of the Assembly, and perhaps not by the deputies themselves. At any rate the masses were convinced that an absolute veto meant the restoration of the ancient order of things.

After the debates had ended, Louis XVI signified his willingness to sanction the August decrees, but he utilized pretext after pretext to avoid accepting the Declaration, the

---

[6] After a short debate the deputies voted on September 21 that the veto might continue during the sessions of two legislatures, but it was to "cease at the second legislature following the one which shall have proposed the law."

unicameral legislature, and the suspensive veto.[7] He fully understood his position, being aware that in deferring the ratification of these measures he could count upon the support of a great many deputies who firmly believed that the National Assembly could not "give the force of law to its decrees without the royal sanction." The Patriots maintained that the monarch had no right to refuse his sanction to the constitutional decrees. Mirabeau declared that the royal veto could not "be exercised when the creation of a constitution is at stake"; and Sieyes denied that the royal sanction was even required, holding that the monarchy existed by virtue of the constitution. This was the view held by the new constitutional committee which was appointed after the resignation of Mounier and his colleagues in the first committee (September 18). The more moderate deputies and the court faction appealed to Louis XVI to call out his troops, while the more determined deputies of the Left realized that it was to their advantage to have the king and the Assembly in Paris. Again, as in July, Louis XVI followed false counsel. On September 14 he ordered the Flanders Regiment to march to Versailles, and once more foreign uniforms were seen on the streets of Versailles and Paris.

In this crisis the Patriots turned again to Paris for aid; and the Paris to which they appealed was again in ferment. The first emigration and the unsettled political conditions had reacted unfavorably upon business. Thousands of unemployed artisans, idle valets and lackeys, grumbling retail merchants, and petty tradesmen whose livelihood had been ruined by the depression crowded the streets. Bread was scarce, speculators active and food prices rising. Hungry mobs of men and women began anew to sack the bakeries. The radical press and stentorian agitators harangued the populace, thrusting the blame for hard times upon the court nobles and other "aristos," and interpreting Louis XVI's refusal to sanction the constitutional decrees as evidence of evil intent against the revolutionary cause. The inevitable consequence of this temper was apparent to Mirabeau, who prophesied that both the king and the queen would meet violent deaths if they persisted in their unfortunate tactics. Louis XVI could not bring himself to accept realities. He took advantage of the agitation in Paris to summon the troops, ostensibly to protect the Assembly against the Paris multitude. The move was most unfortunate, for it seemed to confirm the worst suspicions of the Patriots and the Parisians; and it furnished excellent pretexts to various intriguers who sought to profit from the disorders in the city by urging the crowds to violent action. Some of these worked in the interests of the duke of Orléans, who hoped to be named regent in place of Louis XVI; and it is probable that Mirabeau was involved in this scheme. Others tried to organize a counter-revolutionary movement. Still others saw an opportunity for radical measures. In this turmoil the municipal authorities were helpless. The cure for the disorder lay with the king, but his determination to use the soldiery served not to quiet but to aggravate the disorder.

The "October Days." Presently the Flanders Regiment which the king had summoned entered Versailles. On October 1, at a banquet tendered to its officers by the royal bodyguard, an impromptu demonstration of loyalty to the royal family terminated the evening. Stimulated by the good cheer, the guests drank toasts to the royal couple and trampled the national cockade underfoot, while deliberately omitting toasts to the nation.

---

[7] In a formal letter to the Assembly he wrote: "I approve the general spirit of your decrees [the feudal] and the greater number of articles in their entirety. . . . I have no doubt whatever that I can, with perfect justice, invest with my sanction all the laws that you will pass on the different subjects contained in your decrees."

Paris received the news of that "act of imprudence" on the 3rd of October. The newspapers raised a terrific din of denunciation. The districts, led by two popular agitators, Jean-Paul Marat and Jacques Danton, urged all good men to march on Versailles and bring the king back to Paris. Danton's district appealed to the municipality to send Lafayette to Versailles and demand the recall of the military. On the 4th, the surging crowd in the Palais Royal threatened violent action against the nation's enemies. Thus prepared and organized, the October rebellion needed only a spark to set it off.

Early the next morning after a disturbance at a baker's shop a crowd of women set out for the Hôtel de Ville of Paris to demand bread from the authorities. En route they were joined by the market women, strong-voiced and something less than gentle in their ways. They failed to obtain bread at the Hôtel de Ville, but it afforded them some satisfaction to ransack the building. Presently Maillard, one of the heroes of the capture of the Bastille, gained their confidence, checked their ardor for destruction, and led them off to Versailles. Recruits swelled their ranks all the way to Versailles, but Maillard kept the fiercer of the viragoes in check. A few hours after their departure Lafayette reluctantly sought and obtained permission from the municipality to follow them with the National Guard of Paris. He confessed that he was afraid that the tide would turn in Orléans's favor unless he directed it himself. His conduct during this crisis was characterized by a caution that bordered either on timidity or on conspiracy. There is no doubt that had he not, also, wished the king brought to Paris, he could have taken more energetic steps to inform Versailles of the coming of the mob, or else to prevent the mob's departure from Paris.

On learning of these occurrences Mirabeau attempted to have the session of the Assembly suspended. But the deputies had, that very forenoon, received a temporizing reply from the king on the constitutional measures and they were heatedly discussing the next step to take. When the women arrived, they had already decided to send Mounier at the head of a delegation to the palace and demand an immediate acceptance of the decrees; but on hearing Maillard's complaint about the scarcity of food and the activity of speculators in Paris they decided to present the women's protests with their own demands and appointed a delegation which left late in the afternoon. Meantime the deputies continued their session. Despite constant interruptions from the steadily increasing number of women whom the rain had forced indoors, they remained patient and good-humored under the strain.

Soon the greater part of the mob assembled before the palace, which was defended by the royal bodyguard. Louis XVI, himself, had been hunting, but on his return he received a number of the women and promised them, in writing, that Paris would be provisioned against famine. Confronted by Mounier's delegation, he was most irresolute. At first he contemplated flight rather than surrender to mob pressure; but on second thought he abandoned the idea of flight as savoring of fear and, toward eight o'clock that evening, announced to the delegation from the Assembly that he gave his sanction to the decrees. Toward midnight Lafayette with thousands of troops, composed of National Guardsmen of Paris and volunteers, arrived at the palace. After Lafayette's arrival, which served to end the strain between the royal bodyguard and the National Guard of Versailles, quiet descended upon the palace. Lafayette had taken precautions to guard the palace, but not in sufficient measure. Whether this negligence was due to a false sense of security or to a desire to force the king's hand is uncertain. In the morning some of the more venturesome of the crowd found an unguarded entrance and began to look about. One of the royal guardsmen fired at the intruders. These rose in wrath, forced their way into the inner rooms and dispatched two of the defenders, giving Marie Antoinette barely time to escape into the king's apartments. Several members of the mob were also killed in the fighting. In order to end the mêlée the entire royal family, the king, the queen, and the dauphin, agreed to show themselves to the crowd. Accompanied by Lafayette, they stood out on the balcony of the court. There were loud shouts for Louis XVI, and a few mild cheers for Marie Antoinette, but louder than any other cry was the one: "On to Paris!" At length the king agreed to go, to the great joy of the crowd. That same evening (October 6), after a long noisy journey, the royal family, which had been accompanied by the troops and the delegations from the Assembly, reached the Hôtel de Ville at Paris. At ten o'clock Louis XVI and his family arrived at the Louvre in the Tuileries, his destination and his future home. Ten days later, the Assembly followed him to Paris.

"The baker," "the baker's wife," and the "baker's boy"—as the Parisians, half derisively, half gratefully called the royal family— were now in Paris, safe (the Parisians believed) from their evil advisers; but for all that, bread did not immediately become plentiful in the city. A full month elapsed before Paris saw the last of the long lines of women standing in wait at the bakers' shops. Workers were idle as before and disorders were still common. Therefore the first act of the municipal administration was to restore the semblance of order.

Lafayette, "the hero of two worlds," as his opponents ironically called him, undertook the task of curbing the danger of anarchy. This gave him an opportunity to make capital of the insurrection (which openly, at least, he had opposed) and to advertise his indispensability to the king. The day following the arrival of Louis XVI in Paris, he secretly organized a demonstration in favor of the royal family. He also put pressure on the press to disavow the violence of the preceding days and had Marat condemned by a high criminal court. Though an official inquiry into the insurrection failed to inculpate either Mirabeau or Orléans, Lafayette managed to convince the latter that a brief absence from Paris would be salutary. The duke left for London, ostensibly on a diplomatic mission. As for Mirabeau, his influence was temporarily effaced. The inexcusable hanging of a hapless baker gave the Assembly an opportunity to make provision for martial law against unruly gatherings, and thus order was temporarily restored.

A second emigration followed on the heels of the mob's victory over the king. Mounier, fearing further violence, resigned the presidency of the Assembly and betook himself to Dauphine, but failing to stir up opposition against the Assembly he emigrated. Lally-Tollendal, prominent among the Moderates, also endeavored to arouse sentiment against the Assembly, but he too had little success. Soon a small group of disillusioned liberals, men who had been instrumental in summoning the Estates-General and in denouncing royal despotism, fled their country. The National Assembly had won a great victory, though largely because the masses had come to its aid. Blood had been shed, and the émigrés carried their woes and complaints beyond the frontiers to a Europe that gave heed to their recriminations. For those disciples of Montesquieu and of a limited, constitutional monarchy the Revolution was advancing too rapidly. Those who remained, the Monarchists, or Impartials as they were now called, constituted only a small group in the Assembly, whose influence dwindled steadily until it became negligible. Now that his foremost rivals—Orléans, Mirabeau, and Mounier—were out of the way, Lafayette had his opportunity to guide the Revolution on its course. In a memorandum addressed to Louis XVI he outlined his plans and appealed for the monarch's full confidence.

The Organization of the Assembly. With tranquility somewhat restored, the Assembly settled down in earnest to the stupendous task before it, the reconstruction of France. In this work a beginning had already been made. The August decrees, it was hoped, would destroy feudalism; and the Declaration of Rights and the September decrees had laid the foundations of a constitution. Much remained to be done. Before turning to the accomplishments of the National Constituent Assembly let us first examine in some detail the composition of the Assembly and the organization of the revolutionary forces outside of it which enabled the deputies to bring their efforts to a successful conclusion in September, 1791.

The deputies held their meetings from November, 1789, in a long, narrow building that abutted on the terrace of the Feuillants in the gardens of the Tuileries. Their seats were arranged in tiers in the form of an amphitheater, while near one end of the long riding school (the *Manège)* in which they met was the raised box of the president. The platform of the orators' tribune was opposite it, and the galleries ran all around the hall. Their sessions were open to the public, which permitted excitable or ill-intentioned spectators to interfere frequently in the debates. Yet at all times the deputies expressed themselves freely, and perhaps too freely if the comments of foreign observers at the meetings can be taken at their face value. Ordinarily the galleries contained partisan but well behaved people, whether of the bourgeoisie or of the aristocracy, but after the king's flight in 1791 a rougher element took possession of the galleries and intimidated the deputies with its noise and its threats. Every fortnight a new president was chosen. To facilitate business most of the proposals were prepared in committees, of which there were thirty-one in the Assembly, and presented to the Assembly by the *rapporteur.* Discussions took heated turns, and the uproar frequently kept the deputies from being heard, but the Assembly methodically continued its work.

The difficulties were staggering. While Lafayette's firmness immediately after the October "revolution" prevented the recurrence of violence in Paris, it could not effectively check the more insistent pressure of public and private opinion. Revolutionary sentiment and sentiment opposed to the Revolution were noisily expressed in the Assembly and without. Petitions and demonstrations, threats and incitations to violence, fiery editorials in the newspapers constantly reminded the deputies of the grave responsibilities that rested upon their shoulders. Neither Louis XVI nor his ministers made any efforts to help. They "shammed dead," as one of the deputies observed.

The Assembly had to destroy at the same time that it created. In theory the institutions of the past had been wiped away by the various decrees of the summer; in reality they clung tenaciously to life. It took time to ring out the old and ring in the new. On the one hand the parlements, various subordinate officials, and individual members of the nobility and the clergy strove fiercely to maintain the old order of things. On the other hand the masses took it for granted that the regime of the future had already been established and refused to obey the old royal officials. Many peasants refused to pay taxes and feudal dues. The new communes and the local detachments of the National Guard prevented a complete relapse into anarchy, but they could not prevent the appalling confusion, especially in the rural districts where the peasantry sought to take matters into their own hands. Fortunately for the Assembly, the harvests of 1789 and 1790 were good and the peasants continued in the main to support the deputies. For some time these were free to carry on their work unimpeded, but their accomplishments were compromised in advance because the Assembly was divided against itself.

Parties, in our sense, did not exist. There were no party organizations with officers, official programs, and party funds. The deputies prided themselves on their independence and their individuality. They followed "the promptings of their heart," made alliances that were only shifting and temporary and dictated by the issue at stake. In general, by November, 1789, the Assembly was divided into three large groups or parties whose members voted together and belonged to the same revolutionary clubs. We have noticed that in the very beginning there had been only two groups—those who opposed the Revolution and the Patriots who supported it. But the events of the summer of 1789 broke up the solidarity of the latter and divided them into several groups. On the right of the president's box were the conservatives, the party of the upper clergy and the great nobles who, out of sincere opposition to reforms, systematically obstructed the Assembly's work. The more extreme leaders of that aristocratic faction were D'Es-premesnil and Mirabeau-Tonneau,[8] the younger brother of the great revolutionary orator, whose favorite tactics were to filibuster and rouse a tumult in the Assembly. A more determined foe than the younger Mirabeau was the ambitious and courageous Abbé Maury, a popular preacher and a capable orator, though facile and shallow in his judgments. Cazalès, a chivalrous officer of dragoons under the Old Regime and the greatest orator of the Right, also distinguished himself at first by his clear and vigorous speeches, but as time went on he drew nearer the Left in his sympathies.

Next to these conservatives were the Monarchists or the Impartials, about forty in number and now led by the count of Clermont-Tonnerre and Malouet, a former royal intendant under the Old Regime. They sat in the center, but their views were more conservative. They pleaded a hopeless cause, as circumstances had made their dream of a liberal, constitutional monarchy on the English model impossible of attainment.

The great majority of deputies sat with the Left. With the Left-Center were all the moderates of the Assembly, the Constitutionalists, as they were called on account of the fact that they were largely responsible for the new constitution. Among them, the lawyers Target, Tronchet, and Merlin de Douai became the most conspicuous figures in the debates on the constitution. They also had the services of Sieyes—the "prophet Mohammed"—who was distant and aloof in manner and without talent as an orator, but very influential despite those characteristics, especially in committee work. Among them also were several liberal clerics, such as Talleyrand de Perigord, bishop of Autun and a scheming, unscrupulous aristocrat of great ability, and the Abbé Grégoire, a humanitarian ecclesiastic whose Christian piety often forsook him in the heat of discussion. The affable and ambitious young lawyer, Barère de Vieuzac, a good speaker and an indefatigable worker, was with them; and a number of court nobles of liberal convictions, such as the duke of La Rochefoucauld-Liancourt and the aspiring but irresolute Lafayette.

On the farther left, a little group of young men sat together. They were bound by mutual attraction and by political views, and all wanted to "plow deep" while they had a chance. They were known as the Triumvirate, since they were three in number. One was the young lawyer Barnave, surpassed only by Mirabeau as an orator in the Assembly, a clear-headed person of great sincerity; another was Adrien Duport, a famous jurist of great capacity and brilliance; and the third was the energetic and amiable young noble Charles de Lameth, a veteran, like Lafayette, of the American War of Independence. There was a

---

[8] *Tonneau,* or barrel, was an uncomplimentary reference to his form or perhaps a flattering characterization of his drinking prowess.

slogan that "what Duport thinks, Lameth does, and Barnave says." Alexander de Lameth, the brother of Charles, a good tactician and an authority on military affairs, was also closely associated with the Triumvirate. Finally, there was the Extreme Left, linked with these three men in the early days of the Constituent Assembly but destined to break sharply with them later. Two future members of the Girondin group voted with these radical deputies, Petion, a solemn and somewhat conceited lawyer from Chartres, and Buzot, a temperamental and eloquent Norman. There too belonged the young lawyer of Arras, Maximilien Robespierre. He was somewhat timid at first and unwilling to alienate the more famous leaders, but his confidence and his resourcefulness in debate developed rapidly. Before the Assembly had ended its session, the neat, spectacled Robespierre commanded attention, if not always respect, whenever he took the floor. He had much to learn in the art of public speaking and dealing with men, but his unflinching advocacy of what he considered the popular cause and his undoubted sincerity received recognition, more fully it is true in the Jacobin Club than in the Assembly.

Above all others loomed Mirabeau. His reputation was formed long before 1789, but it was not of a nature to inspire the trust of his fellow deputies, who admired him but could not respect him. He set out to win their confidence, in spite of his turbulent past, in spite of his notorious immorality and venality. We shall find him in every debate—on the constitution, the clergy, finances, foreign policy, social reform. What he had no time or inclination to prepare himself, he inspired his collaborators and lieutenants to prepare for him. He was never ill informed; his words always rang with authority. As a debater he was unsurpassed in the entire Revolution. More than once he turned a hostile demonstration into a personal ovation. Whether he read a speech that some one had prepared for him or improvised one of his brilliant flights, he commanded silence and attention. At first he was perhaps the only deputy who ventured to speak without a prepared manuscript; only later did others attempt to make impromptu speeches and commence real debates. Up to the time of his death the whole course of the Constituent Assembly could be traced through his speeches. He opposed royal despotism, but he advocated a strong monarchy. He described himself in his first note to the king as "the defender of a monarchy limited by law and the apostle of liberty guaranteed by a monarchy."

Revolutionary Forces outside the Assembly. Such was the Assembly, composed of the most distinguished men of France, but men inexperienced in public deliberation. Outside the Assembly were the various revolutionary forces that made its success inevitable. Of these the new municipal administrations and the National Guard that came into being after the fall of the Bastille were perhaps the most powerful. With a few unimportant exceptions they recruited their strength from the bourgeoisie. Lawyers, physicians, men of letters, well-to-do merchants, rich industrialists—the very cream of the liberal forces that had initiated the Revolution—sat in the town halls and filled the ranks of the militia.

In addition to these, the revolutionary clubs and newspapers molded popular opinion in favor of the new administration, though occasionally they presented demands that the Assembly found too radical. Among the clubs the Jacobins with their numerous branches in the provinces dominated all rivals. Officially they were known as the Society of Friends of the Constitution, but they had their more famous name thrust upon them from the fact that their meetings were held in the former convent of the Jacobins, which was only a stone's throw from the *Manège* where the Assembly met.[9] At first only prominent deputies of the Left were members, but early in 1790 the doors of the club were opened to non-deputies as well, until the membership rose to more than a thousand. Later still, when the public was admitted to its galleries, it was not uncommon to see as many as two thousand spectators at the meetings. Soon there arose clubs in the provincial towns and, commencing in 1790, these grew in number to more than four hundred in 1791.

The "Mother Society" at Paris held the affiliated clubs well in hand. The Jacobins of Paris corresponded with the Jacobins in the provinces; struck off pamphlets for their benefit by thousands and distributed them, made recommendations, and received petitions.

Delegations flocked to the doors to extend felicitations or present demands, which the society passed or refused to pass on to the Assembly. In this way the club became the nucleus of the militant and enlightened bourgeoisie. In 1789 and 1790 and in the first months of 1791 the Jacobins followed a moderate, conciliatory policy. They were still debating clubs with parliamentary *organization* and parliamentary ambitions. Their essential purpose was to keep a vigilant eye on the Assembly and to prepare the country for the sweeping reforms that were being made. Their usurpation of legal authority came later, and with it the tendency of committees within each club to assume control of activities. In 1791 the Jacobins of Paris were unquestionably the strongest and best organized force outside of the Assembly, but much of their influence was due to the fact that the deputies who belonged to the club agreed beforehand on their action when a project was brought forward in the Assembly.

For the petty bourgeoisie, the workers and peasants, there existed other societies where initiation fees and dues were cheaper. Among those the most active was the Society of Friends of the Rights of Man and of the Citizen, or more popularly, the Cordelier Club, so called because, like the Jacobins, the members met in an abandoned convent, the convent of the Cordeliers. The Cordelier Club was opened in the spring of 1790. Marat, Danton, Camille Desmoulins, Hebert, Momoro, Fabre d'Eglantine, all of whom came to prominence in 1793, were the leading spokesmen at its crowded meetings. Here one found more spontaneity and less deliberation; no prudent lawyers but impulsive, violent agitators. Of the less influential revolutionary groups, there was the Abbé Fauchet's *Cercle social,* a Masonic-socialistic organization, which had the services of the newspaper *La Eouche de fer,* and Brissot's circle, *Les Amis des noirs,* which advocated freedom and suffrage for the negroes in the French colonies.

But there were also clubs whose members shared less friendly sentiments toward the progress of the revolutionary cause. The *Société de 1789* recruited its members from the more moderate Jacobins, who followed the inspiration of Lafayette, and whose views were expressed in Condorcet's *Journal de la Société de 1789.* The most reactionary club was the group which met under the joint leadership of Mirabeau-Tonneau and Abbé Maury, while midway in political sentiments between the two clubs mentioned was the *Amis de la constitution monarchique,* whose sponsors were the Monarchists of the Assembly. Emigration and the increasingly radical orientation of the revolutionary

---

[9] While the Assembly was still at Versailles, the deputies from Brittany had formed the Breton Club, with which many of the Patriots, deputies from other provinces, were soon associated. After the "October days," the club held its sessions in Paris.

movement weakened these conservative clubs in measure as the influence of their sponsors in the National Constituent Assembly dwindled before that of the Left.

Lastly, there were the newspapers and their enterprising editors, a force of incalculable significance in stirring up political passions. Since the beginning of the Revolution restrictions upon the liberty of the press had virtually disappeared. Deputies, like Bare-re and Mirabeau, founded dailies and reported the debates in the Assembly. An experienced journalist, Panckoucke, in whose salon many deputies were wont to assemble and discuss their work, edited the well informed *Moniteur,* which was sympathetic toward the Constitutionalists. Hosts of ambitious men founded journals, each with its clientele of steady readers. Among the more influential revolutionary newspapers we can cite the *Courrier de Versailles* of Gorsas, the *Patriote jrangais* of Brissot, the *Révolutions de Paris* of Prudhomme and Loustalot, the *Révolutions de France et de Brabant* of the witty, sparkling Camille Desmoulins and last, but not least in popularity and influence, the *Ami du Peuple* of Jean-Paul Marat, a suspicious and embittered physician who was becoming the hero of the Parisian populace. In 1790 the denunciatory *Père Duchêne of Hébert,* with its strong language and honest vulgarity, gained tremendous vogue among the working masses and the soldiers. These journals cost little; they were badly printed as a rule and carried little real news, but everybody read them, even the aristocrats who had many newspapers of their own. Among the newspapers that were hostile to the Revolution one may mention the *Petit Gauthier* and Rivarol's *Actes des Apôtres,* which faithfully echoed the views of the Abbé Maury and Mirabeau-Tonneau.

These were the more tangible means by which the revolutionary gospel was spread. But the spirit of the revolutionists was best expressed in the series of spontaneous fêtes of federation which reached their finest form in the *Fête de la Fédération* in Paris on July 14, 1790. Gatherings of this nature were first held during the crisis of the "Great Fear," when a terrible danger seemed to be hovering over the land. From that small beginning when neighboring villages and cities promised each other aid against their common enemy, the movement broadened and deepened.[10] After the federation of the towns of one province, as in Dauphine and Franche-Comté, came interprovincial federations in January, 1790, and the inspiring fête of the eastern provinces a month later. The National Guard sent their delegates, and representatives came from the civil authorities of the communes. The participants all took a solemn oath to support the new order, to suppress disturbances, to renounce all ancient privileges and distinctions, and to be henceforth "one, immense family of brothers, united under the standard of liberty." At all those fêtes mass was held and the banners of the National Guard were blessed. A great impetus to the federation movement came from the king's public acceptance of the Revolution. On February 4, 1790, Louis XVI appeared before the deputies in the Assembly and promised his complete and unreserved support to the revolutionary program. They were greatly moved, not knowing that he had mental reservations, and in their enthusiasm they rose in their seats and took the oath to be faithful to the nation, the law, and the king.

As the first anniversary of the fall of the Bastille approached, the Assembly decided to join in the movement and to crown it by organizing a national festival. This great national *Fête de la Fédération* was held at the Champ-de Mars in Paris on July 14, 1790. A vast crowd of Parisians, estimated at 200,000, gathered in the colossal amphitheater

---

[10] These manifestations of revolutionary solidarity, of patriotic fraternity, were called *federations* because the *fédérés* were the contingents of the National Guard of the different departments.

Rousseau, Burke, and Revolution in France, 1791

which volunteers had built for the occasion and waited patiently in the rain for the coming of the lengthy procession of celebrants. The *fédérés* from the newly established departments, the deputies of the Assembly, the king and the queen, and Lafayette, who was the master of ceremonies, marched in the procession. The banners were blessed, Talleyrand held mass on the altar of *la patrie* (which had been built in the center of the parade grounds), and Lafayette, after receiving the form of the oath from the king, administered it to the *fédérés*. Then the trumpets blew, rifles flashed in the air, guns were fired, and the enormous crowd repeated the oath after Lafayette: "I swear to be faithful forever to the nation, the law and the king, [and] to maintain the constitution decreed by the National Assembly and accepted by the king. . . ." Louis XVI stood in the gallery and with great dignity swore to maintain the constitution. "Te Deum" was sung and the gathering broke up, cold and damp, but inexpressibly joyful and optimistic. "Today we have a *patrie* and our liberty is assured," wrote one of the *fédérés,* and his expression epitomized the views of the great multitude.

The fête, it is true, also signified the loyalty of the nation to the monarch, as well as the nation's approval of the new regime which had been established. Above all, it symbolized the new consciousness of patriotic allegiance to the nation and to the Revolution. The Federation promised that "fraternity" would not be an empty phrase, that Frenchmen, united as brothers, would defend the revolutionary movement with religious fervor.

THE ACHIEVEMENTS OF THE CONSTITUENT ASSEMBLY

The Constitutional Reforms: The Declaration of Rights. The new constitution which the deputies of the National Constituent Assembly swore that they would create was not drawn up without heated discussion over its numerous articles. The earliest text was voted in the course of a month and a half from August to October, 1789, but many supplementary provisions were subsequently added. Consequently in September, 1790, the Assembly decided to fuse the earliest draft and the later laws into a single organic text. The work was completed, with certain important revisions, in 1791 and accepted by Louis XVI on September 14, 1791. Hence the name, Constitution of 1791, which was given to a body of legislation many of whose provisions were in force as early as 1789.

The voting of the Declaration of the Rights of Man and of the Citizen on August 27, 1789, has already been noted. Whether or not the French Declaration was a literal adaptation from the English models and the Bills of Rights in the constitutions of the various American states (in all probability it was not) is relatively unimportant. The philosophical ideas underlying these declarations were an international commodity of which neither American nor French theorists had a monopoly. There is greater significance in the following observations concerning the French Declaration: (1) Several of its theoretical provisions were ignored or revised in the constitutional legislation of the Assembly. (2) It did not explicitly formulate all the fundamental opinions of the deputies, for it made no reference to economic theories. (3) A number of the provisions were more concerned with practical realities than with absolute theoretical rights. (4) The latent promise of its basic articles enlisted innumerable recruits and adherents to the revolutionary cause from all ranks of the commoners. A careful study of this famous Declaration will throw light both upon the standpoint of its formulators and many aspects of the Revolution.

The complete Declaration which was prefaced to the Constitution of 1791 follows:[11]
[Editor's note: the complete Declaration, which was originally included in this text, has been removed. The Declaration of the Rights of Man and Citizen appears in Appendix A of this booklet.]

The general theoretical principles of French, English, and American liberal thought of the eighteenth century were clearly and vigorously stated in the preamble and the first three articles. These principles which were universal in their appeal, recognizing neither national boundary lines nor distinctions of race, color, or creed, and emphasizing the sovereign nation's right to resist the oppression of irresponsible governments, carried a singular appeal to contemporaries. Applied to a semi-mediaeval society, where caste distinctions were still enforced, they created a conflict between the handful of privileged individuals and the commoners. In this conflict the latter, more than ninety-eight per cent of the nation, saw their opportunity to win the status to which they were entitled by birth and by their native capacities. In the new state of things they found opportunities and careers open to them; wealth or prestige, fame and fortune, for him who would profit by the leveling of barriers. Hence the enthusiastic response of the masses and their quasi-religious defense of the Revolution. If not they themselves, assuredly their children would share in the fulfillment of the promise of a better world. Later, however, many of them became disillusioned, when the Revolution demanded sacrifices and tightening of the belt, when its leaders showed that their interests were not those of the peasantry and the artisans, when they realized that the great opportunities benefited only the superior individuals and maintained the wretchedness of the many.

The deputies of the bourgeoisie who framed the Declaration believed so implicitly that the interests of their class coincided with the interests of the entire nation that they impressed their class fears and convictions upon a document which was intended to be a charter of universal human rights.[12] The fourth, fifth, and seventh articles reveal their preoccupation with guaranteeing individual liberty against despotism. Had they not suffered most from its lack in the Old Regime! Articles twelve, fourteen, fifteen, and sixteen clearly reveal their lurking fear of the monarch. Public agents were to be responsible to the administration, the military power must obey the law, taxes required the consent of those taxed, and the three powers, executive, legislative, and judicial, were to be separated. Article eleven emphasized the need of liberty of speech and the press, a need apparent to authors and readers of revolutionary writings. Since the deputies were afraid or unwilling to alienate the clergy they granted toleration to non-Catholics but not full liberty of conscience (article ten)[13] The sanctity of private property was taken for granted, but it was not defined, for the question of feudal property was not yet settled.

---

[11] F. M. Anderson, *The Constitutions and Other Select Documents Illustrative of the History of France (1789—1901)*, pp. 58—60. Used by permission of The H. W. Wilson Company, publishers.
[12] The negroes in the sugar colonies of the French West Indies had good reason to hope that the Declaration foreshadowed their liberation from slavery. But their champions in the Assembly fought a losing battle against the shipowners and the sugar refiners. Slavery and the slave trade were maintained. On September 24, 1791, the colonial assemblies were empowered to regulate the political status of free negroes and mulattoes. This solution provoked a terrible slave insurrection in Santo Domingo.
[13] The Protestants, who had won their civil rights in 1787, were granted full toleration and political rights in December, 1789. The Jews of southern France gained their political rights in January, 1790, but those of eastern France not before September, 1791.

Neither the rights of association and petition nor of association were recognized, for class or corporate organization was precisely the form of inequality which the revolutionary idea was trying to abolish in order that the individual might be free. The propertyless worker and peasant did become free, but they remained defenseless against their more prosperous fellow citizens. For these sins of omission and commission the radical press scolded the deputies; but in practice it is true that the Constituent Assembly allowed the masses to organize in clubs and to draw up petition after petition. If, in the Declaration and the Constitution of 1791, the bourgeois deputies reserved all power for themselves, they did so because they recognized their own capacities and mistrusted those of the masses. It is a gross anachronism to speak of class consciousness or class warfare in the period between 1789 and 1791, although one may readily grant that the constitutional legislation of the Assembly, generous as it was, discriminated against the lower born. Instances of this discrimination will be shown in the discussion of the new constitution.

The Constitution of 1791. After proclaiming in the Declaration, "Men are born and remain free and equal in rights," the Assembly flagrantly contradicted itself by refusing to grant suffrage rights to all Frenchmen. The constitution divided the population into two classes, active and passive citizens. Only members of the former class were given the right to vote and to serve in the National Guard. The distinction was based upon differences in wealth. To be an active citizen one had to be twenty-five years of age or over and pay an annual direct tax equal in value to three times the local rate of a laborer's daily wage. This provision, which was voted in December, 1789, reflected both the theories of the political philosophers of the century and the fears of the bourgeois deputies. They were afraid that the three million Frenchmen whom they debarred from the polls might be misled either by their own ignorance or by the cunning propaganda of the erstwhile aristocrats. Four and one-quarter million male Frenchmen were thus classified as active citizens. In the ranks of the three million passive citizens there were, in addition to the landless peasants and the artisans who could not pay the required minimum tax, debtors, bankrupts, and wage servants.[14]

The classification of citizens according to their wealth did not end with the distinction between active and passive citizens. That was merely a beginning. The active citizens met in the primary assembly to choose the electors, who met in the chief town of the department and elected the deputies to the assembly, the judges, the bishops, the parish priests, and the members of the local administrations. But to be eligible as elector, the active citizen had to pay a tax equivalent to the local value of ten days' labor; and to be eligible as deputy, he had to be a landed proprietor who paid an annual tax equivalent in value to a silver mark *(marc d'argent),* which was worth slightly more than fifty francs. Out of a total population of approximately twenty-six million, there were not more than fifty thousand citizens eligible to serve as electors, and fewer still who qualified to serve as deputies. In short, political rights were made a monopoly of the well-to-do, for the new constitution did away with privileges based upon birth, but respected and strengthened those arising out of financial prosperity. Protests poured in upon the Assembly against this discriminatory scheme. It was not revised until the very close of

---

[14] As one of the deputies, Duquesnoy, expressed it, "Only property owners are true citizens"; and in the original provision only property owners had been given the vote. But this provision was modified in the final draft.

the Constituent Assembly (August 27, 1791) and then too late, after the primary elections under the Constitution of 1791 had been held.[15]

Although the third article of the Declaration declared that sovereign rights resided exclusively in the nation, the sixteenth article stressed the fact that the separation of powers was essential to a well ordered state. Hence the nation delegated the legislative power to its elected representatives, the executive power to a hereditary monarch, and the judicial power to elected judges. The power to make the laws was given to a single assembly, the Legislative Assembly, whose members were to be elected for two years and whose sessions could not be dissolved by the king. The powers given to the Legislative Assembly made it the strongest political authority in the state. The deputies enjoyed full parliamentary immunity for the free expression of their views. The Assembly alone could initiate and vote the laws of France. While the king was given the right of a suspensive veto over legislation, that veto became invalid if three successive assemblies persisted in voting the same law. Moreover, the veto did not apply to constitutional and fiscal laws, proclamations to the nation, and accusations against individual ministers. Still it is true that the suspensive veto operated practically as an absolute veto because it delayed legislation for several years. The Assembly fixed the tax assessments and controlled public expenditures. Declarations of war and ratifications of peace treaties could not be made by the king without its previous consent. It supervised the ministry and directed the diplomacy of the state.

The executive power was entrusted to a hereditary monarch, but precautions were taken to restrict him in his role of constitutional ruler. Before the draft of the constitution, Louis XVI had been "Louis, by the grace of God, King of France and Navarre." Now he became "Louis by the grace of God and the Constitution of the state, King of the French." He had been the liege lord and the proprietor of the state; now he was the first servant, who was required to swear an oath to be faithful to the nation and the law, to defend the constitution, and to execute the laws. Previously, he could draw without limit upon all the resources of the state. Now he received a civil list, a generous one, of twenty-five million francs annually for his expenses.

In theory, the power that the constitution gave him was of considerable importance; in practice, the exercise of his power was hedged in by many restrictions. He was granted the right to appoint ambassadors, ministers, and a certain proportion of the higher officers of the military forces. He was supreme commander of the army and navy. By his veto power he could effectively delay legislation for a period of several years, but the veto power could not be applied to the most important legislation. He appointed ambassadors, but found the direction of foreign policy largely in the hands of the deputies of the Assembly. He could not select his ministers from the ranks of the deputies, for it was feared that the promise of a ministerial position might either weaken their loyalty to national interests or else strengthen the king's influence over the debates of the

---

[15] The revision of the electoral law came after the king's flight to Varennes in June, 1791. It abolished the eligibility requirement of the silver mark for the deputy, but on the other hand, increased the tax and property qualifications of the electors. The latter were required to be either the proprietors or the usufructuaries of a piece of property assessed on the tax rolls at a rate equivalent to one hundred and fifty to two hundred days' wages. Under certain conditions they were eligible if they paid in direct taxes a sum equivalent to the local value of labor ranging from one hundred to four hundred days. This revision came too late for the elections of 1791, and the elections of 1792 were held under direct manhood suffrage.

Assembly. The Assembly kept a vigilant eye over the six ministers of the king. It decreed that no royal act was valid unless it were countersigned by one of the ministers, who thus assumed responsibility for it. It required these to give an account of their use of funds to the Assembly, and it subjected them to the possibility of impeachment by a special tribunal. The king's administrative power was tremendously weakened by the fact that he exercised it through local bodies in no way responsible to him. Lest the monarch be tempted to use force against the deputies and dissolve the Assembly, the constitution forbade him to station troops within a thirty-mile radius of the place where the sessions were held. Not without some justification could Louis XVI write in 1791: "The King has been declared the supreme head of the administration of the kingdom, yet he can change nothing without the decision of the Assembly." The Assembly was the real master of the state; and this Assembly was to be composed of deputies indirectly elected on the basis of property qualifications. It is no exaggeration to state that the new constitution organized a middle-class government within the framework of a constitutional monarchy.

The Administrative Reforms. The administrative organization was also completely remodeled.[16] The *cahiers* had given indication of the direction that the reform would follow, and the indication was corroborated in the summer of 1789 when the establishment of the new municipalities, or communes, showed that the country strongly demanded the decentralization of the government. The old overlapping and confusing divisions of generalities, provinces, bailiwicks, and *pays d'élections* were abolished completely. A new, uniform, and simple administrative system was established. France was divided into eighty-three departments, each department into districts, each district into cantons, and each canton into communes. It may have been that the deputies created the new departments in the hope of destroying the old particularist spirit of the historic provinces. More likely, the deputies were concerned with establishing a new territorial unit that would make local administration simple and efficient. The departments were small enough for the citizens to reach the chief town *(chef lieu)* and its market in a single day's journey, and numerous enough to be without danger to this central administration. Having adopted these principles, the deputies arranged the delimitation of the new units in the Assembly. In their discussions they were not invariably amicable, but they were realistic and never lost track of the purpose in mind.

With the disappearance of the intendant and the subdelegate, the administrative authority was vested in the hands of the officials elected by the local inhabitants. The new administrative units began to function in the spring of 1790. Except in the case of municipal elections the elections were indirect. Even in the case of municipal elections, where the voting was direct and the voters the active citizens, the poor citizens were excluded from the polls. The central administration had no direct agent of its own in the local administrations. The king could suspend the local authorities, but the latter had the right of appeal to the Assembly against his intervention. Each department, district, and commune had its elected council, which was a deliberating body, and a permanent executive bureau as well. This executive bureau was called a directory in the department and the district and a municipal corps in the commune. Over the latter body the mayor presided. The elected officials inherited all the former powers of the royal intendant. They apportioned and levied the direct taxes, executed the laws, maintained order, and

---

[16] The two decrees of December 14 and December 22, 1789, which defined the extent and functions of the new administrative units, were not properly speaking[1] included in the Constitution of 1791, but they were essential parts of it.

administered schools and poor relief. Other elected officials, the procurators *(procureurs),* represented the state in the different administrative units and served as a link between them and the ministers of the central administration. The canton had no independent political existence and served as the primary assembly for the election of national officials. The decentralization of the administrative organization was most pronounced in the municipalities. Each commune elected its own mayor, its municipal officers, and the local procurator. The term of municipal office was shorter than that of the department or district, fifty per cent of the officers were renewed annually, and the elections were direct. Consequently the political career of the revolutionary municipality was an active one. It was more in touch with political realities than the other administrative units and more democratic in its tendencies. Unlike the larger units, it could summon the National Guard to maintain order and enforce the laws. Except in isolated cases the commune was unchecked in its local administration of national laws.[17]

The reorganization of judicial administration was effected in the same spirit as that of the administrative service of the government. A new hierarchy of elected judges replaced the former magistrates of the Old Regime who had bought their charges. Justice was to be free and within the reach of all citizens. Judicial procedure was greatly simplified. For civil cases each canton had its justice of the peace and each district its own tribunal composed of five judges. Petty cases and misdemeanors were tried locally; more serious infractions of the law came before the district court. In criminal affairs, matters of simple police were entrusted to the communes, more serious cases to justices of the peace in the cantons, and felonies to a special tribunal in each department. There were two elected juries in criminal affairs, one to pass on the case, the other to determine the innocence or the guilt of the accused. There were no juries for civil cases. Provisions were made to insure the accused a fair and open trial, and the penalties were made proportionate to the crime. Most of the old degrading penalties, such as torture, the pillory, and branding, were abolished, but chains and the death penalty were maintained. A procurator represented the king at the various courts, but he could be heard only in special and limited cases and had no power over the procedure. Justice, like the administration of the law, became a sovereign right of the people, even though it still was administered in the name of the king. No appeal courts were established, but by an ingenious arrangement each district tribunal was permitted to review cases of other district tribunals. A supreme court of appeals, the court of cassation, was established to pass on the forms of procedure, but it had no competence over the matter, and it could not interpret the law. Finally, a High Court, also composed of elected magistrates, was established at Paris with competence over cases involving the ministers and high officials and over cases involving treason and crimes against the safety of the state.

The military organization was also reformed, but not so profoundly as the other branches of the government. The presence of an ever-armed Europe, which did not welcome the achievements of the Assembly with excessive enthusiasm, forced the deputies to proceed slowly in this respect. The sale of offices was abolished, the pay of the soldiers was raised, and an incomplete system of promotion based on seniority was introduced. Commissions were open to all, but the appointment of the highest officers of the regular army was left to the king. These reforms were beneficial, but did little to reestablish discipline. The new organization of the National Guard, which was at once a militia and a reserve, took its place beside that of the line troops of the regular army. As a general

---

[17] Paris was given a special law because of its great population and importance, but the organization of the municipality of Paris followed the main lines of the general system.

rule only active citizens could serve in the National Guard. But they numbered from two to three million compared to the one hundred and forty thousand of the line troops. They elected their own officers and wore the prescribed uniform of the nation, blue coat and white waistcoat and breeches. Their flags carried the inscription *Le peuple français. La liberté ou la morte.*

This sweeping reform of the administration had its defects as well as its good qualities. It gave excessive powers to the voters and too little to the king and the central administration. Since all power came from below, the government had slight control over its nominal agents. The reaction against too much centralization, such as France had in the Old Regime and such as it has today, weakened the unity of the nation instead of strengthening it, as the deputies hoped. On the one hand there were too many elections and too many elected officials; on the other, the political experience of the country was slight and the problems overwhelming. If the local officials were chosen from citizens who were hostile to the course of the Revolution, as was the case in 1792 and 1793, or fell under the influence of counter-revolutionary forces, as was true in isolated cases from the very beginning, they could direct the local administration against the Assembly. A political crisis was therefore a potential threat to the stability of the government and to the very existence of the nation.[18]

The Financial Crisis. The financial crisis which had precipitated the Revolution grew steadily worse in the summer months of 1789. The secret opposition of Louis XVI, the intrigues of the aristocrats, the plotting of political schemers, the unappeased hostility of the rural masses, and the accentuation of the economic depression reacted sharply upon the financial situation. The Assembly abolished the taxes of the Old Regime, except the stamp duty and the registration of acts, which the peasants were not paying in any case, and proceeded to reform the system of taxation as the cahiers demanded. Three new direct taxes were substituted for the various direct taxes of the past. Of these the most important was the land tax, since real estate was the principal source of wealth. There was also a personal property tax, calculated according to the rent paid, and a tax upon revenue from commerce and industry. The new direct taxes, like the old indirect taxes, were not paid or were paid only after many protests and much delay. The Assembly was powerless and the new municipalities were unwilling to exercise pressure upon the masses. The treasury was empty and the financial burden of the state higher than ever, as the liquidation of the Old Regime and the establishment of the new administrative system

---

[18] Mathiez, in tracing the roles of the many committees of the Assembly, comes to the conclusion that the decentralization was more apparent than real. He maintains that neither in theory nor in practice did the deputies of the Constituent Assembly intend the separation of powers to become effective until after the Assembly had ended its work. The deputies believed and acted upon the principle that they were extraordinary deputies, representing the nation in all its sovereignty, and endowed with dictatorial rights. "The truth is, that despite the Constitution, the departmental authorities assume no initiative, refer to Paris as before for the slightest difficulties. The only difference is that the committees of the Assembly have replaced the divisions of the Royal Council. The truth is, that the Assembly does not stop with passing- laws but governs, or better still, administers to the smallest detail. . . . The committees of the Constituent Assembly functioned as did later the committees of the Convention." If his views are correct—and they seem plausible—we must revise our conventional interpretation of the constitutional legislation from 1789 to '79 and recognize the fact that the Assembly enjoyed far more real authority over the local administration than historians believed. But, as he says, this authority existed *despite* the constitution and not because of it. *Cf.* Mathiez' critical book review in *Annales historiques de la Revolution française,* janvier-fevrier, 1919, p. 96.

enormously increased the public indebtedness. The interest on the debt and the expenses of the administration amounted to six hundred million francs annually.

To retain the support of the investors in state bonds the Assembly declared against a formal proceeding in bankruptcy, i.e., a repudiation of the internal debt, and it tried various expedients to meet the country's current obligations. Necker, the financial miracle-maker, fell back upon his traditional tactics, which were new advances from the Caisse d'Escompte and new public loans. The loans were voted by a desperate Assembly in August and December, 1789, and again in the spring of 1790, but they were not covered by the public. An attempted direct income tax failed, principally because the administrative organization and the personnel required for the collection were nonexistent. In the fall of 1789 private individuals, municipalities, and corporate groups made voluntary patriotic contributions to the Assembly, but the relief from this source was slight. The Caisse d'Escompte advanced all its available funds to the state, but in November, 1789, the directors of that institution avowed their inability to continue their loans. Eighty-nine million of its one hundred and fourteen million of notes in circulation were already at the disposal of the treasury. Inasmuch as the solvency of the Caisse d'Escompte depended upon that of the state, only part of its note issue being covered by its own reserves and the rest by what the state owed it, Necker proposed that the Caisse d'Escompte be transformed into a national bank. In that way he could increase its capital and have it issue new notes. The Assembly rejected his proposal on the ground that the new issue would not be taken up by the public without additional security, and that their value would be better maintained if they were issued directly by the state. Moreover, if a direct issue were to be made by the state, the interest that the Caisse d'Escompte charged would be saved. But what fresh security could the state offer? "Our patrimony," answered one of the deputies, and the patrimony was the possessions of the church, which on November 2, 1789, the Assembly "placed at the disposal of the nation."

The wealth of the church was estimated from two to four billion francs, an amount sufficient to pay the state debt. The question was whether the state had the right to seize the possessions of the church. Precedents favored alienation. Under Louis XV the Commission of the Regular Clergy had suppressed nine monastic orders and used the property that they possessed for purposes of the common good. Calonne had suggested expropriation before the Revolution, the cahiers had proposed a redistribution of ecclesiastical land, and the Physiocrats had used various arguments against the great wealth of the church, prescribing confiscation as the social remedy.

The debates in the Assembly on the right of the state to take over the goods of the church became heated as soon as Talleyrand had made the specific proposal in October, 1789. The most convincing argument was the legal argument against the church as a corporation, i.e., as a corporate political body within the state, possessing the right to tax the people. Even if the church had the rights of possession, ran the argument, the state still had superior rights, for the church was a corporation, and all corporations held their status by virtue of the law. The church did not *own* property, continued the argument, but *possessed* it for certain purposes only. If the church does not fulfill its duties, the state can take back the property on condition of performing the same services itself. Chapelier, one of the active Breton deputies, put the argument tersely: "It was impolitic for great corporations to possess property." Talleyrand even cited canon law and the decisions of church synods to prove that the lands had been given neither to the clergy nor to the corporation of the church, but for the perpetuation of religious services. By assuming the threefold obligations of the clergy, i.e., education, poor-relief, and worship, the state had the right to take over the lands. Another argument emphasized the luxury and corruption of the high prelates and advocated confiscation as a method of restoring the church to its apostolic simplicity. It was claimed that the great revenues of the clergy were deflected from their rightful purposes. A third argument invoked natural law to prove that society derived no benefit from the church lands which were administered by the clergy, i.e., persons who were not recognized by civil society. This was the argument of efficiency.

The defenders of the existing status, Camus, Champion de Cicé, and the Abbé Maury, brought out the fact that it was legally unjust to deprive a corporation of its property, since property was a social creation, whether owned by an individual or by a corporation.

They even fell back on the Declaration of Rights, which defined property as one of the natural rights. The answer to this was that corporations did not enjoy natural rights. They also maintained that the property had been given neither to the Catholic Church nor to the clergy, but to individual ecclesiastical organizations. They endeavored to show that secularization of the estates of the church would benefit speculators and profiteers and leave the clergy without any visible means of support. But on November 2, the Assembly voted to place the ecclesiastical lands at the disposal of the state, which assumed the obligation of paying the clergy, meeting the expenses of worship, and relieving the poor. Progressives were well satisfied with the Assembly's vote, hailing it as a notable victory over an organization whose privileged status had strengthened reaction and blocked reform. Those who favored a radical reform in the church and the redistribution of its estates were also satisfied. But thousands upon thousands of simple believers were sorely perplexed, even violently shocked by this dramatic turn of events which altered immemorial customs. To them the Revolution seemed to threaten religion.

The Assignats. For a time the Assembly hesitated to use the enormous resources which its vote had given the state. When the last of Necker's expedients failed, it decided on December 14 to place four hundred million francs' worth of ecclesiastical lands on sale. To cover the sale a bond issue in the form of assignats equivalent in amount to the value of the land on sale was floated. A new bank under the control of the Assembly, the Caisse d'Escompte, was established to issue the assignats and to receive the proceeds of all exceptional taxations. The first use of the assignats would be to repay the one hundred and seventy million francs which the Caisse d'Escompte had advanced to the state. These assignats, created on December 19 and paying five per cent interest, were to be exchanged for all interest-bearing state notes and received in payment for the ecclesiastical lands. As soon as the land was sold, they were to be returned to the new bank and burnt. They were not currency; they were treasury bonds redeemable in land instead of in cash.

If the Caisse d'Escompte had succeeded in floating the one hundred and seventy million of assignats which had been assigned to it, the entire operation would have remained a financial transaction. But investors hesitated in the early months of 1790 to accept them. "The public felt no confidence in bonds that were merely problematical promises to sell property the acquisition of which was not free of all mortgages and might give rise to inextricable complications." The notes of the Caisse d'Escompte depreciated six per cent by the spring of 1790.

The Assembly realized that two additional steps would have to be taken if its effort to meet the pressing state debts by means of assignats were to be successful: (1) to declare the church lands national property, and (2) to give the assignats the force of legal tender. By April it had taken the first step. It deprived the clergy of their administration of ecclesiastical property, and undertook to clear off all mortgages and other liens upon the property by assuming the debt of the clergy and the expenses of public worship. Once the state had guaranteed the assignats, the Assembly could advantageously substitute them for paper money. The assignats of the first issue which had not been taken up by investors were called in, and a new issue was floated, virtually with the force of legal tender (April 17, 1790).

Although the decree of April 17, 1790, placed the limit of the amount of assignats that could be issued at the figure of 400,000,000 livres, the success scored by the new emission encouraged the National Assembly to go beyond the limit it set. Assignats, issued now by the state bank (Caisse de l'Extraordinaire), took the place of bank notes. Since their success had wiped out the most pressing state debt, why could not the state wipe out its entire debt by issuing additional assignats likewise secured by the national land! A strong minority group of deputies tried to oppose the projected policy, advancing irrefutable financial arguments against increasing the number of assignats in circulation. In time they saw the accuracy of their forecast revealed. They foresaw the partial avowal of bankruptcy that would ensue, the depreciation of national paper money, inflation, speculation, higher prices, decrease of consumption and production, and a serious economic crisis; but the majority in the Assembly was adamant to the appeal. For a month the deputies debated the question until on September 29 the Assembly voted the payment of the debt of the state and clergy in non-interest-bearing assignats. At the same time it raised the limit of issue of assignats from 400,000,000 to 1,200,000,000 livres. Subsequent decrees raised the issue of assignats up to the alarming total of 1,800,000,000 livres. For this circumstances were partly to blame. The deputies foresaw the difficulties, but they saw no other solution of the financial problems. In May and June, 1790, the National Assembly took over the royal domain and appropriated 25,000,000 livres for the king's annual expenses; in July, 1790, it took over the maintenance of the church. By those two measures the deputies added more than a billion livres to the debt of the state. And, more important still, they pinned the highest hopes on the political consequences of their measures.

One alternative proposal had been made, that non-circulating bonds, bearing five per cent interest, be issued to cover the sale of the additional land that was offered. It was rejected. Without an additional issue of assignats, rightly argued Mirabeau, Chapelier, and Montesquieu, who were the spokesmen of the majority, the public land would not and could not be sold. The sale of the land was the important matter. The sale of land had to be facilitated if the twofold goal of the Assembly were to be realized; viz., (1) the cancellation of the *entire* state debt (and not merely the most pressing obligations), and (2) the creation of a widespread group of land purchasers, who, willy-nilly, would become defenders of the Revolution and the constitution. Montesquieu voiced the prevalent optimism when he said: "The assignats will be the connecting link between the private interests of the individual and the general interests of the state; the very adversaries [of the assignats] will become proprietors and citizens through the Revolution and for the Revolution." And another deputy vividly correlated the sale of the national land with the constitutional labors of the Assembly: "It is a question of strengthening the Constitution, of curbing the hopes of its enemies, of binding them to the new order of things by self-interest."

To a very great extent the political hopes of the deputies were realized. "Self-interest" even more than patriotism induced a large body of Frenchmen to open their pocketbooks and buy national property. As proprietors of land which the Revolution had placed on the market, the purchasers were chained to the revolutionary chariot and were obligated by enlightened calculation to defend the new order against a counter-revolution which would nullify their purchases. In this respect the decision to place the confiscated land on sale and to issue assignats was a political success. However, it must also be noted that the plan of sale and the success of the sales themselves were reflected in and modified by the vicissitudes of the factional political struggles and the political divisions of the country. Such occurrences as the flight of the king, the emigrations of the nobles, the war (from 1792 on), had direct bearing upon the financial question.[19]

The economic and financial consequences of the assignat policy were less happy. The state debt was not canceled. For a passing moment—a very brief one, however—the assignats supplied an artificial stimulus to production, since the big business men quickly disposed of their assignats, investing them in land and in merchandise. Eventually that operation resulted in higher prices. The first issues were in high denominations, 1000 livres, 300 livres and 200 livres, but later issues in 1791 touched as low as 50 livres and 5 livres. By a decree of the Assembly on May 17, 1790, the exchange of metallic currency for paper money was made legal. The paper money depreciated at once, and the rift between specie and paper money rapidly grew wider. The Assembly hesitated a long time before it came to its decision to issue the smaller denominations, for the deputies realized that the hardships of depreciation would in that fashion be transferred to the working population. But the disappearance of specie made the decision inevitable. Coin gradually became more and more scarce in France, because the mercenary troops were paid in specie, as were debts to foreign bankers and payments on foreign imports. Émigrés also carried specie out of the country, and hoarding completed the disappearance of metal currency. The practice of banks, business houses, and regional and local administrations (as in Germany from 1921 to 1924) of issuing private paper money, as well as the depreciation and the final repudiation of private paper money ruined private fortunes, encouraged wild speculation in land as well as in assignats, discouraged thrift and sober living, and created a panic psychology. There were other contributory causes to the fall of the assignats. The country was flooded with counterfeit money that was manufactured by criminals in France and by émigrés out of France. Instead of burning the assignats as they were received by the treasury, as had been prescribed by the decrees, the Assembly not only delayed the return of the assignats by giving the purchasers of land a long period of time for payment, but actually reissued them in smaller denominations. A certain amount was canceled by the treasury, but 980,000,000 livres in assignats were still in circulation in May, 1791, and 1,700,000,000 a year later.

The official tables of the depreciation of paper money tell the tragic story of its declining value. By the end of 1791 the assignats had fallen between twenty and twenty-five per cent; in the following spring (1792) the assignat in Paris had lost almost forty per cent of its nominal value. Abroad, at London, Amsterdam, Geneva, and Hamburg, the depreciation was still more marked, the assignat being quoted at a loss of fifty to sixty per cent. There were two periods, in the summer of 1792 and again during the Terror (1793-1794), when the assignat recovered part of its face value, but on the whole the decline was constant until 1796, when this paper money was entirely repudiated.

---

[19] The experiences of different countries of Europe after 1918 enable the student or today to appreciate more fully the influence of political developments upon financial policy.

Agrarian and Economic Measures. The agrarian policy and the economic reforms of the Assembly disappointed the masses as sorely as its fiscal policy. The agrarian policy was expressed in the deputies' treatment of the question of the feudal dues and in the procedure adopted to regulate the sale of ecclesiastical land. While the August decrees abolished the tithe outright, they did not do away *in toto* with the feudal rights. The first clause, which stated that "the National Assembly hereby completely abolishes the feudal system," was sufficient for the peasants, most of whom could not read and paid no attention to the qualifying clauses if they could read. The qualifying clauses distinguished between feudal rights which were to be abolished without indemnification and those which were to be redeemed by monetary payment. Pending their ultimate redemption the latter were to be collected by their owners. When the noble and his feudal lawyer made their appearance to explain the decree and collect the dues, the peasants refused to pay, maintaining that they were being cheated. They sent protests to the Assembly and supplemented their words with deeds of violence against nobles and their chateaux. Indeed, the disturbances of the fall and winter of 1789 and of the spring of 1790 were more extensive and more profound than the peasant insurrections prior to August, 1789.

In the spring of 1790, the Assembly's committee on feudal dues made its recommendations, which were voted by the deputies. The committee was composed entirely of jurists, "a soviet of lawyers," says one historian. Two categories of feudal dues were established according to their supposed origin. Those dues which were assumed to have arisen from the exactions of nobles and the usurpation of the state were classified as *personal* rights. They included servitude, hunting and fishing rights, right of warrens and dovecotes, of justice, banalites, and personal corvées. These were to be abolished outright without compensation. Those which were assumed to have arisen from the concession of land in perpetuity by the lord to the peasant were classified as *real* rights. They included all land rents (*cens and champart*), all real corvées, lods et ventes, and all dues which had been commuted into money payments. These, which were the most lucrative of the noble's rights, were to be repurchased from the proprietor.

The procedure adopted for the redemption of the real rights placed the burden of proof squarely upon the peasant. In the absence of a legal title, proof that a noble had been in possession of his land for the preceding thirty years was sufficient to validate his rights. While the capitalization of the dues was not unduly high, nor the time limit for redemption too brief, there were several exacting provisions. All arrears in payment had to be made good. Annual dues and dues of mutation had to be redeemed together. The principle of solidarity of redemption was established, so that no one peasant might redeem his dues unless all other tenants of the same fief also redeemed theirs or unless he paid for them all.

Neither the actual course of history during the Middle Ages nor the principles of feudal law justified the policy established by the Assembly. The peasant's instinct, which told him that the whole feudal system hung together, was more correct than the complex distinctions of the jurists. Protests rained in upon the deputies. "Never," says Professor Sagnac, who has made a careful study of the feudal legislation, "have laws let loose a more lively indignation." Under the circumstances redemption was well-nigh impossible. Through all of 1790 and 1791 the peasants vented their opposition in rioting, looting, and attacking the National Guard which were sent to enforce the legislation and quell the disorder.[20]

The peasants expected more from the sale of the ecclesiastical estates than they had derived from the legislation on the feudal system, but again they were doomed to disappointment. The richer peasants and even those peasants who owned small plots took advantage of the terms of sale to increase their holdings, but in general the landless peasant did not realize his dream of acquiring a patch of land for himself and his family. The terms of the sale were not difficult to meet, at least for those who had some financial resources; and former nobles, ecclesiastics, bourgeois, and the richer peasants, including many who bought for speculation, took advantage of them. This ready response was not necessarily motivated by patriotic sentiments, for many a shrewd purchaser saw the economic wisdom of exchanging depreciating assignats for something as tangible and solid as real estate. In a later chapter we shall consider the extent of bourgeois and peasant purchases, but here it is sufficient to note that in failing to satisfy the legitimate land hunger of the rural masses, the National Constituent Assembly chilled the revolutionary enthusiasm of innumerable lowly individuals who had hailed the events of 1789. To all the petitions of the landless peasantry for the division of large estates, the free use of the commons, the abolition of *métayage*, and the governmental regulation of the grain trade, the deputies turned a deaf ear. They were prisoners of their economic views and of the inexorable necessity of raising great sums of money to satisfy the claims of the creditors of the state.

The economic liberalism of the deputies explains their measures concerning trade and industry, which were of a piece with their legislation concerning the feudal dues and the sale of national land. They abolished the grievous internal customs which had stifled trade within the kingdom. They also abolished the guilds which still hampered trade and industry by denying the workingman the right to use his tools and his initiative for his own benefit, and they laid down the new principle that "every person shall be free to engage in such business or to practice such profession, art, or craft as he shall find profitable." Partly in consequence of their measures and partly in response to other circumstances, they brought about an artificial prosperity which favored the display of individual initiative and the employment of capital funds. Internal and foreign trade was flourishing, and factories were busy. For a few months in the spring of 1791 there was heightened production and consumption. Business men, anxious to get rid of their assignats, made heavy investments and repeated purchases of commodities, all of which stimulated manufactures. But the boom did not last long. The decline of the assignats and the concomitant rise in prices on the one hand, and the growing unemployment, caused in part by the decline of the luxury trades, tended to produce an economic crisis. The Parisian workingmen went on strike for higher wages. Their cause was ably seconded by the petitions of the newly formed popular societies of the capital. This blending of the demands for economic relief and political equality frightened the middle-class deputies, whose response to the demands was the famous Chapelier law of June 14, 1791.

---

[20] In a recent study, a French historian takes the attitude that the legislation of 1790 was not unreasonable, and that its provisions would gradually have been met, at least in the department of the Gironde. The feudal dues were completely abolished without any compensation whatsoever in the course of 1792 and 1793.

Fearful lest the movement lead to the restoration of the abolished guilds in a new form, the deputies forbade any kind of association among people engaged in the same trade for the defense of their "alleged common interests." As Jaurés has amply shown, theoretically this law ignored class distinction. Employers as well as employees were forbidden to form trade associations, while the terms of the labor contract were to be arranged between the individual employer and the individual employee. From their own point of view the deputies were consistent in preventing corporative associations of workingmen, for they believed that such associations, indeed any corporate groups at all, represented an attack upon the liberty of the individual. But in denying the workers the right to form unions for collective bargaining, in refusing them the right to go out on strike, and in prescribing heavy penalties for violations of these provisions, the Assembly manifestly showed its fear of the workers' strength. Such protests as were made against the Chapelier law came largely from the democrats of the popular societies, who found in it an excuse to redouble their campaign against the property qualifications of the electoral system. Once the disfranchised workers gained political rights, they reasoned, such discriminatory legislation would become impossible. The conservative deputies retaliated by denouncing the democratic agitators as anarchists who wished to destroy all property rights. Thus a breach was opened between the Constituent Assembly and certain sections of the people, and the way was prepared for a continuance of the unrest.

The Civil Constitution of the Clergy. The first reforms of the Constituent Assembly made the remolding of religious society imperative in order to harmonize it with the new civil society. To the deputies, who had been educated by the clergy, a separation of church and state was unthinkable. Moreover, the execution of its financial reforms gave the Assembly no alternative to regulating the affairs of the church. The legislation concerning the tithes and the ecclesiastical lands forced the state to assume the financial obligations of the Galilean Church. Those obligations were many and burdensome—the clerical debt, the expenses of the cult, relief of the poor, and support of education and hospitals. To cut down those obligations seemed absolutely necessary to the deputies who were struggling with the problems of putting France on a stable financial basis.

Other motives, however, besides financial considerations lay behind the early religious policy of the Constituent Assembly which culminated in the celebrated Civil Constitution of the Clergy (July 12, 1790). These motives were derived from the political traditions of the Old Regime and from the teachings of the *philosophes* which, paradoxically, had been accepted by many of the lower clergy. The political traditions emphasized the subordination of the church to the state and the independence of the Gallican Church from the authority of the papacy. The cahiers of the clergy agreed that a reform of the Gallican Church was in order. On the other hand the *philosophes* in general agreed that the state could not exist without religion. Rousseau voiced one of the strongest convictions of the political philosophers when he wrote, "Those who would treat morality and politics apart will never understand anything, either about the one or about the other." It is true that the *philosophes* would have preferred a civil religion to Catholicism. But the new revolutionary idealism was developing into a civil or patriotic religion, and parish priests encouraged their parishioners to fuse the new revolutionary religion with Catholicism by quoting Holy Writ to justify the articles of the Declaration of Rights. Of the deputies in the Assembly, many were partisans of the natural rights philosophy of their age, but an overwhelming majority was also profoundly Catholic. Their religious reforms were in no sense an attack upon Catholicism or Christianity; their measures were an effort to associate the clergy with the Revolution. They were fully aware that no one could interpret their decrees to the unlettered masses so well as the local priest.

At first the lower clergy applauded the religious enactments. But the refusal of the deputies, in the spring of 1790, to declare Catholicism the state religion made them lend a willing ear to the complaints of the upper clergy. At that moment Catholicism was the only religion supported by state funds. The Catholic Church kept all civil records and controlled education and poor relief. Why then did the revolutionaries lay themselves open to an accusation of hostility to religion, particularly when so many of them were loyal Catholics? The answer is that they could not help themselves. In the first place, to declare Catholicism the state religion would be to undo their own work, for the Declaration of Rights had already granted religious toleration, and a decree of December 24, 1789, admitted Protestants to all civil and military offices. In the second place, the deputies could not violate those philosophical convictions which lay at the basis of the Declaration of Rights.

The first great reform measure concerned the regular clergy. Demands for a reduction of the number of monastic establishments had been made before 17895 after the Declaration of Rights was voted, the existence of the regular clergy was doomed. Many of the monks themselves had petitioned the National Assembly to abolish the monastic orders. After a provisional suspension (October, 1789), the deputies definitely suppressed all monastic vows and abolished those establishments which required them on February 13, 1790. They gave the members of the religious orders the choice of accepting a pension and reentering civil life or retiring to one of the designated monastic houses which the law set aside for them. As all future monastic vows were forbidden and no new houses could be founded, the monastic system was doomed to extinction. But no compulsion was put upon the regular clergy. Most of the nuns remained in the educational or charitable institutions until the end of 1792, while the majority of monks did not leave until 1791, to become teachers, librarians, administrators, or priests. There was no pronounced opposition to the decree of February 13, 1790.

The turn of the secular clergy followed. The first ecclesiastical committee of the Assembly, appointed August 12, 1789, was strengthened in February, 1790, by the addition of fifteen new members, and on April 21 it submitted a plan for the reform of the constitution and practices of the clergy. The majority of the committee were "Gallican" (defenders of the national liberties of the Catholic Church in France against the papacy); none of them were outstanding Jansenists or representatives of the *philosophes*. The members were convinced that long precedent had given the state the right to reform the clergy, and that the reform should be effected without the intervention of the pope. The plan was peacefully discussed, article by article, in the Assembly and became law on July 12, 1790. The name applied by the committee to its body of measures, the Civil Constitution of the Clergy, marked its determination not to interfere with the dogma of the Catholic Church, but merely to record the *civic* nature of religious functions.

Since a decree of the National Assembly had divided France into eighty-three departments, each department being further subdivided into districts and cantons, the desire of the committee to end the old chaotic ecclesiastical divisions of France was greatly facilitated. The number of bishoprics and archbishoprics was reduced from one hundred and thirty-nine to eighty-three, each department being made an Episcopal diocese, presided over by a bishop. Instead of the old archbishoprics, there were to be ten metropolitan districts in each of which the bishop of the leading city was to serve as metropolitan. Similarly, the parishes would be redivided on new and simpler lines, the very large ones reduced and the small ones increased in size. All cathedral chapters were to be suppressed and all benefices without duties abolished. A permanent Episcopal council, composed of the vicars of the seminaries, was to ratify the decisions of the bishop. Inasmuch as the priests were public officials salaried by the state, they like all other functionaries were to be elected. The same departmental electors that chose civil officials were to elect the bishops, and the district electors were to elect the parish priests.[21] There was to be a revision of salaries, both for the bishops and the lower clergy, so that the excessively high remuneration of the former and the pathetically meager salaries of the latter would be remedied. The bishops were to be instituted by a senior bishop or a metropolitan, and they were forbidden to appeal to the pope for confirmation of the election. However, they might address a letter to him as "the visible head of the Universal Church in testimony of the unity of faith and communion" which united them. Thus the primacy of the papacy was recognized, but its jurisdiction denied. And thus the Catholic Church in France would become a national church, free from the absolute rule of the pope and at one with the civil state in its sentiments of liberty and progress.

The deputies were far from anticipating the hostile reaction that greeted the Civil Constitution of the Clergy. They were not aware of having exceeded their rights. They had abolished the Concordat of 1516, suppressed the plurality of benefices (August 4-11, 1789), and done away with annates; and the papacy had made no protest. Were they not, moreover, in making the church subordinate to the state and transforming the functions of religion into civic duties, applying the eighteenth century philosophy of enlightenment? In *The Social Contract,* Rousseau resolved the natural functions of religion into the ordinary moralities— civic duties—which would be supported and controlled by the state. "The function of the state," wrote the atheist D'Holbach, "is to make good men; the function of religion is to make good citizens." Mirabeau proclaimed that "the service of the altar is the public function."

The French clergy, however, with their traditions of Gallican liberties behind them, took another view of the matter. They were not content to win independence from Rome merely to lose it to the state. The several bishops who were deputies abstained from voting on the Civil Constitution. One of them, Boisgelin, the archbishop of Aix, stated categorically that the measure could not be binding unless it received canonical consecration. The Assembly refused to allow the bishops to form a national council which would take the necessary canonical measures to consecrate the decree, for fear that the counter-revolutionary ecclesiastics would use that council against the revolutionary movement; and by its refusal throw the responsibility of canonical consecration upon the pope. To this Civil Constitution the king could not apply his veto power, for the decree was constitutional in character. His only alternatives were to accept or reject it. Rather than risk his newly regained popularity and the opportunity to strengthen his powers, Louis XVI decided, first, to ratify and publish the Civil Constitution (July 22), and then to appeal to Pope Pius VI for his consecration.

Negotiations dragged for several months. After declaring that he was going to examine the decree, the pope later gave clear signs that he would reject it in its then existing form. But the decree, even if revised, would not have been acceptable to him, for it weakened his disciplinary control over the French clergy. Besides, the deputies had no intention of revising the Civil Constitution. On this side, the pope had a political ax to grind. His subjects in the enclave of Avignon and the Comtat-Venaissin were in full revolt and

---

[21] This meant that even Protestants, Jews, and freethinkers might cast their votes in church elections.

demanded annexation to France, invoking in support of their aims that doctrine of popular sovereignty which the pope had secretly condemned. The émigrés and Bernis, the French ambassador at Rome, urged him to reject the decree.

Ecclesiastical Opposition to the Assembly. In the meantime the application of the Civil Constitution was being essayed in France, but with slight success. The cathedral canons continued to officiate. The suppressed bishops kept their jurisdictions. Several bishops and priests died, and the voters elected their successors. Sharp protests were raised. Sporadic violence in some parts of the country and indifferent neglect elsewhere complicated the situation. To end the confusion, to force the clergy to commit themselves for or against the reforms, the Assembly determined to use compulsion. On November 27, 1790, it decided that all the ecclesiastics retained in their functions would be required to take an oath to the as yet unfinished constitution, which meant specifically a pledge to support the Civil Constitution of the Clergy. All those who refused to take the oath would be reputed to have renounced their office and would be replaced by other clerics. If the priests who refused to take the oath continued to exercise their former functions, they would be prosecuted under the law. Otherwise they would be pensioned.

Pope Pius VI continued to play for time, but on December 26, Louis XVI gave his sanction to the decree on the clerical oath. He sanctioned the decree on the advice of Boisgelin, who himself intended to refuse to take the oath. Boisgelin advised the king to give the impression that his acceptance was forced. In that case his conscience would still be clear, for a forced action did not bind it. The general opinion prevailed among the deputies that the great majority of the clergy would take the oath. But that opinion was wholly erroneous. Only seven bishops took the oath, among them Talleyrand, Grégoire, Lomenie de Brienne, and Gobel, the future bishop of Paris. The percentage of lower clergy that took the oath is more difficult to establish, for some took it "with reservations" and others retracted their oath later, when the pope formally condemned the Civil Constitution. According to the most careful estimates, slightly more than fifty per cent of the parish priests and vicars refused to take the oath.

The pope's solemn denunciation of the religious enactments in March and April, 1791, made the situation irremediable. Pius VI condemned not only the Civil Constitution, but also the abolition of the tithes, the suppression of the annates, and all the principles of the Revolution. By this papal action France was cut in two. Over vast stretches of territory force alone could impose the new law. Slowly, the scales fell from the eyes of the deputies. They had tried to create a national church and had succeeded only in creating two churches, one for the adherents of the revolutionary order, the other for the supporters of the ancient scheme of things. The opponents of the Revolution quickly seized the opportunity that presented itself—"to fish in muddy waters," says Madelin. In his forty-third note to the king Mirabeau urged him to push the deputies to measures still more extreme. Here, he thought, was the great chance to discredit the Assembly and put Louis XVI at the head of the revolutionary movement.

The advice was not wholly necessary. At first the Assembly was reluctant to apply the decree about the clerical oath. It allowed many of the refractory clergy to perform their religious functions, in some cases, for almost two years after the acceptance of the decree, and it accorded the dismissed clergy a pension of 500 livres. That conciliatory policy was further strengthened by the slowness with which the new church was organized. Only Talleyrand and Gobel agreed to institute the new bishops into office. Those in turn consecrated others until by April, 1791, sixty new bishops were instituted.

The resistance of the lower clergy and the indignation of the faithful made the conciliatory policy impossible. The dismissed parish priests continued to perform the religious services, while their flocks resented the intrusion of the new clergy. Millions of pious souls still took communion with their "good priests" and followed them into chapels, hospitals, barns, vacant churches. If they addressed themselves to the juring priest for a baptism, or a marriage ceremony, or a burial—for only the new constitutional clergy kept the civil records—they repeated these services secretly with the refractory priest whom they knew and loved. The latter was a martyr for his devout parishioners. He no longer received a salary, his dwelling was taken from him, and the authorities denied him the use of his church, but in spite of these privations he said mass, preached sermons, and administered the sacraments to his flock.

Not infrequently the revolutionary clubs and the National Guard had to be called to install the new parish priests. In some instances the latter also took it upon themselves to break up the services of the nonjuring clergy. Private chapels were raided and sacked; fighting took place in the very sanctuaries. As Easter approached (in 1791) the hostility grew more acute. All available steps were taken to prevent opposition to the religious organization.

The last effort of the Assembly to extend toleration to the dissidents also failed. It decreed on May 7, 1791, following the example already established by Talleyrand for the department of Paris, that the nonjuring clergy could hold services publicly, in full liberty, in any of the suppressed churches. But the disillusioned deputies speedily learned that they could not legislate tolerance into social custom. The decree of toleration was disavowed in practice. The constitutional clergy refused to accept the new ruling. They had risked all, physical danger, the fulminations of the pope, and the freedom of their conscience, in rallying behind the revolutionary law, and they had no intention of submitting quietly to a measure which would make their official services useless. Without the firm support of the administration they could not exist, for their churches would be deserted in favor of the tolerated refractory priests. Secondly, the public authorities refused to apply the decree of toleration on the justifiable ground that the church services of the refractory clergy provoked counterrevolutionary disturbances. To maintain the course of the Revolution, they alleged, both the civil and the religious laws of the state had to be observed, and all those who opposed the law proscribed and prosecuted.

To a large extent the reasoning of the public authorities and the clubs was justified by circumstances, for violence was not entirely on the side of the revolutionary adherents. The constitutional priests had as little safety, or less, in strongholds of the nonjuring clergy as the latter had in those regions where sentiment was hostile to them. Originally and fundamentally a religious protest, the opposition of the faithful Catholics to the impious law gradually became a counter-revolutionary war against the Revolution, a war fomented and led by staunch royalists and "aristocrats" of all shades. "The confessionals [of the refractory clergy]," wrote the departmental authorities of Morbihan, in Brittany, on June 9, 1791, "are schools where rebellion is taught and commanded." The religious laws did more than any other single act of the Constituent Assembly to develop the counter-revolution. They forced the refractory clergy and their millions of followers into the opposition.

THE COUNTER-REVOLUTION AND REVOLUTIONARY EXPANSION

The Counter-Revolutionary Movement. The "October days" had virtually made Louis XVI a prisoner at the Tuileries. The Assembly no longer feared that he would have recourse to troops, but the Left suspected that in all other ways he would employ his personal influence against the Revolution. The aim of the more resolute deputies, therefore, was to defeat that possibility by weakening his executive power. On the other hand Lafayette, whom the events of October had made the dominant political figure in France, endeavored to strengthen the royal prerogative. He knew that the masses regarded him with awe and respect, and he dreamed of becoming the Washington of France and the real power behind the throne. Neither the king nor the queen liked him, but in order to win time for their own plan they pretended to place themselves under Lafayette's tutelage. Louis XVI gave him command of the regular troops in the immediate vicinity of Paris and expressed confidence in his "mayor of the palace." At the same time the monarch addressed a secret communication to his Bourbon relative, Charles IV of Spain, protesting firmly against all the arbitrary actions of the Assembly. "I owe it to myself," he wrote, "to my children, to my family, to my entire house, to combat the degradation of the royal prerogative which long centuries have confirmed in my dynasty."

Lafayette was no tyro at the game of practical politics. He subsidized a political press and made a bid for the support of the revolutionary leaders. The road to Mirabeau's support lay through his ambition and his purse. His ambition was fixed upon a ministerial position and his purse was open for the payment of his enormous debts. The Assembly, which recognized his ability but suspected him because of his shady past, defeated his ambition by its unfortunate decree of November 7, 1789. This measure denied the king the right to select any of his ministers from among the deputies of the Assembly, but it is apparent that the decree aimed primarily at Mirabeau. Thereupon Mirabeau showed himself receptive to various secret intermediaries of Louis XVI, who brought him into closer contact with court circles. Lafayette and Mirabeau were jealous of each other, yet they were in substantial agreement in their policy of strengthening the king's executive powers.

For his part, Louis XVI detested Lafayette and despised Mirabeau. Yet he tried his utmost to bring the two rivals together in order that they might serve his interests. In all likelihood, despite his appeal to Charles IV of Spain, the king had not yet abandoned confidence in legal means of strengthening his executive powers. On February 4, 1790, shortly after the flurry of a madcap royalist intrigue fomented by his brother, the count of Provence, he appeared very unexpectedly before the Assembly. In his speech, which had been prepared by Necker and Lafayette, he disavowed all plots against the revolutionary cause, loyally accepted, both for himself and for his consort, the new regime, and summoned all citizens to follow his example. Sincere as he undoubtedly was, for the moment at least, the king had no control over the course of events. The enemies of the Revolution, the so-called "aristocrats," made capital of the popular impatience with and grievances against the National Assembly. The court party circulated pamphlets in which they stressed the shortcomings of the revolutionaries and endeavored to win over the various groups of malcontents to a reactionary policy. Their spokesmen in the Assembly and their counter-revolutionary press heaped ridicule upon the patriots. Dismissed functionaries, impatient peasants fuming over the legal perpetuation of the feudal land dues, the aggrieved clergy, all were grist for the counter-revolutionary mill.

The first measures of ecclesiastical reform in the fall of 1789 and the spring of 1790 gave the "aristocrats" an opportunity to cloak their counter-revolutionary activities under the veil of religion. As Easter approached in 1790, the secret agents of the émigré count of Artois redoubled their activity. "Easter week," wrote one of Artois's agents, "is the time when the bishops and priests can profitably lead back their errant subjects to the true religion and to the king. I hope that they will appreciate their interests and those of the state sufficiently clearly not to neglect this opportunity; if they work together, success seems certain." In the Assembly several hundred deputies filed a protest against the religious decrees. That protest had no echo in most of France, but in the south of France and in Alsace, it served to unleash the ill restrained jealousy and hatred between the Protestants and the Catholics, for there the various measures of the Assembly were falsely represented as the work of Protestants and infidels. In Alsace, the religious animosities covered a variety of grievances against the revolutionary government. The menace of civil war in Alsace, moreover, was particularly dangerous, for the lay and ecclesiastical princes were appealing to the head of the Holy Roman Empire against revolutionary France. In the south of France (the Midi), religious intolerance went hand in hand with economic rivalries in the cloth and silk trades. Disturbances began in April, 1790, and lasted for several months with great loss of property and life. In a skirmish at Nîmes on June 13, three hundred people were killed, most of whom were Catholics and royalists. In Avignon, which had revolted against the political authority of the pope, there were violent conflicts between the partisans of the old rule and the leaders of the new who wanted to have Avignon incorporated into France.

Louis XVI still sought legal and constitutional ways of regaining his lost prerogatives. He had no part in stirring up the civil war in the Midi and saw in its failure only an added reason to follow Lafayette's instructions. Lafayette, in common with most of the moderate leaders, was frightened by the interminable disorders and was more determined than ever to strengthen the monarch's executive powers. In his comment on a memorandum that Lafayette submitted to him the king wrote (April 16): "I promise Monsieur de Lafayette fullest confidence in all measures concerning the establishment of the Constitution, my legitimate authority . . . and the restoration of public tranquility." At the same time Louis XVI came to full terms with Mirabeau. On May 10 he promised the deputy 200,000 livres for the payment of his pressing debts, 6000 more a month for his expenses, and notes for a million livres payable at the close of the Assembly. Mirabeau's duties were to strengthen the royal authority and advise the king in his conduct. Having already taken money for his services to various individuals, most recently to the duke of Orléans and the count of Provence, Mirabeau found himself in no novel role when he became the secret agent of the crown.[22] His new relations with the court did not constitute treason to the cause of the Revolution. He had never made a secret of his royalist convictions, and he firmly believed that France could have tranquility only under a monarchy, but a monarchy whose king sincerely accepted the achievements of the Revolution. Therefore, in essaying to prevent both a counter-revolution and a more radical orientation of the revolutionary movement, Mirabeau was paid, as Lord Acton says, "to be of his own opinion."

An early opportunity presented itself for the fulfillment of Mirabeau's program in the dispute between England and Spain over control of Nootka Sound and Vancouver Island

---

[22] The nature of Mirabeau's relations with the court is best revealed in the three volumes of *Correspondance entre Mirabeau et le comte de la Marck* (Paris, 1891).

in the Pacific Ocean. The Assembly spent several weeks in May, 1790, debating the question as to whether France was bound by the terms of the Family Compact of 1761 to come to the assistance of Charles IV, the Bourbon ruler of Spain. But the deputies also considered the grave question of the diplomatic powers of Louis XVI; namely, his right to declare war and ratify peace. In these debates the best speakers of the Right and the Left took part; for the former, Maury and Cazalès, as well as Malouet of the Center; for the latter, Duport, Alexandre Lameth, and Barnave. Mirabeau employed all his oratorical skill to aid the cause of Louis XVI, but it proved unavailing. The deputies voted to limit Louis XVI's power over the military forces of the nation and reduced his diplomatic prerogative to conducting negotiations, which were subject to the ratification of the Assembly.

Perhaps if Mirabeau had prevailed in the debates and succeeded in strengthening the executive power of the king, Louis XVI would have been more willing to accept the Revolution. The deputies' vote prevented the outbreak of war between France and England, but it temporarily discredited Mirabeau, especially with the Jacobins of Paris. He made a desperate effort to convince Lafayette that the use of force against the radical deputies was in order, but again he failed. Lafayette guarded his popularity too jealously to risk it in a futile gesture. The Fête de la Fédération was approaching, and he intended to capitalize it for himself. The Fête de la Fédération on July 14, 1790, was, as we have noted, an impressive ceremony which seemed to mark the harmonious unity of all Frenchmen. Lafayette might well have considered it a personal triumph, for he received wild acclaim from the spectators and shone in all his glory. For a brief interlude after July, 1790, there was a lull in the counter-revolutionary movement, but once the enthusiasm of the Fête had died down, the struggle was resumed with even greater vigor. Military dissensions grew sharper, and the religious conflict was aggravated.

Political and Economic Radicalism. "That fête poisoned the spirit of the troops," sorrowfully wrote General Bouillé, meditating over the tumultuous reception received by the regulars and the National Guard *(fédérés)* in Paris on July 14, 1790. It did indeed spread revolutionary sentiment among the troops, but the troops were prepared to receive it. In the six months from January to July, 1790, one could have traced the progressive breakdown of all discipline in the regular army. The more determined aristocrats among the old officers had emigrated; those who remained either maintained a sullen resistance to the democratic current in the troops or else tried to take advantage of the relaxed discipline by heading this opposition. At heart all of them realized their impotence to stop their men from undermining their authority. The regular troops, like the members of National Guard, had taken the oath of allegiance to the nation and were at the disposal of the local government. Like the National Guard the regulars joined the clubs and Masonic lodges. The minister of war realized that the situation was dangerous, but beyond penning eloquent notes to the Assembly, did little to remedy it. The Assembly passed the responsibility of action to the king, recommending the formation of a new army. But an armed Europe gave Louis XVI sufficient cause for hesitation before so vast an undertaking.

Soon mutinies occurred in the principal garrisons of the kingdom, at Toulon, Brest, Strasbourg, and elsewhere. In all the mutinies, Lafayette and the Assembly had tried to steer a middle course, to maintain discipline in the ranks without alienating either the support of the officers or the loyalty of the troops. But Lafayette was a militarist by profession. To support discipline he was not loath to use force. In August, 1790, the garrison troops of Nancy in Lorraine rebelled against their commandant, an action which had the gravest consequences.

The situation at Nancy did not differ from that in any of the other garrison towns. The officers were showered with threats and insults by the zealous patriots, denounced for their aristocratic birth, and hindered in the execution of their commands. The troops were wooed by the revolutionary clubs, and their heads were filled with the intoxicating fumes of the new gospel of equality. They protested against the quality of their rations, demanded that the expense accounts be verified, and not infrequently refused to obey the orders of their superior officers. The officers met those manifestations with the only means at their command, which was military punishment. The Nancy affair got out of hand when the Assembly, under Lafayette's instigation, voted to repress the mutinous troops. In spite of Barnave's opposition, it ordered General Bouillé, Lafayette's cousin and the commander of the Army of the East, stationed at Metz, to march on the rebels at Nancy and suppress the insurrection. He gathered a small army of regular troops and National Guardsmen and cut his way into the city. Some thirty of the rebels were hanged, more than forty condemned to the galleys, and the revolutionary clubs closed. Bouillé's soldiers maintained law and order at the point of the bayonet. At first, the entire country approved of Bouillé's step. The king wrote him a congratulatory letter in which he intimated very plainly that Bouillé's popularity might soon stand the monarchy in good stead. The Assembly and the Jacobins felicitated his National Guard for its vigorous repression of anarchy. The National Guard of the capital held memorial services for the loyal troops that had fallen in the strife. But before three months had passed, the Assembly retracted its praise for Bouillé, and reopened the doors of the Jacobin Club of Nancy. More than ever, during September and October, discipline was relaxed and dissension rife. Lafayette's popularity was waning fast, while Mirabeau was under a cloud; and, despairing of their aid, Louis XVI made ready to appeal to the great powers for intervention.

Precisely at this moment the religious war began in earnest. The schism among the clergy, caused by the enforcement of the Civil Constitution, gave a great impetus to the counter-revolutionary movement. Twenty thousand National Guardsmen, inspired by their attachment to the monarchy and their religion, answered the call of their leaders and marched to the camp of Jalès in the Midi. The cross was their banner. Their leaders, who were counterrevolutionary agents of the émigrés, priests, and nobles, issued a manifesto that "they would not lay down their arms until they had reestablished the king in his glory, the clergy in their estates, the nobility in their prerogatives, and the parlements in their old functions." For six months, the camp remained organized, until the Assembly dissolved it by force. The departments in the Midi were not the only ones to resist the application of the religious laws. The pope's anathema against the entire Revolution stiffened the resistance of the northern departments, of the west (Brittany and the Vendée), and particularly of the east, where the contact with the émigrés and the Germanic states was closest.

To make the situation still more critical, Louis XVI cast his lot with the refractory clergy. As we have noted, he had never sincerely accepted the reforms of the Revolution, and least of all, the ecclesiastical legislation. A year had passed since the October uprising, and all constitutional attempts to increase his powers had failed. In the meantime the new administration had painfully come into being: the municipalities were functioning, the courts were organized, the monastic establishments and the religious chapters were being shut down, and plans for the sale of national land well under way. His self-appointed mentor, Lafayette, was daily losing ground against the sweeping democratic forces of the newspapers and the popular clubs. Soon the sections of Paris (the sixty electoral districts had been replaced by forty-eight sections) forced Louis XVI to dismiss almost his entire ministry and accept a new one of less pronounced royalist views. At that juncture the king was forced to sign the decree on the clerical oath (December 26, 1790), secretly protesting as he did so that he would rather be king in Metz than king of France under such tyranny.[23] The bitter hostility between the juring and the refractory clergy and their respective followers contributed indirectly to the growth of an anticlerical faction. But the more immediate consequence was to accelerate the growth of a democratic and republican movement.

This movement developed outside the Assembly and against the desires of most of the deputies.[24] In its political aspects it was a demand for universal suffrage and for an end to the distinction between active and passive citizens. The centers of political agitation were the club of the Cordeliers (opened in April, 1790) and the fraternal societies in the forty-eight sections of Paris. The petty bourgeoisie led the movement at the Cordeliers, but the passive citizens who made up most of its membership supplied the energy. Petty traders and dealers, artisans, hawkers and criers, journeymen and apprentices, in short the greatest proportion of the Parisian citizenry, attended the meetings of the popular societies. Under the leadership of the Abbé Fauchet and a Freemason journalist, Nicholas de Bonneville, a group of mystic Christian-Socialists met weekly to listen to an exegesis on Rousseau's *Social Contract*. Bonneville preached direct government in his newspaper, the *Bouche de jer* and Marat, in his *Ami du peuple,* seconded the appeal. The radical press launched a republican campaign against the monarchy to which Brissot, the future leader of the Girondins, Danton, Robespierre, and Camille Desmoulins gave guarded support. Sharp reproaches were directed against Lafayette, the deputies of the Right, and the refractory clergy. Somewhat more indirectly, this republican agitation was also preparing the masses to accept the belief that war against kings and aristocrats was the sole means of perpetuating the reforms of the Revolution.

Along with the movement for more radical political reform there developed a movement of social and economic protest against the policy of the Assembly. The peasants had unceasingly manifested their discontent since 1789, but early in 1791 the working-men of Paris recorded their protest against unemployment, rising prices, and the inflation of paper money. There were strikes in the printing establishments and in the building trades. Both groups of malcontents, peasants and artisans, looked to the state for the satisfaction of their grievances. If those who clamored for more sweeping political reform were successful, radical social and economic reform was certain to follow.

This prospect greatly troubled the more moderate bourgeois deputies. Their anxiety over the radical movement was shown in their support of Mirabeau's campaign for social conservatism. Suspected by only a mere handful of deputies Mirabeau engaged upon a campaign of propaganda and bribery that made an art of political corruption. Fully utilizing the court money at his disposal, he bought newspapers, bribed deputies, silenced some republican leaders, and had conservative pamphlets distributed in great profusion. He regained his popularity with the electorate of Paris and his influence with many of his

---

[23] Metz was the headquarters of Bouillé's army.

[24] In the Assembly hall Robespierre pressed his demand for the inclusion of the passive citizens in the National Guard, for he saw that the poorer citizens would greatly strengthen their political influence if they obtained the legal right to bear arms.

colleagues in the Assembly. Even Marie Antoinette regarded him more favorably. But he died on April 2, 1791, his plan unconsummated. His funeral was the occasion for a great ovation to his memory, and his remains were deposited in the Pantheon. All Paris grieved over his untimely death. Perhaps, as many historians have thought, he alone was capable of saving the monarchy, but one may challenge the validity of this view. It is far more likely that Mirabeau's death saved him from the discomfiture and chagrin of seeing the pressure of events defeat his plan. His desperate expedient of provoking extreme, radical utterances in order that these might discredit the Assembly was not likely to succeed. Contrary to his advice Louis XVI had already made up his mind to flee toward the eastern frontier. Mirabeau's scheme contained no fundamental remedy to allay the discontent of the radical extremists or to placate the grievances of the disgruntled conservatives. His death helped make his reputation for statesmanship; but more immediately it gave various other deputies an opportunity to lead the debates.

For the next few months the apprehensive Assembly tried to throw back the wave of radical proposals. The deputies extended toleration to the refractory clergy and passed or attempted to pass measures against the democrats, such as the continued exclusion of passive citizens from the National Guard, prohibition of collective petitions, and the expulsion of the Cordeliers from their meeting place. In measure as Robespierre gained recognition as the defender of the poor, so Barnave stood out as the champion of the propertied class which had carried through the Revolution. In May, 1791, Barnave suffered a reverse by losing a long debate with Robespierre over the question of granting the vote to the colored population of Santo Domingo. The decision to grant the franchise to the mulattoes which ultimately brought on chaos in the French part of the island was a triumph of theory over fact, of idealism over expediency. Its immediate consequences were to strengthen the resolution of the moderates like Barnave to keep the revolutionary movement within bounds.

Shortly after this debate, while the reporter of the constitutional committee was discussing the organization of the next legislature, Robespierre made a motion which filled his opponents with joy. He proposed, and the Assembly decreed, that the members of the present Assembly should not be eligible to the next. Robespierre and the democratic deputies believed that they were saving the coming legislature from the continued presence of the obstructive deputies of the Right; the moderates and conservatives were delighted to save the coming legislature from the continued presence of the deputies who proposed to give a more radical turn to the Revolution. Wise and disinterested, Robespierre's motion assuredly was not. While it brought him added renown, the democrats claimed a triumph over the deputies of the Right. The greatest blow to the latter was the dramatic flight of Louis XVI. On June 20, the king and the royal family fled from Paris toward the eastern frontier. Were the sovereigns of Europe ready to intercede in his behalf?

Revolutionary Propaganda and International Problems. At first the liberals of Europe had given an enthusiastic welcome to the French Revolution. Liberal Europe was greatly interested in French affairs, for French philosophical ideas and the analogous doctrines of the German *Aufklärung* had spread over a large part of the Continent. French was still the universal language in Europe, and French civilization still maintained its hegemony on the Continent. From the reports of tourists and more or less permanent residents in France as well as from the information given out by Frenchmen living abroad, the different countries of Europe knew that the judicial aristocracy of France had led the struggle against irresponsible despotism. The fall of the Bastille was at first unwittingly represented in Europe as the work of that aristocracy. Hence an additional reason for the universal approbation that greeted that memorable event. But the disorders in the country districts and the attacks upon the chateaux rapidly disillusioned most European sympathizers.

Gradually the sovereigns of Europe began to realize the danger of the revolutionary movement. This danger lay in the extension of its universal principles, in particular of the Declaration of Rights, beyond the French frontiers and in the possibility that certain national groups might attempt to apply those same principles. In fact those revolutionary principles were extended beyond France through the conscious and unconscious propaganda of enthusiastic Frenchmen and equally enthusiastic nationalists of other European countries. The numerous Frenchmen resident in various cities of Europe, tourists, business men, political refugees, liberal supporters of the French movement who flocked to France from all corners of Europe, all served as agents for the spread of the revolutionary gospel. The "pilgrims of liberty," as the first foreign visitors who came to Paris were called, joined in the political debates of the Assembly. The political refugees from Holland, Switzerland, and Belgium formed clubs for the purpose of bringing on a revolutionary movement in their native lands. The Freemasons of France helped spread revolutionary propaganda into Savoy and the Rhineland.

The revolutionary propaganda was a failure in eastern and southern Europe. Russia and Hungary were protected against the revolutionary infection by their distance from France. In these countries isolated individuals declared themselves partisans of the French, but they had no influence over the masses. In Italy, support of French reforms was slight and superficial, while it was almost nonexistent in Spain and Portugal.

The propaganda was much more effective in England and the Germanies, where the intellectual movement before the Revolution had prepared the liberals. From the point of view of the French, England and the Germanies were of strategic importance. As neighbors of France they could crush the extension of the Revolution by their hostility, while by their support or neutrality they could allow it to develop. Many illustrious Germans hailed the first conquests of the Revolution. It found a supporter in Herder, the chief exponent of German nationalism. The poet Klopstock, the philosophers, Kant, Fichte, and Humboldt, as well as other publicists and professors, approved of the early events. The bourgeoisie of several cities also responded favorably to the news from France, while the peasantry along the Rhineland followed the example of their French neighbors by refusing to pay feudal dues and partaking in violent riots against their landlords.

The bishopric of Liege also responded to the contagious influence of French disturbances. There was a demand for the curtailment of the privileges of the bishop, who fled to Treves at the first visible signs of reform. The peasantry and the artisans joined the revolutionary movement, while the more moderate elements appealed to Prussia, which sent in troops to maintain order. A second revolution took place in the Austrian Netherlands in 1789, the first one having been suppressed in 1788. Here too the inspiration came from France, and the leaders were returned refugees who had been living in France. The returning refugees gained popular support, roused the country, and expelled the Austrian troops from Brussels in December, 1789. The German-speaking cantons of Switzerland were also affected, largely because of their nearness to Alsace, while next door to the Swiss cantons the revolutionary propaganda was effectively spread in Savoy. There were no violent disturbances in England because the response to the Revolution came from the intellectuals rather than from the masses. Fox, Sheridan, and

Bentham were among its first defenders. Pitt also viewed the early events with satisfaction and thought that the overthrow of the Old Regime would be followed by the establishment of an orderly constitutional monarchy. With the French government occupied with the Revolution, he hoped for a period of peace in Europe and an opportunity to reduce taxes at home and introduce the reforms that had long been proposed. The most active apologists of the French Revolution in England were the dissenters and nonconformists, who hoped to utilize the attack upon arbitrary government and privilege in France to gain fuller religious rights in their own country as well as to further the cause of parliamentary reform. They formed new societies or revived old ones and entered into correspondence with the French revolutionary clubs, particularly with the Jacobins of Paris. The most famous of these societies was the Revolution Society of 1688, which sent a congratulatory address to the National Constituent Assembly in 1789 and celebrated the first anniversary of the fall of the Bastille in 1790.

The fatal weakness of the revolutionary propaganda was that it aroused an intellectual reaction in the countries that it penetrated. The summer and autumn disturbances in France during 1789 frightened the faint-hearted supporters in England and the Germanies. The French émigrés aggravated the fears of the timorous. They established themselves wherever a relative or a protector agreed to receive them—at Turin, at Rome, at Koblenz, Worms, and elsewhere on the Continent. They were most numerous on the Rhineland, where the prince of Condé had collected a small army at Worms in the domains of the elector of Treves. Though they were not popular because their mode of life was, or seemed, scandalous to their more sedate hosts, they made a deep impression with their exaggerated accounts of atrocities and their insistence that all the evils in France resulted from the work of a handful of scoundrels. The failure of the revolt in the Austrian Netherlands also turned sentiment against the French. The revolutionists fell out after their expulsion of the Austrian troops in December, 1789, and became involved in strife between the landed interests and the clerical group on the one hand and the democratic element on the other. An effort to form a federal republic was defeated, and the irreconcilable social and religious differences among the inhabitants brought on a violent struggle which ended with the victory of the privileged classes, the flight of the democrats, and the discrediting of the entire movement because of its attendant violence and bloodshed.

The liberals of Germany still professed their allegiance to the principles of the Revolution, but with many reservations and restrictions. They became more discriminating and less frequent in their praise. Moreover, the loose political confederation and the old local traditions and regional activities in the German-speaking countries greatly weakened the force of the French appeal. Revolutionary propaganda made only slight headway east of the Rhine. The hostile reaction developed most sharply in the countries subject to the influence of the Catholic Church. Bavaria, Sardinia, the states of Italy, Spain, and Portugal took careful precautions against secret societies, revolutionary propagandists, and the communication of revolutionary ideas and ideals. In March, 1791, a cordon of troops was stretched along the Pyrenees to ward off "the French pestilence."

England did not escape the reaction. Anglican churchmen and landed proprietors led the van in denouncing what they regarded, justly or otherwise, as atrocities across the Channel. The most eloquent and the most influential of the critics was Edmund Burke, whose famous *Reflections on the Revolution in France* created a sensation upon its publication in November, 1790. Its effect upon public opinion both in England and on the Continent was marked, though one of the unforeseen consequences of its publication was the barrage of angry rejoinders that it drew from capable pens. The Rejections is important also because it was the first methodical indictment of the basic natural rights philosophy of the French Revolution, as well as an impassioned statement of the conservative position. For the natural rights of man of the eighteenth century thinkers Burke substituted the historic rights of nations. He believed—and his views were followed by many nineteenth century of inculcating civic morality and respect for political liberty; that such necessary political virtues could arise only from the interplay of established interests. But his criticism of the deeds of the Constituent Assembly and the French people was unfair, because it was grounded upon insufficient information and inadequate understanding of conditions in France both before and after 1789. Among the many replies provoked by his book, the most outstanding were the polished *Vindiciae Gallicae* of the Scot, Sir James Mackintosh, and the blunt, stirring *Rights of Man* of Thomas Paine. The first part of the latter work appeared in 1791 in a cheap edition, and its large sale had much to do with the new interest of the English lower middle classes in the French Revolution.

The political effects of Burke's rhetorical denunciation of the French experiment and his eloquent defense of British institutions and tradition were the strengthening of the Tory majority in Parliament and the weakening of the efforts for parliamentary reform and the abolition of the Test Act. The Whigs split into two factions, the more numerous led by Burke, the other by his old friend and political disciple, Charles James Fox. The governing classes were beginning to show such horror of reform that every effort to carry through the schemes which William Pitt himself had advanced somewhat earlier was regarded askance. The masses followed Burke and William Pitt, whose appeal to history aroused their British patriotism. The parliamentary following of Fox was so slight that it has been called the "weakest and most discredited opposition" that England had ever known. For a full generation England labored under the dread of political and social change, and no improvement was to be recorded until after the Napoleonic period. "Philosophical radicals" like Jeremy Bentham, Joseph Priestley, or William Cobbett (only after 1806) might express their sympathy with some of the revolutionary ideas, but, for all the influence that these ideas exercised upon British institutions from 1789 to 1815, the Revolution might never have taken place. Burke himself advocated an armed crusade, after first proposing that the English government should establish a pacific blockade against the French revolutionary propaganda. The pope's formal anathema against the Revolution in the spring of 1791 gave added force to Burke's proposal against the "French barbarians."

The Assembly was anxious to avert war with the great powers, and on May 22, 1790, the deputies voted the pacifistic decree by which France renounced all wars of conquest and promised to refrain from using her troops against the liberty of other peoples. Mirabeau protested bitterly that that decree forced "France to disarm before a Europe still in arms," but it kept the peace. Soon, however, there arose between revolutionary France and the European sovereigns problems involving questions of territory and basic conceptions of international law.

As early as September, 1789, the German princes in Alsace sent protests to the head of the Holy Roman Empire against the feudal decrees, the abolition of foreign ecclesiastical jurisdiction within France, and the abolition of the tithes. Later they protested against the confiscation of the ecclesiastical estates. Legally their various rights had been secured to them by international treaties (Münster and Ryswick) and by separate agreements with the French kingdom; but on the other hand it would have been difficult for the National Constituent Assembly to treat princely rights in Alsace (which was part of political France) differently from, or more leniently than, the rights of other privileged individuals within France. While the Assembly denied the legal claims of the German princes, among whom were the electors of Treves, Mainz, and Cologne, the bishop of Basel, the duke of Wirtemberg, and the margrave of Baden, it offered them a money indemnity which the princes refused. The Assembly finally took the position, in November, 1790, that Alsace was French, not by virtue of the treaty of Westphalia (1648), but because the Alsatians felt that they were French and desired union with the French. The dispute hinged on even more vital considerations for the German princes than their rights under international law, for the immediate question as to the effect of the revolutionary reforms in Alsace upon their own neighboring states was involved. The princes demanded that the empire reassert its full rights over Alsace, claiming that France had forfeited its sovereignty of that province by ignoring the reservations made in the treaties concerning Alsace. In December, 1790, Emperor Leopold II supported their claims in a sharp note to the French government which went unheeded.

The papacy too had cause for complaint against the Assembly. Ever since the fourteenth century Avignon and the Comtat-Venaissin had been under the temporal rule of the popes, forming a little papal state within France; but in June, 1790, the more radical inhabitants of Avignon rebelled, expelled the papal legate, and demanded annexation to France. Would revolutionary France accept the invitation, particularly after its decree of the preceding month solemnly renouncing wars of conquest? The deputies of the Left, with Robespierre as spokesman, insisted that that decree allowed the nation, rather than the political ruler, to decide its destiny. Hence the annexation of Avignon would not be conquest, but the satisfaction of the expressed desires of its inhabitants. Slowly the Assembly allowed itself to be convinced. In April, 1791, its diplomatic committee reported that Avignon belonged by right to France and advised its incorporation with France, with an indemnity to the pope. The proposal was rejected, and Avignon was left for months to the warring factions within its territory. By September of the same year, however, Avignon was formally annexed to France. Thus a new principle of international law, was adopted, the application of the democratic doctrine of popular sovereignty in the field of international relations. To the great powers, France's action ruptured all existing diplomatic bonds between the Revolution and Europe. It seemed as though France gave herself the right to annex, peacefully, any state that desired a revolution against its sovereign. In the words of Gaxotte, a historian hostile to the Revolution, "Instead of being an incident of internal French politics the Revolution was going to become a cosmopolitan venture, a universal religion threatening not only the form but the very existence of all states."

Projects of Intervention and the Flight of the King. If the monarchs of Europe did not then unite in a crusade against France, it was because they thought France too weak to carry out her pretensions. Her military forces were of no moment, her finances were in disorder, and her government had broken her alliances with Spain and Austria. The renunciation of all wars of conquest, the refusal to aid the Belgian revolutionists, the evident desire to defer decisive action on Alsace and Avignon, all pointed to France's helplessness. The Austrian alliance was broken in fact "not in name, and the Family Compact with Spain had been severed by the Assembly in May, 1790, when the deputies failed to come to the aid of Spain against England in the Nootka Sound controversy. France "was destroying herself," wrote Mercy-Argenteau, the Austrian ambassador.

Both Louis XVI and the émigrés appealed to the powers to intervene, the former secretly and the latter openly. To arouse Europe against the Revolution became the sacred duty of these embittered crusaders who had voluntarily exiled themselves from their native land. From Turin, which he made his headquarters, the count of Artois sent emissaries to Rome and Madrid to win support for his intrigues in southern France. Calonne, now the leading spirit among the émigrés in the Rhineland, hoped to use Condé's supporters at Koblenz as the spearhead of a Prussian army of intervention. Needless to say, the émigrés were of dubious value to Louis XVI; the royal princes were less concerned with him than with a counter-revolution which would benefit them. Breteuil, the secret agent of Louis XVI, warned the Emperor Leopold II against the count of Artois, and Louis XVI and Marie Antoinette disavowed the latter's schemes.

The émigrés stopped at nothing short of the entry of foreign troops into France and a full restoration of the Old Regime. Louis XVI, on the contrary, wanted the intervention to end with a military demonstration at the frontier. His object was to intimidate the revolutionists with the spectacle of the powers of Europe united against them. He had no desire to become the prisoner of Artois or any other émigré leader. Even before the passage of the decree of the Civil Constitution of the Clergy he had already appealed for assistance at the courts of Madrid and Vienna. The ecclesiastical legislation strengthened his early decision; it did not determine his action. In October, 1790, Louis XVI commissioned Breteuil to take full measures leading to the kind of intervention that he had in mind. Bouillé, the loyal general who had quelled the Nancy insurrection, received word to hold his troops in Lorraine in readiness for action, while Count Fersen, the secret lover of Marie Antoinette, began to draw up careful plans for the flight of the royal family. The traditions of the seventeenth and eighteenth centuries supported intervention. Louis XVI considered himself the incarnation of the state and felt free to use whatever means he deemed best to protect the state against its enemies. The émigré nobles, in the spirit of vassals rallying to the support of their overlord, gave their loyalty to the *prince,* not to the nation. Hence they did not think of themselves as betraying or deserting their country, but as defending the rightful ruler against his rebellious subjects.

As late as the summer of 1791 the sovereigns of Europe were not prepared to listen to appeals for intervention. The dynastic rivalries of the great European powers which had in part precipitated the interminable wars of the eighteenth century were still acute during the early years of the French Revolution. Not until Austria and Prussia began to compose their differences (at the Congress of Reichenbach in July, 1790), not until Austria concluded peace with the Ottoman Empire while Russia was concluding peace both with the Ottoman Empire and with Sweden, was there any possibility of a European intervention in French affairs. Even then the governments of Austria and Prussia paid as much attention to the situation in Poland, where Catherine the Great of Russia was planning a second partition, as they did to the French Revolution.

The monarch most eager to intervene in behalf of Louis XVI and the émigrés was the Hohenzollern prince Frederick William II, the sorry successor of Frederick the Great on the throne of Prussia (1786-1797). But his conditions were that Austria join Prussia and that he receive territorial compensation on the Rhine for the expenses of intervention, while Austria was to seek compensation in Alsace and Lorraine. The emperor Leopold II (the brother of Marie Antoinette) still hesitated, despite the fact that the settlement of his domestic and foreign affairs now permitted him to intervene in France. Perhaps his earlier experience as an enlightened despot in Tuscany made him less hostile than other rulers to the course of events in France. As late as the spring of 1791, he still turned a deaf ear to Frederick William II, to Artois, and to Breteuil, the accredited representative of Louis XVI, and to the repeated appeals of Marie Antoinette. Catherine urged him on, but he knew that she "was racking her brains" to divert Austria from Poland. Then, more or less abruptly, he agreed to consider the Prussian proposal of intervention. He had received a letter from Marie Antoinette in which his sister announced the imminent flight of the royal family to the eastern frontier of France. At a secret conference held at Mantua, May 20, 1791, Austria, Prussia, several secondary German states, and Spain reached a general agreement to come to the aid of the Bourbons in France.

Secret preparations for the escape from Paris had been going on since December, 1790. Various incidents connected with these preparations led not a few revolutionists to suspect that mischievous plans were afoot, but nothing definite was known. The Assembly took its precautions against the rumored flight. Louis XVI gave credence to the rumors by preparing to spend the Easter season (1791) at Saint-Cloud, outside of Paris, but the National Guard and a large crowd of Parisians stopped his carriages in the courtyard of the palace, and the royal family was obliged to reenter the Tuileries. This incident is still shrouded in some mystery. Louis may have been sincere in his desire to escape the services of the constitutional clergy and take communion with a nonjuring priest at Saint-Cloud, but Lafayette alleges in his memoirs that the entire affair had been arranged in advance so as to enable the king to prove to Europe that he was a prisoner in his own palace. The crowd, at any rate, was convinced that, once the royal family reached Saint-Cloud, it would continue directly to the frontier.

After this affront Louis XVI and Marie Antoinette were more determined than ever to escape from Paris. In order to gain time for the fruition of his plan the king tried to quiet public suspicion by agreeing to the proposals of the Assembly. He consented to hear mass said by a constitutional priest. Requested to address a circular letter to the French embassies on the Continent, he obeyed, stating in the letter that he was perfectly free and had accepted the revolutionary program without any reservations. But he also took the secret precaution of instructing Breteuil to disavow all his public utterances. Count Fersen completed the preparations for flight by June 20, and that night the royal family made its escape from the palace. The objective was Montmedy, a small town near the Luxemburg frontier. General Bouillé, whose troops could be counted on, was to send cavalry detachments from Metz along the road toward Paris in order to convey the refugees to the frontier. Suspicion was to be averted by explaining to the local inhabitants that a consignment of great value was en route from Paris which required the protection of Bouillé's regiments.

The count of Provence left by another route and reached the Austrian Netherlands without any trouble. But the royal family was less fortunate. Valuable time was lost in starting and there were further delays on the road. The fugitives made such slow progress, and the presence of the royal troops aroused such suspicion that Bouillé's officers decided not to wait any longer and led their men away from the main road. Though the king was recognized at several points of the journey, the only person who dared give the alarm was Drouet, the postmaster at Sainte-Menehould. When the heavy traveling carriage reached Varennes, it was delayed again to wait for the relay of post horses. Meanwhile Drouet had galloped through the Lorraine woods from Sainte-Menehould to Varennes and given the alarm. The road was barricaded, and the authorities arrested the entire party. Louis XVI acknowledged his identity and was detained to await orders from Paris. Early the next morning (June 22) couriers arrived from Paris, bearing the Assembly's orders to seize the monarch. The return trip to Paris was tragic. Hooting, menacing crowds blocked the road and threatened the royal family with violence. Midway, Barnave, Petion, and Latour-Maubourg, the three deputies whom the Assembly had sent out to escort the king to Paris, met the royal carriage. On the 24th of June the convoy passed through the silent streets of Paris. The silence was ominous, and the soldiers guarded the streets of the capital. With marked relief the royal couple heard the grilled gate of the Tuileries swing shut behind them.

Appendix E: Kates, "Introduction" to *The French Revolution: Recent Debates and New Controversies*

Kates, Gary. "Introduction".in *The French Revolution: Recent Debates and New Controversies* (London, 1998), pages 1-20

"What? You have something *new* to say about the French Revolution?"

That was the reaction of one of my graduate school professors when he heard that I intended to write a doctoral dissertation on the French Revolution. Indeed, it is a sensible reaction. After all, whole forests have been cleared to make way for the historical literature on the French Revolution, as a trip to any decent college library will demonstrate. There, the casual stroller will discover stacks and stacks of books on every conceivable topic. Perhaps no other even in history has attracted so much attention.

Much of the problem with studying the French Revolution involves sorting through what others have said about it. Ever since Edmund burke and Thomas Paine first argued about the Revolution's meaning, the debate on it has seemed almost as interesting as the event itself. That debate, of course, has spilled over into neighboring disciplines: political scientists, philosophers, sociologists, literary critics, and art historians have all given the French Revolution prominent weight in their fields. The French Revolution is perhaps the closest thing historians have developed to a litmus test: one's stance on the French Revolution inevitable reveals much about one's deepest ideological and political convictions.

This book deals only with a small, but significant, part of that debate: the quarrels that have captivated professional historians since the Revolution's 1989 bicentennial celebration. After all, since historians devote their entire careers to developing an expertise by way of its archives and bibliographies, they are perhaps in the best position to comment on the Revolution's significance and meaning.

The study of the French Revolution by professional historians (as opposed to philosophers, writers, or journalists) is hardly a century old, barely half the temporal distance from the Revolution itself. It began with the Centennial celebration of 1889, when the Paris City Council awarded its first chair of History of the French Revolution at the Sorbonne to Alphonse Aulard (1849–1928). Since then, the holder of this chair has been acknowledged as the dean of French Revolutionary studies.

Aulard's writings promoted democratic republicanism buttressing left-wing political parties of the Third Republic. Aulard had no sympathy for the monarchy. In his view, the despotic abuses of the Ancien régime justified the violent uprising of 1789. Aulard admired the courage of the Constituent Assembly deputies, but in the end, he thought that they sheepishly balked from confronting a recalcitrant king and a treasonous queen. The Constitution of 1791, a flawed document in Aulard's eyes that allowed the monarchy too much power, was weakened by the king's flight to Varennes in June 1791. The courage of Georges Danton and the other Paris militant activists pushed the Revolution beyond the halfway point. Aulard praised their efforts which culminated in the insurrection of 10

August 1792 and the declaration of France's first democratic republic based upon universal male suffrage. For Aulard, the establishment of a republic under the National Convention marked the zenith of the Revolution.[1]

After World War I, Aulard was challenged by his most gifted student, Albert Mathiez (1874-1932). Influenced both by the recent victory of Bolshevism in Russia, as well as by the awesome legacy of French socialist leader Jean Jaurès (himself an important historian of the Revolution), Mathiez rejected Aulard's beloved Danton as a corrupt bourgeois politician and, instead, defended wholeheartedly Robespierre's efforts to save France through the Terror. Mathiez's Marxism was pragmatic; but his defense of the Terror was nonetheless passionate and had great influence upon a generation of historians from Europe and the United States. In perhaps his most brilliant book, *La vie chère et le movement social sous la terreur* (The Cost of Living and Popular Movements During the Terror [1927]), Mathiez argued that the cost of living for ordinary Parisians improved more during the Terror than at any other time. In Mathiez's view, Robespierre was not a dictator hungry for arbitrary power, but a democratic politician responding to popular pressures from Parisian workers. Unfortunately, the gains of those sans-culottes were temporary; and, while the Revolution counted on their support, its bourgeois leaders turned against Robespierre and renounced the sans-culottes participation and demands.[2]

Mathiez's influence was especially great because of the Société des Etudes Robespierristes (Society of Robespierrist Studies), the organization he founded that published documentary collections, books, and most importantly, the scholarly journal *Annales historiques de la revolution française.* By Mathiez's early death in 1932, the *Annales* had established itself as the premier journal of record for French Revolutionary historiography. Mathiez's successors closely followed the master: Georges Lefebvre (1874-1959), Albert Soboul (1914-82), and Michel Vovelle (b. 1933) all combined the Sorbonne's Chair of the History of the Revolution, and the editorship of the *Annales historiques,* with a commitment to Marxism usually demonstrated by membership in the French Communist Party. Consequently, in the century since the founding of Aulard's Sorbonne chair, the academy of French Revolutionary scholars has been dominated by left-wing socialists committed to a particular way of seeing the Revolution and to a special set of contemporary political values.

As it solidified into its own sort of orthodoxy, this Marxist interpretation could be summarized in the following manner: the French Revolution was not simply a political struggle from (evil) absolute monarchy to (good) democratic republicanism, but represented a deeper shift from feudalism to capitalism. The Revolution was led by an alliance between bourgeois élite (owners of liquid capital), and popular classes (artisans and peasants), against the landowning nobility. The greatest success of such an alliance occurred in 1789, but after that it began to show signs of strains. By the summer of 1791, revolutionary events were marked by class conflict between the capitalist bourgeoisie and the popular classes. This struggle produced an urban political movement led by the sans-culottes, whose vision of a truly social revolution influenced nineteenth-century radicalism. The Terror represented the pinnacle of the sans-culottes movement in which the Jacobins established (albeit temporarily) the first modern democracy in a major

---

[1] Paul Farmer, *France Reviews Its Revolutionary Origins: Social Politics and Historical Opinion in the Third Republic* (New York, 1944), pp. 61-6; James L. Godrey, "Alphonse Aulard," *Some Historians of Modern Europe,* ed. Bernadotte E. Schmitt (Chicago, 1942), pp. 45-65.
[2] James Friguglietti, *Albert Mathiez, historien révolutionnaire* (Paris, 1974).

European state. Thus the French Revolution was essentially a class struggle in which one class was destroyed (the nobility), one class was awakened (the sans-culottes), and one class won control of the state (the bourgeoisie).

In England and the United States, there was less of a commitment to Marxism among French Revolutionary scholars. Historians such as J.M. Thompson (1878-1956) or Louis Gottschalk (1899-1975) were not known for their political activism or party labels. Still, it is remarkable how easily a watered-down version of French Marxism spread throughout Anglo-American college texts between 1930 and 1970. Just as Gottschalk championed Mathiez's work in the 1930s, so R.R. Palmer (1909-) translated Lefebvre's most accessible book into English shortly after World War II.[3]

To be sure, there were some important differences between the Anglo-Americans and the French. During the 1930s, for example, Harvard historian Crane Brinton (1898-1968) adopted a skeptical position in his influential *Anatomy of Revolution*. In his view, the French Revolution was achieved by "moderates" who bravely fought the forces of the Ancien régime, and busily tried to construct a regime based upon the noble virtues of liberty and equality. Such "moderates" were unable to halt the Revolution's surge toward war and anarchy, and the result was "the accession of the extremists," whereby freedom turned sour. Thrown off course by Danton, Robespierre, and the Jacobins, the Revolution toppled from liberty to tyranny.[4]

Outside of the historical academy there was a rich tradition stemming from Edmund Burke that viewed the Revolution itself as wholly unnecessary and, in fact, counterproductive for the establishment of liberty. Among scholars, their voices were isolated and ignored.

But no longer. During the past twenty-five years, there has been a transformation of enormous magnitude in the scholarship on the French Revolution. This change—one is tempted to call it a revolution—has been marked by the almost total collapse of the orthodox Marxist interpretation, and a range of sharp attacks on virtually all of its major points and approaches. The broad teachings of Mathiez, Lefebvre, and Soboul are today, even in France, discredited. Considering how monolithic orthodox Marxist interpretations of the Revolution had become since the 1920s, some sort of challenge within academia was inevitable—but if the attached was expected, the complete collapse of the Marxist paradigm was a surprise.

Alfred Cobban (1901-68), a distinguished professor at the University of London, deserved credit for breaking the first window (if not throwing the first stone) in the Marxist house. During a 1954 lecture, Cobban questioned whether the Revolution was led by a rising bourgeoisie. Analyzing those leaders of the Third Estate who opposed the king and aristocracy in the Estates-General, Cobban noted that only 13 per cent were merchants, manufacturers, or financiers. This revolution was not, in fact, made by a capitalist bourgeoisie. Rather, Cobban argued that the greatest number of leaders came

---

[3] Georges Lefebvre, *The Coming of the French Revolution,* trans. R.R. Palmer (Princeton, 1947). Because of his popular college text, *A History of the Modern World,* Palmer is probably the most influential historian of the French Revolution. Palmer's highly sympathetic view of the Terror is presented in *Twelve Who Rules: The Year of the Terror in the French Revolution* (Princeton, 1941).

[4] Crane Brinton, *The Anatomy of Revolution* (New York, 1965 [originally published 1938]).

from the ranks of local, petty public officials—administrators, prosecutors, judges, and the like—hardly capitalists, and hardly people who had no connection to the Ancien régime. Cobban agreed with the Marxists that the French Revolution was a social revolution, but it was one of "notables" no of capitalists.[5]

Beyond Cobban's graduate students, few colleagues paid much attention to his insights until his research was reworked into a book in 1964. By that time, his efforts were helped greatly by George Taylor of the University of North Carolina, whose important articles in mainstream journals added much empirical ammunition to the revisionist stockpile. Just as Cobban had robbed the Revolution of angry revolutionary bourgeoisie, Taylor demonstrated how the investment patterns by bourgeois and noble families were remarkably similar.[6] By the 1970s, when Colin Lucas published his now-classic article reprinted in this volume, the Revisionist school had become an entrenched minority among French Revolutionary scholars.

No matter what is written about the French Revolution in England or the United States, it is really only France that counts. Revisionists would thus remain an iconoclastic minority until they could mount a beachhead in France. That occurred dramatically with the 1978 publication of François Furet's *Penser la Révolution française* (translated into English as *Interpreting the French Revolution*). Despite its turgid prose, the absence of new archival material, and an idiosyncratic structure, no other book has shaped the research agenda for French Revolutionary scholarship in the 1980s and 1990s more than this one.[7]

Furet (1927-1997) attached the Marxist "catechisme," but he did much more than translate Cobbanite Revisionism for a French audience. Until Furet's book, most Revisionist attacks had come from social and economic historians who disputed the Marxist version of class struggle. Furet, on the other hand, hoped to restore "to the French Revolution its most obvious dimension, the political one, and of focusing attention … in the ways of legitimating and representing historical action."[8] In Furet's hands, this meant a return to political theory and intellectual history. By studying more carefully the meaning of revolutionary rhetoric, historians could recapture the profound ideological change that occurred in how Frenchmen thought about politics. Furet ignited new interest in the cultural history of the Revolution, which had diminished into an isolated corner by the mid-1970s. Almost overnight that oldest of problems—the relationship of the Enlightenment to the French Revolution—was resurrected into a burning issue for debate and controversy.

Furet argued that advanced democratic ideas of certain Enlightened philosophers such as Jean-Jacques Rousseau became the heart and soul of the French Revolution. Democracy here did not mean governing by consent, or even respecting individual human rights. Rather, wrote Furet, the Revolution embraced a radical ideology of popular sovereignty so that any abuse of power could be excused so long as it was achieved in the name of *the*

---

[5] *The Social Interpretation of the French Revolution* (Cambridge, 1964). The 1954 lecture was reprinted in Cobban's *Aspects of the French Revolution* (New York, 1970), pp. 90-111.

[6] George V. Taylor, "Types of Capitalism in Eighteenth-Century France," *English Historical Review 79* (1964): 478-97; "Noncapitalist Wealth and the Origins of the French Revolution," *American Historical review 72* (1967): 469-96.

[7] François Furet, *Interpreting the French Revolution,* trans. Elborg Forster (Cambridge, 1981).

[8] *Ibid.*, p. 27.

people. In short, democracy meant the power of a national state to defeat those who opposed its will. Consequently, Furet argued that the trajectory of the Revolution from its first day was toward the state using democratic ideology to rule in a despotic manner: that is, without regard for human rights. That process culminated, of course, in the Terror, which was the pinnacle of revolutionary democracy and dictatorship.

Just as Furet interpreted the early years of the Revolution as a kind of prologue to the Terror, so he viewed the Napoleonic Empire as its epilogue. Napoleon did not so much turn against the Revolution as consolidate its radical principles. Like the Jacobins of the Year II, Napoleon abused the rights of the people while acting in their name, and he continued the Revolution's bent towards administrative unity and political centralization. While he led the army to new glories, the campaigns he waged and the armies he championed had their roots in the war begun by the Jacobins in 1792 and 1793. For Furet, the Empire was but a late state of the Revolution, with few fundamental differences.

Furet's attitude towards the revolutionary era is profoundly conservative. France becoming a democracy did not mean that its people became free: it meant that the collection French People was sovereign, and that each individual was subservient to it. Politicians who thought of themselves as democratic claimed to speak in the name of the whole people. Dissent was at best distrusted, since it could lead to factional strife that undermined unity. For Furet, the Terror was not an accidental phase of the Revolution but, rather, emblematic of the entire Revolution. Unlike Crane Brinton, who believed that circumstances had thrown the Revolution off course after a moderate phase filled with notable achievements, Furet argued that the Revolution was radical from the state, and its early achievements were only a mirage.

During the 1980s, as the bicentennial celebration approached, Furet followed up this suggestive essay with a series of more solid historical works. Many of them were joint projects from conferences and colloquiums, where he and his allies presented their approach to the Revolution in a more comprehensive but rarely systematic fashion. By 1989 Furet had become arguably the most important historian in the world of the French Revolution.[9]

Furet's ascendancy not only furthered the demise of Marxist historiography but also gave greater visibility in France to Anglo-American scholarship. Furet is perhaps the first major historian of the French Revolution to speak fluent English—and, given his unabashed admiration for the United State, he also enjoys speaking it at every opportunity. Furet is also perhaps the first to accept a permanent appointment at an

---

[9] For his most concisely doctrinaire statement see the introduction to *Les Orateurs de la revolution française, tome 1: Les Constituents,* ed. François Furet and Ran Halevi (Paris, 1989). See also *L'Héritage de la revolution française,* ed. François Furet (Paris, 1989); *Terminer la revolution: Mounier et Barnave dans la révolution,* ed. François Furet and Mona Ozouf (Paris, 1991); *Le siècle de l'avènement républicain,* ed. François Furet and Mona Ozouf (Paris, 1993); *Dictionnaire critique de la révolution française,* ed. François Furet and Mona Ozouf (Paris, 1988; English trans. Arthur Goldhammer, Cambridge, MA., 1989); François Furet, *Le Révolution* (Paris, 1988; trans. Antonia Nevill, Oxford, 1992 as *Revolutionary France 1770-1880).* See also the series of conference proceedings organized by Keith Baker, Colin Lucas, and Furet, *The French Revolution and the Creation of Modern Political Culture,* 4 vols (Oxford 1987-93), which include several important articles by Furet and his colleagues.

American university—for much of the 1980s and early 1990s, he had a regular visiting appointment at the University of Chicago.

It is no wonder then that many of Furet's earliest and strongest supporters came from scholars working in the United States. Among them is Keith Baker, who introduced Furet to Chicago. In a series of brilliant articles, Baker has done much to revitalize the intellectual history if the Revolution by carefully tracing how certain Rousseauian strands of Enlightenment political ideology mutated into revolutionary Jacobinism. For him, as for Furet, the key conduit was the Constituent Assembly deputy, priest, and pamphleteer, Emmanuel-Joseph Sieyes, "the theorist who had done more than anyone to interject Rousseauian notions of national sovereignty into the assembly's debates."[10]

The influence of Rousseau upon the French Revolution has been among the most heated debates in the eighteenth-century studies, and no one has discussed this problem with more sensitivity and erudition than Baker. In 1762, Rousseau had set forth his theory of the general will in his small but difficult book, *The Social Contract.* In contrast to other Enlightenment thinkers such as John Locke, David Hume, or Thomas Jefferson, Rousseau believed that politics was largely the process of discovering the will of the nation. If a member of that nation was found in a small minority of citizens who were dissenting from the national will, Rousseau advised the citizen to drop such views and gladly yield to the majority of citizens. No citizen, argued Rousseau, had a right to go against what a nation wants for itself. Such a doctrine may be democratic (in the sense of being populist), but it clearly poses serious problems for protecting the civic rights of minority groups.

According to Baker, the Revolution's free-fall into Rousseauian democracy was not the product of 1792-3 when the nation was at war, but was the result of deliberate decisions made by the National Assembly as early as the summer of 1789. At the end of one well-known lecture delivered as part of a bicentennial commemoration in 1989, Baker argued that by accepting Rousseau's theory of the general will as the basis for rejecting an absolute royal veto in 1789, the Constituent Assembly "was opting for the Terror."[11]

Like Furet, Baker placed the Terror squarely at the center of the revolutionary process. The Terror was not some detour away from the Revolution's true goal: it was the outcome of the Constituent Assembly's repeated adoption of Rousseauian political principles. After reading Furet and Baker, it seemed impossible to condemn the Terror as a temporary deviation from some political norm. In Baker's view, the Terror occurred not only because of what happened in 1792 or 1793, but because of the way in which political power and violence had been reconceptualized in 1789.

Furet and his collaborators also differed from earlier Revisionists in one very significant manner: they undermined the very foundations of Liberal historiography. Since the early nineteenth century, most historical writing was done by those who championed the great events. Liberals, or Whigs, believed that the French Revolution, when taken as a whole, was necessary to move France and Europe from a pre-modern to a modern society. For Liberals, the Old Regime had become so ossified and paralyzed by its own internal contradictions that, by the late eighteenth century, only revolutionary change could

---

[10] Keith Michael Baker, *Inventing the French Revolution: Essays on French Political Culture in the Eighteenth Century* (Cambridge, 1990), p. 295.

[11] *Ibid,* p. 305.

resolve France's grave problems. BY the mid-twentieth century, the notion of the Revolution as an agent of progress, despite its great faults, was shared by virtually all of the academic historical community, from Cobban to Soboul. If Anglo and American historians often accepted the views of French Marxists, it was because they shared fundamental attitudes about the nature of the Revolution as an agent of liberty. [12]

At the center of the Liberal approach to the Revolution is a periodization that separates a moderate and constructive early phase of the Revolution (1789-92) form the more radical and violent period that followed (1792-94). Liberal historians typically point to the great achievements of the early phase (passage of the *Declarations of the Rights of Man and Citizen,* abolition of feudalism, reorganization of the judiciary and administration, freedom for Protestants and Jews, etc.) as demonstrating the virtues of revolutionary change. Correspondingly, they typically explain away the excessive violence of the Terror by noting the grave circumstances that led to its establishment: war, economic dislocation, and counter-revolution.

To declare that the Terror was conceptualized or originated in 1789 is to say that the Revolution never went through a "moderate" phase: the entire political dynamic from the Tennis Court Oath through the death of Robespierre can be viewed as one great era in which the state wielded unprecedented authority in the name of the people, but usually not to their benefit. Indeed, in the hands of many recent Revisionists, the entire Revolution is viewed as one gigantic imposition forced in the backs of the peasants, who, of course, made up more than three-quarters of the population. "The violence was all rather senseless," remarks Donald Sutherland. [13] The French Revolution wasn't worth the trouble.

This conclusion would have surprised Alfred Cobban, the British historian who began revisionism forty years' ago. For Cobban, the Ancien régime was so beset with contradictions and structural problems that nothing short of revolution could reform the country; nor was the Revolution itself all senseless violence. The construction of a liberal political order, based upon respect for human rights and religious toleration would have been impossible without the clashes of 1789 and the achievements of the Constituent Assembly. For Cobban, the Third Republic was unthinkable without the first, even if the original model had its defects. [14]

The turning of recent French Revolutionary historiography against its Liberal foundations is startling. Certainly, the ascendancy of Neo-Conservative ideas in England and the United States have provided much fodder for recent Revisionism. Usually former Liberals themselves, Neo-Conservatives in the 1960s and 1970s turned against the whole idea of revolutionary change as itself illiberal. Associating the revolutionary process

---

[12] On the Liberal foundations of Marxist historiography, see George Comninel, *Rethinking the French Revolution: Marxism and the Revisionist Challenge* (London, 1987).

[13] Donald Sutherland, "The Revolution in the Provinces: Class or Counterrevolution?," in *Essays on the French Revolution: Paris and the Provinces,* ed. Steven G. Reinhardt, *et al.* (College Station, TX, 1992), p. 116. see also his *France 1789-1815: Revolution and Counterrevolution* (New York, 1985).

[14] For Cobban's more liberal views, see his *In Search of Humanity: The Role of the Enlightenment in Modern History* (New York, 1960), esp. Parts 4 and 5. For all his liberalism, however, Cobban was certainly no cheerleader for the Revolution and sometimes adopted a more critical posture. See, for example, "Local Government During the French Revolution," in *Aspects of the French Revolution* (New York, 1968), p. 130.

with fanaticism (read Bolshevism and later Iranian Islamic fundamentalism), Neo-Conservatives gave up their Rousseau for copied of Burke and de Tocqueville: progressive change occurs, they now argued, slowly and outside of institutions controlled by the state. Any efforts by the state to push through large-scale social or political programs were bound to lead to violations of property and civil liberties.[15]

Since the early 1950s, Neo-Conservative thinkers have had their own pet history of the French Revolution. In his 1952 classic, *The Origins of Totalitarian Democracy,* Jacob Talmon argued that they French state became a "totalitarian democracy" during the Terror in the sense that its social programs were designed to alter the course of every citizen's life, producing a secular version of a messianic age. In Talmon's view, such a state would become a harbinger for twentieth-century experiments on both the political right and left. Talmon traced the idea of totalitarian democracy back through Sieyes to certain key Enlightenment figures, Rousseau most prominent among them. While Talmon's history was attacked by Liberal historians—even his own PhD advisor Alfred Cobban dismissed his argument—the book succeeded in associating Rousseau with the Terror.[16]

Talmon's intellectual history has much in common with the newer approach of Furet. Both Talmon's and Furet's approach privilege political theory and the spread of ideas; both see a direct line from Rousseau through Sieyes and Robespierre; both associate Rousseauian democratic ideas with a collectivism that quickly turned oppressive; both, in short, see the Terror as the essence of the Revolution and view it as harbinger of Bolshevism and Fascism. Talmon's methodology is primitive in comparison to that of Furet and Baker, whose perceptive investigations into discourse theory have significantly advanced the field. In contrast, Talmon's method tends to distort Enlightenment ideology by projecting twentieth-century meanings onto eighteenth-century ideas. Only the most extreme historians writing today, such as Raynauld Sécher, extend Talmon's view by arguing that the Terror culminated in a genocidal campaign in the Vendée resembling twentieth-century horrors.[17]

Whether in it solder form from Talmon, or its more sophisticated version from Furet, Neo-Conservative Revisionism had clearly become the ascendant interpretation of the historical establishment in England, France, and the United States by they 1989 bicentennial celebration. In France, despite Michael Vovelle's semi-official position, it was Furet whom the media anointed "King of the Revolution," and who seemingly made an appearance at every academic conference and numerous French television shows.[18] In the United States, the best illustration of Revisionism's popularity was the enormous success of Simon Schama's mega-history of the Revolution, *Citizens*, which exaggerated further Furet's arguments into slogans that at times echoed Margaret Thatcher if not Burke:

---

[15] Irving Kristol, *Neo-Conservatism: Selected Essays 1949-1995* (New York, 1995).

[16] J. L. Talmon, *The Origins of Totalitarian Democracy* (London, 1952). The book has been reprinted several times in paperback and had been translated into French, German, Hebrew, and Japanese. For Cobban's criticisms, see his *Rousseau and the Modern State,* 2nd ed. (London, 1964), pp. 29-31, and *In Search of Humanity*, pp. 182-5.

[17] Raynauld Sécher; *Le Génocide Franco-Française: La* Vendée-*Vengé* (Paris, 1986). See Hugh Gough, "Genocide and the Bicentenary: The French Revolution and the Revenge of the Vendée," *Historical Journal 30* (1987): 977-88.

[18] Steven Lawrence Kaplan, *The Historians' Feud* (Ithaca, 1994).

The Revolution did indeed invent a new kind of politics, an institutional transference of Rousseau's sovereignty of the General Will that abolished private space and time, and created a form of patriotic militarism more all-embracing than anything that had yet been seen in Europe. For one year, it invented an practiced representative democracy; for two years, 'it imposed coercive egalitarianism ... But for two decades its enduring product was a new kind of militarized state ... The terror was merely 1789 with a higher body count.[19]

Since the bicentennial celebration, the most important developments in the historiography of the Revolution have been Neo-Liberal challenges to the position laid out by Furet and his colleagues. In this volume, we have selected four articles that seek to critique Furet's approach to the Revolution. While each of the authors approaches the Revolution differently, and while none would regard themselves in any kind of formal school with the other, we can nonetheless see the beginnings of a shared set of attitudes that may be classified as Neo-Liberal. First, unlike Revisionists, Neo-Liberal interpretations do not minimize the oppressive character of the eighteenth-century nobility. The aristocracy is seen as a distinct political group with interests separate and opposing those of commoners. Second, Neo-Liberal arguments insists that the period of the Constituent Assembly was substantively different (i.e., more moderate and more constructive) than the Jacobinism of the Terror. Third, Neo-Liberal interpretations claim that the collective violence of the Revolution's early years (such as that surrounding 14 July 1789, or even 10 August 1792) was often purposeful and necessary to the establishment of a liberal and free state.

These Neo-Liberal historians challenge the view that the Revolution was primarily a failure. A rising bourgeoisie may not have started the Revolution, but the revolutionaries successfully destroyed the Ancien régime and refashioned a society that made a nineteenth-century liberal state possible. Some scholars, such as Colin Jones, are even willing to resurrect the notion that the Revolution did indeed involve a transition to capitalism. Still, the new approach to social cleavages seems different than Marxism, if only because Neo-Liberals define class more in terms of specific professions and occupations with varied social interests than in terms of a solid group with political interests. There is not much idealization among the Neo-Liberals of either the sans-culottes or the Committee of Public Safety. In comparison with this burgeoning Neo-Liberalism, recent Neo-Marxist responses to Revisionism have not yet made much of an impact.[20]

Alongside the Neo-Liberal response to revisionism, the other significant recent trend in French Revolutionary scholarship has been the maturation of women's and gender history. Until the 1970s, few general histories or document collections on the Revolution included much information about women, feminism, or gender. This omission changed in the 1970s with the rise of a contemporary feminist movement; and it was clearly American feminists who set the pace toward a new history that took into account the fate of women and used gender as an analytical tool. One of the first articles in a major journal to deal with the topic was authored not by an established scholar, but by a female

---

[19] Simon Schama, *Citizens: A Chronicle of the French Revolution* (New York, 1989), pp. 184 and 447.

[20] Neo-Marxist works include Comninel, *Rethinking the French Revolution;* E. J. Hobsbawm, *Echoes of the Marseillaise: Two Centuries Look Back on the French Revolution* (New Brunswick, 1989); and Morris Slavin, *The Left and the French Revolution* (Atlantic Highlands, NJ, 1995).

American graduate student obviously inspired by the women's movement.[21] When in 1979 three American feminist historians published a collection of primary documents devoted to French Revolutionary women, a new research agenda was established for the field.[22]

Unfortunately, that research did not filter down into college classrooms with any great speed, perhaps because of the traditional nature of much of the historical profession. Of course, the new research made us realize that women participated in every major event in the Revolution. We learned more about the movements of street women during the great events of the Revolution (such as the October Days), as well as the influence of élite women in the clubs and presses of Paris. Unfortunately, however, that did not necessarily mean that this feminist-driven researched changed the way that other specialists or college teachers approached the Revolution. Curiously, by classifying the new research as "women's history," it became possible for many historians to ignore or marginalize such research, and continue teaching their subject along the same old lines. Some professors muttered that knowing about women's participation was one thing; discovering how that participation changed the fundamental character of the Revolution was quite another. This kind of attitude seems to have been especially true in France, where Furet's recent general text as well as his and Mona Ozouf's *Critical Dictionary* ignore women, feminism, and gender.[23]

During the last decade or so, feminist-inspired historians have addressed this challenge by shifting research from studying women as such to exploring how gender might be used fruitfully as an analytical tool. Instead of identifying women as the primary subject, recent feminist historians have widened the scope to include revolutionary discourse, policies, events, and culture—interpreted through the lens of gender. Benefiting from the advances made in other fields, such as literary criticism and gay and women's studies, historians have become interested in how the Revolutionaries refashioned gender roles for both men and women and, correspondingly, how ideas regarding manhood and womanhood influenced the way revolutionary statesmen conceived of the new regime.

For example, historians have long known that women were formally excluded from organizing political clubs by the National Convention during the fall of 1793. But it has been too easy to see Jacobin attitudes as prejudicial, old-fashioned, and out of character with their more democratic political beliefs. Nonetheless, recent work shows that Jacobin ideas about women may not have been old-fashioned or prejudicial at all; when looked at from the perspective of gender, they may have been part of an effort to articulate a new and daring view of politics, in which both "men" and "women" are redefined in contrast to aristocratic gender roles: "Each sex is called to the kind of occupation which is fitting for it," the Jacobin deputy Amar declared on behalf of the Convention. "Man is strong, robust, born with great energy, audacity, and courage," while women are destined for "private functions." Historians who use gender as an analytical tool teach us that Amar is

---

[21] Jane Abray, "Feminism in the French Revolution," *American Historical Review* 80 (1975): 43-62.

[22] *Women in Revolutionary Paris, 1789-1795*, ed. Darline Gay Levy, Harriet Bronson Applewhite, and Mary Durham Johnson (Urbana, 1979).

[23] Furet, *Revolutionary France; Critical Dictionary,* ed. Furet and Ozouf. For more general reflections on women's historiography see Joan Wallach Scott, *Gender and the Politics of History* (New York, 1988), pp. 15-50; and Karen Offen, "The New Sexual Politics of French Revolutionary Historiography," *French Historical Studies* 16 (1990): 909-22.

not making an old-fashioned statement about women, but rather, he is formulating a new (if dark) vision about how gender roles will function in modern republican politics.[24]

If we are to make sense of Amar's political program, we must learn how Jacobins like him used gender to differentiate one group of citizens from another. No on has pioneered this path more successfully than Lynn Hunt. In a study from the early 1980s, Hunt explored why the Jacobins replaced Marianne with Hercules as the anthropomorphic symbol of the French nation. What did it mean for the French nation to be represented by a man instead of a woman? In the article on Marie Antoinette reprinted in this volume, Hunt demonstrates how attitudes towards the French queen reveal much about the ways in which French Revolutionary leaders hoped to shape sexual roles in the new republic.[25]

Of great importance in shifting the lines of research from "women" to "gender" is the recent work of an American feminist political scientist, Joan Landes. Grounding her research on the theories of German social theorist Jürgen Habermas, Landes argued that the crucial factor for women during the French Revolution was not their participation but rather their formal exclusion from political life altogether. Women were not simply forgotten or ignored by the Revolution's new leaders. Rather, "the collapse of the older patriarchy gave way to a more pervasive *gendering* of the public sphere." The lines between public men participating in civic life and domesticated women caring for family and children alone, argued Landes, were more purposively drawn by the Jacobins than ever before.[26]

Landes blames this development of Jean-Jacques Rousseau. His reformulation of political culture included a devastating critique of gender roles under the Old Regime. Elite women, Rousseau claimed, had overstepped their natural bounds and had attained entirely too much power and visibility, especially in Paris and Versailles. Indeed, in Rousseau's view, the feminization of the Old Regime nobility threatened to undermine any semblance of order and morality. The solution, Rousseau argued, would be to divide gender roles much more rigidly than had ever been the case for the French aristocracy. "The theorist of democratic liberty," Landes wrote of Rousseau, had "a profound mistrust of women such that he would deny them the most elementary political rights."[27]

---

[24] Amar's speech is reproduced in *Women in Revolutionary Politics*, pp. 213-17.

[25] Lynn hunt, "Hercules and the Radical Image in the French Revolution," *Representations* 1 (1983): 95-117, and included in her *Politics, Culture, and Class in the French Revolution* (Berkeley, 1984), pp. 87-119. Other recent examples of this approach to gender history include Madelyn Gutwirth, *The twilight of the Goddesses: Women and Representation in the French Revolutionary Era* (New Brunswick, 1992); Geneviève Fraise, *Reason's Muse: Sexual Difference and the Birth of Democracy*, trans. Jane Marie Todd (Chicago, 1994); Christine Fauré, *Democracy Without Women: Feminism and the Rise of Liberal Individualism in France,* trans. Claudia Goodman and John Berks (Bloomington, 1991); and Dorinda Outram, *The Body and the French Revolution: Sex, Class and Political Culture* (New Haven, 1989).

[26] Joan B. Landes, *Women and the Public Sphere in the Age of the French Revolution* 9Ithaca, 1988), p. 2. For criticisms of Landes's work see especially Dena Goodman, "Public Sphere and Private Life: Toward a Synthesis of Current Historiographical Approaches to the Old Regime", *History and Theory* 31 (1992): 1-20; and Keith Michael Baker, "Defining the Public Sphere in Eighteenth-Century France: variations on a Theme by Habermas," in *Habermas and the Public Sphere*, ed. Craig Calhoun (Cambridge, MA, 1992), pp. 181-211. Goodman and Baker tend to criticize Landes more for her understanding of Habermas than for her analysis of how gender roles changed during the Revolution.

[27] P. 67.

Landes thus argued that the new "bourgeois political sphere"[28] was in many ways more regressive that what élite women had experienced under the Old Regime. Indeed, far from gaining political rights during the French Revolution, Landes claimed that the Old Regime showed far more toleration for public women than did its republican counterpart. From Landes historians learned, perhaps for the first time, that the omission of women from the *Declaration of the Rights of Man and Citizen* was not a prejudicial oversight, but rather, they were excluded because the Republic had been conceived as an exclusively masculine public space.

Landes sees her work as a contribution to left-wing feminism's critique of contemporary patriarchal limitations on female political power. Under the influence of Australian political theorist Carole Pateman, both Landes and Hunt hope to expose the patriarchal roots of liberal democracies, in order to prod them to initiate more radical change that would further empower women.[29] However, it is one of the great ironies of recent historical scholarship that this left-wing feminist scholarship has so far been more fruitfully developed by Neo-Conservative Revisionist scholars than by anyone else.

Revisionists and the new feminist scholars share two essential attitudes about the Revolution: first, both groups believe that the revolution marked a step backwards for women's rights. Second, both give credence to the ideas of Jean-Jacques Rousseau—it was his highly contentious ideas that gave rise to new notions of female domesticity.

The best example of the appropriation of feminist history for Neo-Conservative purposes is found in Simon Schama's *Citizens*, which arguably incorporated more recent scholarship on women than any other recent general history. Using Hunt's research on Marie Antoinette, Schama depicted the 1793 trial of the queen as merely one facet of "the stormiest phase of sexual politics in the Revolution." For Revisionists, the Jacobin attack on Marie Antoinette and other public women such as Olympe de Gouges and Madame Roland, as well as the general closure of female political clubs in 1793, are emblematic of a pervasive Rousseauian democratic despotism.[30]

In fact, this convergence of what might be labeled "feminist revisionism" is what makes possible the outlook of Olwen Hufton's piece in this volume, "In Search of Counter-Revolutionary Women." Hufton sees the Revolution primarily as an attempt by big-city fold to control the masses of poor rural peasants, who were not so much counter-revolutionaries in the ideological sense, but simply wanted to get out of the political steamroller. When that became impossible, women had to fend for themselves, devising their own imaginative strategies for undermining Jacobinism in the countryside. "By

---

[28] P. 204.

[29] Carole Pateman, *The Sexual Contract* 9Stanford, 1988).

[30] Schama, *Citizens*, p. 800. Along the same lines, see Patrice Higonnet, "Cultural Upheaval and Class Formation During the French Revolution," in *The French Revolution and the Birth of Modernity*, ed. Ferenc Fehér (Berkeley, 1990), pp. 69-102. For a Neo-Liberal response to this line of thinking, see Suzanne Desan, "'Constitutional Amazons': Jacobin Women's Clubs in the French Revolution," in *Recreating Authority in Revolutionary France*, ed. Bryant T. Ragan, Jr, and Elizabeth A. Williams (New Brunswick, 1992), pp. 11-35; and the introduction to *The French Revolution and Human Rights: A Brief Documentary History*, ed. Lynn Hunt (Boston, 1996).

looking at gender roles in the counter-revolution," Hufton hopes to "convey how it was possible for women to subvert the Revolution in the home and one the domestic front."[31]

The irony of a feminist revisionism shows just how much historical writing reflects greater trends operating in contemporary culture. After all, despite stereotypes that suet up a mythic struggle between a Left that champions revolutionary struggle and a Right that seeks to prevent any major social change, today's college students and faculty across the political spectrum are generally highly skeptical about the efficacy of any revolutionary change, and at the same time, deeply committed to a civic culture that promotes equal opportunities for women and men. It is only natural and appropriate that their own political convictions influence how they perceive the French Revolution.

Sometimes new students of the Revolution—and veteran scholars as well—grow weary at the noisy debates over its meaning and place in history. Most historians choose their field not because of a fondness for theory or political polemics, but usually because of a love to study the documents themselves. Yet, the historiography of the French Revolution is so monumental that it often threatens to intimidate the young researcher. Is it really necessary to pay close attention to polemics among historians and other partisans? Why isn't it possible to simply ignore the various schools of historical thinking, and to study the Revolution without becoming embroiled in its historiography?

Without historiography scholars would not know how to go about their business. We would be like travelers lost in the forest without a map—all the trees might look alike, and we would not know which path to travel. Instead of thousands of trees, we have primary source documents. And the first problem confronting the historian is deciding which document to investigate and what questions to ask about it. Without a rigorous historiography that compels us to think critically about our approaches, our political views, and our rhetorical strategies, we would have only our prejudices and our passions on which to rely. As in the nineteenth century, history without historiography might still be worth reading as literature, but it would rarely be considered part of the social sciences.

François Furet is right that "the French Revolution is over." We live in another age, and the problems of the late eighteenth century are no longer our own. Nevertheless, the legacy of the achievements and failings of that age are still with us. The French Revolutionaries dreamed of a world (like ours) dominated by democratic republics. They tried—and ultimately failed—to figure out what duties a democratic government had towards it citizens, and what responsibilities it had towards its neighbors. Our era may not be theirs but surely how we choose to write about their early efforts will help shape how our readers think about our own political problems.

---

[31] Olwen H. Hufton, Women and the Limits of Citizenship in the French Revolution (Toronto, 1992), p. xxiv.

Appendix F: Recommended Reading

In addition to materials cited elsewhere in packet, the following works are recommended:

GENERAL TEXTS

Hunt, Lynn and Censer, Jack. *Liberty, Equality, and Fraternity: Exploring the French Revolution* (Penn State, 2002); also on line at http://chnm.gmu.edu/revolution/index.html

Hunt, Lynn, ed. *The French Revolution and Human Rights* (Boston, 1996).

Doyle, William. *The Oxford History of the French Revolution,* 2nd ed (New York, 2003)

Lefebvre, Georges. *The Coming of the French Revolution,* trans. R. R. Palmer (Princeton, 1972)

Schama, Simon. *Citizens: A Chronicle of the French Revolution* (New York, 1989)

SCHOLARLY MONOGRAPHS

Andress, David. *Massacre at the Champ de Mars: Popular Dissent and Political Culture in the French Revolution.* Woodbridge, Suffolk, 2000. Solid analysis of the radical democratic movement in Paris during the summer of 1791.

Blum, Carol. *Rousseau and the republic of virtue : the language of politics in the French Revolution.* Ithaca, NY, 1986. Concentrates on the Jacobin left between 1792-1794.

Censer, Jack Richard. *Prelude to Power: The Parisian Radical Press, 1789-1791.* London, 1976. Particularly good for understanding the relationship between journalism and politics .

Kates, Gary. *The Cercle Social, the Girondins, and the French Revolution.* Princeton, 1985. Analysis of one radical club.

Kennedy, Michael L. *The Jacobin Clubs in the French Revolution: The First Years.* Princeton, 1982. Concentrates more on the establishment and character of provincial clubs than on the Paris Jacobins.

Loomis, Stanley. *The Fatal Friendship: Marie Antoinette, Count Fersen, and the Flight to Varennes.* London, 1972. Popular fiction based on historical fact.

McDonald, Joan. *Rousseau and the French Revolution, 1762-1791.* London, 1966. Explains the influence of the *Social Contract* in relation to his other work.

Murray, W. J. *The Right-Wing Press in the French Revolution, 1789-1792*. London, 1986. A counterpart to Censer's book, focusing on the influence of journalism upon counter-revolution.

Price, Munro. *The Road from Versailles: Louis XVI, Marie Antoinette, and the Fall of the French Monarchy*. New York, 2003. Gracefully written and very well informed.

Rose, R. B. *The Making of the Sans-culottes: Democratic Ideas and Institutions in Paris, 1789-1792*. Manchester, 1983. Excellent for understanding the theories of the revolution's first democrats.

Rude, George. *The Crowd in the French Revolution* (Oxford, 1959). A classic study.

Tackett, Timothy. *Becoming a Revolutionary: The Deputies of the French National Assembly and the Emergence of a Revolutionary Political Culture (1789-1790)*. Princeton, 1996. Among the most important books on the early years of the French Revolution.

Tackett, Timothy. *When the King Took Flight*. Cambridge, MA, 2003. An engaging narrative laying out the story in all its dramatic details.